DATE DUE			

D

A
HISTORY OF THE
AMERICAN LIBRARY
ASSOCIATION
1876–1972

A History of the American Library Association

1876-1972

DENNIS THOMISON

AMERICAN LIBRARY ASSOCIATION
CHICAGO
1978

Library of Congress Cataloging in Publication Data

Thomison, Dennis, 1937–
   A history of the American Library Association,
1876–1972.

   Includes index.
   1. American Library Association—History. I. Title.
Z673.A52T48   020'.622'73   77-27966
ISBN 0-8389-0251-0

Printed in the United States of America

To My Mother,

Juanita Lapinski,

whose love and encouragement
were always there.

CONTENTS

FOREWORD

Many professional or educational associations mark a significant milestone in their history by publishing an "in-house history" glorifying the association and calling attention to the virtues and contributions of its leaders. The American Library Association has probably done that less than most associations, primarily because librarians don't take their professional history very seriously, but also because there is a vast amount of fundamental research yet to be done before anything like a definitive history can be written. For instance, only in the last three years have the ALA Archives been reasonably accessible to scholars. In 1973 they were transferred from Chicago to the University of Illinois where, thanks to a substantial grant from Beta Phi Mu, they are now being organized for use. The future library historian should fare better as a result of this decision; doctoral students are already finding the archives a major source for their dissertations. Encouragement for former ALA presidents to preserve their records either at Illinois or elsewhere will also add to the sources available for historical research.

Whatever the promise for the future, ALA, like many kindred associations, enters its second century with all too little work done to record its growth and development. There are too few substantial biographies of library leaders, and, for the most part, the various divisions and subunits of ALA lack even good memoirs or reminiscences upon which basic chronologies can be built. Much of the work that has been done has concentrated upon the early period with less attention to developments after 1900, except for Peggy Sullivan's excellent *Carl Milam and the American Library Association* (1976). There are standard biographies of William Frederick Poole, Charles Evans, and R. R. Bowker, but no really adequate biographies of

Justin Winsor, Melvil Dewey, or Charles A. Cutter. Even good historical articles are rare, though the *Journal of Library History* has provided encouragement to several library historians.

Under these circumstances, the association is fortunate that Dr. Dennis V. Thomison, Associate Professor of Library Science at the University of Southern California, has revised his doctoral dissertation for publication. It was originally written to cover the period 1876–1957, but he has added a chapter to cover the events of fifteen more years, bringing his story to a conclusion with the retirement of David H. Clift as ALA Executive Director in 1972. Admittedly the bulk of his work is from printed sources, but no one could write an ALA history any other way at the present time. As Thomison himself recognizes, his may not be the definitive history of ALA, but I predict that it will be the standard history for some time to come. Thomison's volume provides the basic framework for a definitive history as well as much information that one could discover elsewhere only with great difficulty.

Moreover, no one can claim that Thomison's book is an "in-house history." He is critical of many of ALA's positions through the years and is not hesitant to point out where he thinks the association went astray. As is true of any such work, others will take issue with his interpretations, and he will be criticized for what he has left out as well as for what he has included. Still, despite Thomison's somewhat negative tone, I believe that his work is useful and his analysis worthwhile. ALA *has* often spent too much time on organizational problems, and the members and their governing bodies *have* too often failed to take positive steps that were clearly needed. Yet ALA has also been in the forefront of professional advancement, and the victories in achieving status, standards, and legislation are also part of the story. ALA watchers will find the debates on successes, failures, and recurring questions familiar and interesting. They can and will draw their own conclusions, with Thomison's work doubtless being used to buttress arguments on both sides of organizational arguments. "Ça plus change. . . ."

In my own writing of articles to commemorate the ALA centennial, I have often used Dr. Thomison's dissertation with considerable profit. Those who continue to work on library history involving association activities will find it an indispensable point of departure. Meanwhile, ALA councilors, officials, and would-be officials might well study persistent issues that Thomison has identified and ask the question, Must we really roast this chestnut again?

EDWARD G. HOLLEY, *Dean*
School of Library Science
The University of North Carolina
at Chapel Hill

INTRODUCTION

In 1876 the American Library Association was formed by a few men and women who saw the need for an organization dedicated to libraries and librarians. The stated purpose of that new group was very simple: to promote library interests in the United States. Over a period of almost 100 years, the concept of the association has changed considerably, although the basic purpose has perhaps stayed the same. From a small organization with a very simple structure, it has developed into a huge, complex association of 28,754 personal members in 1976. This is the story of that development, from the very beginning to the conclusion of David Clift's tenure as executive director in 1972.

The association was, and is, a product of its time. Its origin came during a period of American history when many professional and educational associations were being formed and when urbanization of American society was drawing librarians closer together. Like many other groups of professionals, ALA met annually during its formative years but accomplished very little between those conferences. For this reason, the history of the association during this early period is basically a record of these meetings. Over the years, ALA activities gradually expanded, but it was World War I that encouraged the organization to become an active, viable association that achieved national recognition. There were reverses and setbacks after the war, but ALA would never again be the sleepy little organization it once was.

At the close of this study in 1972, ALA was also a product of its time. Perhaps reflecting the times, it was divided, insecure in certain respects, yet always confident in its own ability to achieve success. There was a developing awareness of social responsibilities, but not to the extent or at the speed desired by many of its members. The association had a real sense of pride in itself; yet, after almost 100 years of existence, it still was not quite sure what a professional association ought to be doing. It was divided in so many ways that its membership often wondered how it managed to stay together; yet basically most members seemed convinced that it ought to remain one organization. At the close of its first century, ALA was aware of its many accomplishments, but it was acutely conscious of its many deficiencies and failures, too.

As with any historical study, this book may be criticized for what it has omitted as well as for what it has included. It was not intended to be a complete history of every aspect of the life of ALA. The author has selected what he believes to be important, interesting, and significant in the mainstream of the history of the association.

Some aspects were chosen for more detailed treatment because they help to show the atmosphere of the times and the relationship of librarianship to what was happening elsewhere. Some topics and some individuals received rather slight treatment because there is very little information available about them. In part, this is because time and people have been unkind with the archives of the association. Many records have been destroyed or dispersed, and their absence was severely felt in writing this history. It also seems apparent that record keeping was very sporadic during the early years, and most officials had little interest in, or feeling for, preserving the history of their organization.

Other subjects, such as education for librarianship, received brief treatment because of the existence of extensive studies by previous researchers. These studies are noted where appropriate rather than attempt to repeat their valuable research. Finally, in a general history such as this, it was not possible to develop in detail the growth of the component parts. Thus, the divisions and affiliated organizations are discussed only in their relationship to ALA. Each division and affiliated organization may well deserve a separate study to do it justice.

This study has time limitations as well. It begins with an unsuccessful organization in 1853, because at least the seeds for later establishment were sown at that time. The study ends in 1972, at the close of the David Clift tenure, in order to provide some natural break as well as to furnish at least a minimal degree of historical perspective.

Where it has been possible, the main dependence in this work has been on the archives of the association, now largely located at the University of Illinois but also housed in part at headquarters in Chicago. The correspondence of some of the early officers has been preserved, and so have the official records of the association. Special mention should be made of two very important collections of materials. One is a scrapbook containing many of the letters, circulars, and telegrams concerned with the conference of 1876. There is also an extensive collection of materials, including confidential correspondence, dealing with ALA's role in the selection of the Librarian of Congress in 1939. Minutes and proceedings of the executive board and Council are also at the headquarters library. These accounts were seldom verbatim, however, and so it was necessary to depend on unofficial accounts. The two journals that have served as official journals of ALA—*Library Journal* and the *ALA Bulletin (American Libraries)*—have provided a considerable amount of detail. While personal interviews did not form an important source of information, some interviews were held, and the author corresponded with individuals to clarify certain points.

It should be made clear that this is not intended to be a definitive or authorized history of the association. A truly comprehensive account of ALA's story will have to await further research on individuals and the component parts of the association. Furthermore, basic source materials for the period 1957–72 were not made available to the author. For this important span of time, reliance was on secondary sources and the proceedings of the council and executive board. This policy, too, will have to be changed by ALA leadership before the much-needed comprehensive history of the association will be possible.

The author would like to acknowledge the valuable assistance provided by Raymond Kilpela, Katharine Laich, Martha Boaz, William Wilson, and numerous other colleagues who by their advice and encouragement contributed to this book.

1

THE FOUNDING OF THE AMERICAN
LIBRARY ASSOCIATION

*A*lthough the American Library Association was founded in 1876, its origins can be traced back to the first convention of librarians, held in 1853.[1] At the time of this meeting, it was the intention of those in attendance that there should be annual meetings and that a permanent organization should be established. In both respects, this convention failed; but the idea was implanted in the minds of librarians. Twenty-three years later, the time was more propitious; other similar associations had been formed, and ambitious leaders were emerging in the library field. The convention is significant, then, not for what was accomplished during its sessions, but because it was the progenitor of the more famous conference of 1876.

The first printed suggestion that a national convention of librarians should be held appeared in *Norton's Literary Gazette and Publishers' Circular* (hereafter referred to as the *Gazette*). This was on July 15, 1852, in an editorial apparently written by the publisher, Charles B. Norton, a New York bookseller who was especially concerned with library interests. A year elapsed and much persuasion was necessary before the convention of 1853 occurred. After the initial call was made, the major impetus for the meeting came from Prof. Charles C. Jewett of the Smithsonian Institution. He was a highly respected librarian and has been called the "ablest and most zealous of the early American reformers in the methods of library administration."[2] Others, such as Daniel Coit Gilman of Yale, Seth Hastings Grant of the New York Mercantile Library, and Reuben A. Guild of Brown University, also promoted the idea. After a considerable amount of correspondence on the subject among the leading librarians of the country,

1

the *Gazette* in May, 1853, made a formal proposal that librarians meet in New York in September. Although the suggestion aroused favorable comment among librarians, Jewett soon became worried about the possibility of an embarrassingly small response. One month before the meeting was to be held, he wrote to his friend Grant:

> Since the call was published, I have seen but very few who would be likely to take an interest in the convention. I have found some, on whom I had counted, who seem unwilling to take any active part. The fact is our fraternity are generally very quiet, unostentatious men, not accustomed to public speaking, or fond of exhibiting themselves.[3]

Jewett wrote to librarians in this country and abroad in an effort to interest them in attending the convention. When Norton was in Europe, he attempted to persuade the great English librarian, Sir Anthony Panizzi of the British Museum, to attend. Panizzi wrote to a friend that he had a great desire to do so, but the expense was too great for him, and his trustees refused to subsidize the trip.[4]

CONVENTION OF 1853

The concern over a possible small response to the convention call was unnecessary. When the librarians met on September 15, 1853, there were eighty men present, representing forty-seven libraries.[5] Jewett, as the "leading spirit" of the convention, was elected president, and Grant was elected secretary. In his opening address, Jewett outlined the rather simple purpose of the convention:

> It is not, so far as I know, proposed to accomplish any end by this Convention, beyond the general one expressed in the call, of "Conferring together upon the means of advancing the prosperity and usefulness of public libraries," and of seeking mutual instruction and encouragement in the discharge of the quiet and unostentatious labors of our vocation. . . .[6]

As Jewett pointed out in this speech, this was actually not the first convention of its kind ever held in the world. However, according to Jewett, the earlier gatherings had been made up "primarily of 'dilettante,' not practicing librarians." The librarians at the 1853 convention were for the most part from the northeastern part of the country, but there were representatives from as far away as New Orleans and San Francisco. In addition to librarians, there were historians, lawyers, professors, and ministers present.

Prior to the convention, the *Gazette* had published a comprehensive list of subjects that might be considered by the librarians. This list was divided into the following categories: The Library: Its Character; The Library Building: Points to Be Observed; and Library Management. The few days of the convention did not offer enough time to allow a thorough consideration of all the items proposed, but the list was apparently meant to ensure that the delegates would have enough material to justify a meeting. In this the planners were successful, for there were long and often heated debates over the proposals presented.

Most of the problems considered have been resolved by now, but some are still of importance and interest to librarians today. One of the proposals that proved impractical in the short run was Jewett's plan for printing the catalogs of the major libraries of the country for general distribution. He suggested that stereotype plates might be used to reproduce the catalog information from various libraries, resulting in the production of inexpensive catalogs and bibliographies. Although metal plates were desirable, the need for economy had led him to experiment with plates of clay and shellac, which were less expensive. Jewett believed these materials to be more resistant to wear than metal and thought there would be no appreciable loss of quality in printing even over a period of years.[7] William Frederick Poole of the Chicago Public Library dismissed the idea as "Mr. Jewett's mud catalogue" but others saw a tremendous potential in the concept, and the delegates approved the plan unanimously. However, when the invention was finally put into operation, the shrinking and warping of the clay plates prevented success. Nevertheless, the same principle was later incorporated in the production of catalogs by using metal plates. An integral part of Jewett's plan was the use of a uniform set of catalog rules, which he himself both collected and devised. In addition, Jewett's attempt at codification was the first of several efforts in this country to standardize library practice in the cataloging of books.

Several other topics discussed during the convention deserve mention. Charles Folsom of the Boston Athenaeum presented a proposal for a "card catalogue," which was actually a series of punched slips of paper on a string. Many librarians saw the desirability of having a manual of accepted library practice. *The Librarian's Manual*, published by Reuben Guild in 1858, was probably a result of this expression. Samuel Osgood, a Unitarian minister, suggested in a speech that popular libraries should be established throughout the nation. The Reverend Edward Everett Hale, representing the Worcester, Massachusetts, Young Men's Christian Association library, seconded the suggestion but pointed out that the term *public* referred to subscription libraries, not public libraries in the modern sense of the term. In addition, Poole's periodical index was on display, and the librarians formally approved plans for the second edition of this index. At the end of the meeting, it was voted to form a permanent organization and to meet the following year in Washington.

Throughout the convention, it was obvious the librarians intended to establish a permanent organization. In fact, President Jewett had said in his opening address,

> I unite most cordially in the hope which I have heard expressed this morning, that the Convention may be the precursor of a permanent and highly useful organization.[8]

Before the end of the convention, a committee of five members was appointed to make arrangements for the next meeting. Several matters were referred to committees with instructions to report back at the 1854 meeting. Thus, there is conclusive evidence that the librarians fully intended to meet again.[9]

Nonetheless, the committee charged with making arrangements failed to do so, and a second meeting was never held. Authors and historians of the period have offered several explanations for this failure.[10] The immediate reason was that, in July of 1854, Jewett left his position at the Smithsonian Institution. As a result, Jewett—the most influential librarian at the 1853 convention, a member of the arrangements committee planning the second meeting, and the only resident of Washington on the committee—was no longer in a position of authority. Norton of the *Gazette* later encountered financial difficulties and was unable to continue his active promotion of library interests. Other reasons for not meeting later were probably the financial crisis of 1857, the events leading to the Civil War, the Civil War itself, and the Reconstruction era. Taken together, these circumstances would have been enough to prevent librarians from meeting again very soon.

The convention of 1853 was in several important respects a failure. The librarians were unsuccessful in their attempt to found a permanent organization, and they were not successful in stimulating a second meeting. There were, however, some important indirect results of this meeting:

1. An informal arrangement was made among librarians for the regular exchange of reports and circulars.
2. Librarians had the opportunity to learn about the systems of classification in use in the various libraries.
3. The resulting publicity in newspapers was entirely favorable and helped to establish a climate friendly to library development.

4. Folsom's crude "card catalogue" was explained to other librarians.
5. A considerable number of librarians became personally acquainted and more aware of each other's problems.
6. Although no permanent organization resulted, the precedent was established for holding national meetings of librarians. This precedent contributed to the founding of the American Library Association when the timing was more propitious.

CONFERENCE OF 1876

Immediately following the convention of 1853, there was general agreement that the meeting had been highly successful. During the twenty-three years that elapsed before a second national meeting of librarians was held, it is possible that librarians wrote to each other about the convention and about meeting again, but there is no record of this. But as the American centennial year of 1876 approached, it apparently occurred to a number of librarians that another national meeting would be appropriate.

It is, of course, now difficult to determine the point of origin for the idea of librarians holding a second conference or convention. There were many librarians still living who had attended the 1853 meeting, and apparently the spirit of that meeting had not entirely dissipated.[11] It might also be pointed out that a number of associations had already been formed, including the American Book Trade Association, and the time seemed ripe for this type of cooperation. Moreover, many professional meetings were scheduled during the centennial celebration in Philadelphia, and it seemed logical for librarians to go along with the trend. If the later word of Melvil Dewey, librarian of Amherst College, can be accepted, he had had in mind for several years the formation of a national organization of librarians and the establishment of a library periodical.[12] Therefore, while it is difficult to determine precisely who was really responsible for the meeting, there were a number of leaders who became interested in the possibility of a meeting. The time also seemed to be very appropriate for the formation of an association of librarians.

The first suggestion in print that a conference should be held was apparently an anonymous letter in the March, 1876,[13] London *Academy*. The writer commented, "In these days of International Congresses, it is strange that no attempt should have been made to convene a Congress of librarians." The letter was noticed by Frederick Leypoldt of the *Publishers' Weekly* and reprinted in that journal on April 22, 1876. Charles Cutter, librarian of the Boston Athenaeum, also referred to the letter in the April 20, 1876, issue of the *Nation*.

One of those who read the letter in the *Publishers' Weekly* was Melvil Dewey at Amherst. On May 16, 1876, he left for New York to talk over his various plans with Leypoldt and Richard R. Bowker, also of the *Publishers' Weekly*. Dewey's diary indicates the date of the meeting as May 18, but the discussion apparently occurred on May 17.[14] The result of the meeting was an agreement to issue a call for a national library conference. On May 17, Leypoldt and Dewey sent a letter to Justin Winsor of the Boston Public Library, enclosing a preliminary call. Several days later, a similar call went out to other librarians, but this time it was signed by Leypoldt, Dewey, E. L. Jones of the *American Catalogue,* and William I. Fletcher of Hartford, Connecticut. Fletcher's name was added, without his knowledge, at the suggestion of Dewey. In this regard, Dewey wrote in his diary for May 18, 1875,

> I told them that Fletcher of Hartford who was the most promis-
> ing of the young librarians was in favor of such a convention, and
> would surely sign the call as soon as it was offered to him, indeed
> from what he told me I should think it safe to put his name down
> on the list as in favor of the project.

As a matter of fact, it was not "safe," for Fletcher's superior at the Watkinson Library in Hartford refused to let him attend the meeting. This situation proved very embarrassing to Dewey, and he wrote in his diary on May 20, "we got into an awkward little hole" over the mistake.

The call sent out was simply a suggestion that "efficiency and economy in library work" would be promoted by such a conference.[15] It recommended August 15, 1876, in Philadelphia as a practical time and place for a meeting. It noted another call would be issued in the near future and asked all librarians who were willing to sign such a call to write Melvil Dewey at the *Publishers' Weekly* office. The response from this announcement was quite favorable, but there were several problems. According to Justin Winsor, unless the librarians met in Boston, it would be practically impossible for him to attend. Although Dewey wrote in his diary that "Poole & the Boston people were all agreed to sign without knowing more of the character of the project. . . ," Poole was not at all willing to add his name to the call. In a letter to Winsor, Poole grumbled first of all about being contacted by telegram. He added he would have to know more about the meeting and "who is at the bottom of it before giving the use of my name."[16] Six days later, Poole again wrote to Winsor to say he had received a circular from Leypoldt and was surprised to see it indicated Winsor's support for the conference:

> Is this authorized? I inferred you were not for the plan from your note to me. They want my name. I have not given it, for it looks to me as if there were axes to be ground. Leypoldt says you will be asked to draw up a circular. I have written to Leypoldt that when you do this he is authorized to append my name to it.[17]

Another librarian who posed a problem for the conference planners was Ainsworth R. Spofford, the Librarian of Congress. Although he expressed the opinion that conferences were "mere wordy outlets for impracticables and pretenders," Spofford thought it might be possible to attend the proposed meeting.[18] He was not, however, willing to sign his name to the call. Poole transmitted this information to Winsor in Boston, with the added comment, attributed to the president of Amherst College, that Dewey was a "tremendous talker, and a little of an old maid." As if to finish the discussion about attending the conference, he closed with the comment, "It won't pay for you and me to attend that barbeque."[19]

Fortunately, other librarians were more enthusiastic about the proposal. Important leaders such as Reuben Guild, Henry A. Holmes of the New York State Library, and Lloyd P. Smith of the Library Company of Philadelphia indicated their support. The significant exception was still Poole. Dewey realized the importance of having his signature, so he not only wrote to Poole, but he also asked Charles Cutter to write Poole a letter of reassurance. Cutter wrote of Dewey that he was "no imposter, humbug, speculator, deadbeat, or anything of the sort," but of course Poole had never indicated that he believed this to be true of Dewey.[20] In his letter, Dewey reassured Poole that the only reason he was so prominent in the planning of the conference was that no one else was willing to do all the necessary work without compensation. He ended his letter in an almost pleading manner:

> We can't do without you and feel satisfied. Your name is always mentioned among the very first, and it would look all wrong not to see it in the list we now have.[21]

Apparently the coaxing was effective, for between June 5 and June 10 a second call went out to librarians regarding the proposed conference, and this time Poole's name was included among the signers. Indeed, Poole was soon writing to Dewey with suggestions, and hinting that Spofford, the only major librarian who had not signed the call, might easily be persuaded to join in the planning.[22]

At the suggestion of a number of people, the time of the conference was changed to October 4–6. Another printed call that went out on June 28 included the names of many prominent librarians and was signed by Winsor, Poole, Smith, and Dewey. In addition, Cutter commented in the *Nation* on June 27, "the profession is awakening to a sense that it is a profession" and in need of a permanent organization such as other professions had already established. The response to this call, and perhaps the additional publicity, was reassuring. Even Spofford responded, saying he would be able to be present and would be willing to present a paper.

The problem of providing full or partial stenographic reports of all meetings led to an argument between the strong-minded Dewey and the equally strong-minded Poole. Poole was against the idea because of the cost, as he explained in a letter to Winsor on September 18.

> I am somewhat in doubt whether we want full reports. It will be a premium offered to loquaciousness. And who is to bear the expense? Our librarians cannot do it. Please apply a breaching to Dewey and hold him back.

Poole prevailed in this argument, but Dewey only reluctantly gave up the idea. Later, as one of the secretaries at the conference, he complained about the additional work this entailed.

The day of the conference arrived, and 103 librarians assembled in the rooms of the Historical Society of Pennsylvania. Winsor was elected president, while Spofford, James Yates, Poole, and Smith were all elected vice-presidents. Since stenographers were not hired, Dewey, Charles Evans of the Indianapolis Public Library, and Guild acted as secretaries. The general plan was to have a paper presented, followed by a general discussion. Among the topics covered were cooperative indexing, cooperative cataloging, injuries to books from gas and heat, sizes of books, branch libraries, novel reading, and public relations. The practical emphasis of the conference was shown in the policy of allowing general questions, with prominent librarians stating how they had solved the problems.

The influence of Dewey was everywhere at the conference, as can be seen in the committee reports and in the transcripts of the general sessions. Perhaps the best example of this influence was in the action taken on the question of book sizes and how they were to be noted in catalogs. Charles Evans had delivered an excellent paper on "Sizes of Printed Books," which caused considerable discussion and resulted in the appointment of a committee to investigate the possibilities. Before the close of the conference, Evans, as chairman of the committee, reported to the assembled librarians. He indicated the committee members recommended that book sizes be noted in centimeters. Since Dewey was active in metric reform, which he believed would be adopted by the entire world in a short time, it was obvious who was behind the proposal. Poole arose to object, saying he had been a committee member but was not aware of this decision. Dewey explained:

> It will shed some light on the remarks of the gentleman from Chicago if I say that during the session of this committee last evening a very small minority felt constrained to retire—shall I say it?—to smoke. It was during the absence of this small minority that the report presented was unanimously adopted by the committee.[23]

The "small minority" had been outmaneuvered, and the committee report was adopted without further comment.

A paper that has often been overlooked, but which at the time probably created much discussion, was presented by Samuel S. Green, librarian of the Worcester (Massachusetts) Free Library. Green advocated closer personal relations between librarians and their public, a new concept for the time.[24] The *New York World* on January 3, 1877, went so far as to suggest that all public librarians and their assistants should be required to pass an examination on the contents of Green's address.

In addition to the reports and the speeches given, there were other benefits derived from the conference. The special report *Public Libraries in the United States of America,* the first truly national survey of libraries, was brought to the conference from Washington by its editor, Samuel R. Warren.[25] The cataloging rules of Cutter, which actually formed Part II of the national survey edited by Warren, were made available for perusal; in fact, they were so available that the twenty-five copies brought to the meeting "for display only" were said to have lasted about that many minutes. The secretary, probably Dewey, noted that this was a good illustration of the warning to "beware of specialists who are prone to carry off the volumes which they most thoroughly appreciated."[26] The first version of Dewey's decimal classification system was presented to the public at this conference, and Dewey answered questions raised by librarians. Several committees were established to consider means of cooperation, and this augured well for the future.[27] Above all else, a forum had been established. There was now an organization with meetings where common problems could be discussed, new ideas proposed, and friendships sealed. Unlike the convention of 1853, the 1876 meeting established an organization that proved to be permanent, and the momentum continued. The American Library Association had been established by resolution during the final session of the closing day of the conference.

A pleased Melvil Dewey wrote about the success of the conference several months later. He believed that it had been a triumph beyond the hopes of even the most ardent proponent. He added this prediction of one of the oldest librarians: "Through all coming time 1876 will be looked upon as the most eventful year in the history of libraries." In addition, Dewey said it was the year in which librarians took their place among the recognized professions.[28] The *New York World,* in summing up the conference, said that 1876 was the year in which the American library became what it ought to be: an essential factor in solving the educational problems of the country.[29]

THE START OF *LIBRARY JOURNAL*

The year 1876 had also seen the arrival of the first periodical devoted to librarianship. This was the *American Library Journal,* whose first issue was dated September 30, 1876. On the masthead, Melvil Dewey was listed as managing editor and F. Leypoldt as publisher. The name was changed to *Library Journal* in the September, 1877, issue. The date of the first issue, and its contents, show that the new publication was not a result of the birth of the new association, but instead preceded it. An editorial stated:

> The Committee's programme for the Philadelphia Conference is printed elsewhere. It will be seen that discussions on the more important library topics will be opened by papers from the leading librarians of the country. . . . There is no lack of inducement for librarians to attend; and as it should be the most profitable three days of their library life, it is scarcely to be supposed that any Board will refuse to grant leave of absence, not the least important outcome of this meeting should be the proposed national organization.[30]

The same issue also carried a brief sketch of the development of the idea of the new periodical. According to this short history, formal plans had been made for its publication at the May, 1876, meeting of R. R. Bowker, Frederick Leypoldt, and Melvil Dewey. Thus it is easily understandable that Bowker resented the later statements that *Library Journal* was an achievement of ALA. Bowker was more willing to accede to Dewey's claim to be the originator of the idea, although he clearly did not agree with the claim. On the final day of the conference, after the formation of ALA had been accomplished, it was moved that the *American Library Journal* be considered the organization's official publication. The proceedings of the meeting do not indicate that this resolution was passed, but apparently it was, because the

February 28, 1877, issue added the words "Official Journal of the American Library Association" to the masthead.

Although the *Library Journal* did benefit somewhat from its designation as the official publication of ALA, the magazine received no direct subsidy. The subscription list was small, and the struggle for mere existence was constant. Libraries in general had suffered from the extended period of depression following the panic of 1873, and they found even the low subscription price a burden. With the resumption of specie payment in 1879, there was a general resurgence of prosperity in the country.

For some time, however, it seemed as if the improved economic conditions had come too late. In a cautious note in December, 1879, the publisher announced that the *Library Journal* would be continued through 1880. The statement expressed the hope that "the efforts of the friends of library progress will be more actively exerted in its behalf."[31] Two months later, the "Title Slip Registry," a feature of *Library Journal,* was discontinued. In June, 1880, the publisher announced that *Library Journal* was to be suspended. A loss of $2,500 had been incurred in the publication, and the publisher felt that the lack of support from the library profession meant it was futile to continue. Most of the features appearing in *Library Journal* would henceforth be included in the *Publishers' Weekly,* according to the announcement. At some future time, when the growth of public library interest warranted it, the publication would be resumed.

This announcement created considerable protest and sympathy among librarians and led to the resumption of *Library Journal* with a July-August, 1880, issue. Frederick Leypoldt replaced Bowker as editor, with Melvil "Dui" also listed as an editor.[32] Although the editors promised only to complete the volume, in December it was announced that publication would be continued for another year. Thus, the periodical seemed to have survived its worst period of inadequate financial backing and deficient circulation.

SUMMARY

Librarians made an abortive attempt in 1853 to establish their own professional organization but did not actually do so until 1876. Credit for proposing ALA cannot be given to any one individual, since the idea seemed to have occurred to a number of people at the same time. But Melvil Dewey was certainly the guiding force in the planning and success of the Philadelphia conference of 1876. This conference established the professional organization, set up a committee structure to insure continuity, and set a pattern that was followed in future ALA meetings. This pattern included (1) a dependence on well-established, often older, librarians for the leadership;[33] (2) the presentation of papers of a practical nature to stimulate thought and discussion; and (3) the use of a committee structure to provide investigation in depth for the benefit of librarians.

The profession was fortunate also in the establishment of its own periodical, the *Library Journal,* in 1876. Although an independent operation, it was tied to ALA as the official publication. *Library Journal* contributed to the esprit de corps in the profession, to the body of knowledge of library science, and to the communication of news of interest to librarians. Hampered by inadequate financing, as was ALA, the new periodical managed to continue publication after a very brief interruption. In doing so, it may well have contributed to the survival of the association itself, since the periodical created publicity, provided a means of easy communication, and added to the common bond among librarians. The close relationship between the association and *Library Journal* continued until the establishment of the *ALA Bulletin* as the official publication of ALA in 1908.

At this point in the summary, it would be appropriate to suggest reasons why the 1876 conference was successful, whereas the 1853 meeting failed to produce a permanent organization. The United States had changed significantly in the period between conferences. In 1853 the divisive issues leading to the Civil War were uppermost in the minds of the people. By 1876 the Reconstruction period was almost over. The nation was about to embark on a long period of comparative sectional harmony and economic growth. An urban life style was rapidly replacing the rural society of pre–Civil War America. Libraries were becoming more numerous and more important. In 1853 there were about 500 libraries; in 1876 there were 3,700. Transportation was also improving, and so it was easier for librarians to meet with one another. The founding and success of other professional organizations undoubtedly helped lead to the establishment of ALA. Already established were such groups as the American Medical Association in 1847, the National Education Association in 1857, and the American Dental Association in 1859. Soon to be formed were the American Bar Association (1878) and the American Economic Association (1885). The period, an era of growing nationalism, seemed to be especially favorable for the establishment of professional groups. The *Library Journal* provided the publicity and constant encouragement to continue the efforts. Finally, the 1876 conference had energetic leaders like Winsor, Dewey, and Bowker. These men, and others, provided the momentum that enabled the conference to develop into ALA.

2

DECADE OF ESTABLISHMENT

*L*ibrarians at the Philadelphia conference had chosen as the first ALA president Justin Winsor, who was undoubtedly the best-known figure in the library world at that time. At the time of the conference, he was superintendent of the Boston Public Library, but in 1877 he resigned in a salary dispute with city officials and became librarian of Harvard University. In both positions, as well as with ALA, he displayed a remarkable talent for administration.[1] In addition, he was a historian and later served as president of the American Historical Society. As president of ALA, he was described by a member of the first conference in the following manner:

> He wears his years [45] lightly, although he is a tireless worker. No other person in the room has so dignified and impressive a presence as he. . . . Like nearly every other man present, he is not smooth shaven . . . but he wears his well-trimmed beard and moustache with the air of a man of the world.[2]

Winsor, the vice-presidents, and Dewey as secretary were named to act as an executive committee or board and were charged with the responsibility of drawing up a constitution. This document was printed in the *Library Journal* of March 31, 1877, and was characterized by the editor as "admirably brief and clear. . . ."[3] Two points in this first constitution are especially worth noting. First, it called for the membership of the association to elect an executive board of five members. This group had the power to select additional members and was to elect officers of ALA from the executive board thus constituted. The board was also given the task of naming committee members from its own membership.[4] The executive board was given full authority to act for the association between conferences in all matters on which the board was in unanimous agreement. The spirit of democracy, then, does not appear to be strong in this constitution, but at least the leaders provided a check on the executive board's authority to act for the association.

An unusual amount of committee activity grew out of the initial meetings at Philadelphia. A very strong spirit of friendliness and cooperation is evident in the reports of progress made by the several committees. The committee concerned with book sizes was an example of this cooperative spirit. Its members recommended the substitution of letters for the numerical symbols then in use in describing the sizes of books. It suggested the use of the letter Q for 4° (quarto) O for 8° (octavo), and D for 12° (duodecimo). The committee reported it had also reconsidered the use of centimeters instead of inches in cataloging information. It will be remembered that, at the Philadelphia conference, Dewey had successfully maneuvered ALA into adopting the metric system. After considering the question, committee members declined to make a change.

> They find on investigation that even the opponents of the metric system acknowledge that it is soon to come into general use in this country. . . .[5]

Not surprisingly, one notes that Dewey was a member of this committee, along with James L. Whitney and Charles A. Cutter. At this time, progress was also noted on a new edition of Poole's *Index to Periodicals*. William Frederick Poole had produced two editions of this index, the basic periodical index of the nineteenth century. He had then indicated that if a new edition were to be produced, it would have to be a cooperative venture. Librarians at the Philadelphia conference had expressed a strong interest in additional indexing. Dewey had noted that Amherst College Library was spending fifty dollars each year in supplementing Poole's work. After Poole outlined the problems he had encountered in his first two editions, librarians agreed to undertake a new edition on a cooperative basis. A committee was formed to establish policy and to make plans. It reported the initial findings in January, 1877. The committee decided to establish a uniform set of rules for indexing, to limit the indexing to English language periodicals, to issue supplements at five-year intervals, and to continue the subject-only indexing of the first two editions.[6] Poole also reported that he had found an associate editor in William I. Fletcher.[7]

Several months later, the cooperative committee, with Dewey as its secretary, announced the first major project of ALA. This was a proposal to provide libraries throughout the country with library supplies of good quality at low prices. A common problem at this time was the lack of sources of supplies of a uniform quality; so the suggestion of the committee was timely. The committee also announced that a unique financial arrangement had been made: any profit derived from the project was to accrue to ALA, and any loss would be absorbed by Dewey. This supply department was headquartered at Dewey's address in Boston for a period of one year. During that time, there was some criticism of ALA for being engaged in a commercial venture. The result was that the relationship was ended, although the service was continued. Subsequent names of this supply department were the Readers' and Writers' Economy Company and the Library Bureau.

An early *American Library Journal* editorial on standardization and cooperation had unknowingly prophesied internal dissension in the new organization. This article was unsigned, but it had all the earmarks of the managing editor, Dewey. It stressed the need to arrive at "agreement upon certain points," such as book sizes, abbreviations, form and order of titles, and other problems facing the librarian. According to the author of the editorial, after library procedures were agreed upon and approved by ALA, the organization could concern itself with other matters.[8] This emphasis on uniformity was characteristic of Dewey, and it would lead to many bitter debates later on.[9] At this time, however, the spirit of cooperation was too pervasive to allow differences of opinion to hamper library progress.

CONFERENCE OF 1877

This cooperative spirit was still evident several months later, when President Winsor opened the 1877 conference with remarks that illustrated the general positive attitude of the librarians.

> I think we meet with a confidence greater than last year, and with the feeling that a good work has begun, and well begun. Our purpose then was undefined as compared with our present aims. We have fostered a fellow-feeling that has been helpful to each other. . . . We have vindicated the profession before the ordinary, working-day world.[10]

This conference was meant to be a working meeting; so there were few papers presented. Topics included the problems of fires in libraries, the distribution of public documents, discounts on book purchases, accession records, and the spread of disease by books. Winsor reported on the recently established telephone network between the central library of Boston and its branches. He also commented on a new machine that had recently become available.

> I have experimented somewhat with typewriters. I never succeeded in getting any satisfactory work.[11]

It was at this conference that internal strife first surfaced. The problem was uniform title entries, including the question of capitalization in titles. Dewey was for the omission of capitals and wished to have the association endorse this position. On the opposite side was William Frederick Poole, who said:

> I wish to say that I do not propose to be bound by anything that this Association may do in this matter. I do not regard it as an essential matter; it is simply a matter of taste. The Association ought not to prescribe any special rule in this matter, no more than it ought to say what kind of a necktie a male shall wear. . . . I propose to stick to the old English system, and to use it until we get ready to write a small "I" for the personal pronoun.[12]

But Dewey believed that it was necessary for the organization to set policy on this and other questions of standardization. He said that as secretary he received many letters from librarians asking for advice on procedures. The replies given would carry more authority if they represented decisions made by the association, according to Dewey. His motivation was, of course, farther reaching than this. Dewey was very systematic and well organized. It was his desire that libraries should be organized uniformly for the convenience of patrons, and this would only be possible if all libraries adopted similar policies. Sanction of ALA would encourage uniformity among librarians.

Poole was not alone in opposition to Dewey, but he was the leader. Thus, it was Poole who was characterized as the "Martin Luther of the Conference" in an editorial in *Library Journal*. This editorial was unsigned, but was probably written by the managing editor, Dewey. It pointed out that

> The Association is not a mandatory body, nor does it assume infallibility. The difficulty against which Mr. Poole . . . frequently protested, has therefore no existence: it is not expected that large existing libraries should revolutionize existing systems for the sake of ideal but inconvenient uniformity. But a uniform system, for the value of those who can conveniently use it, is none the less desirable.[13]

INTERNATIONAL CONFERENCE
OF LIBRARIANS

Following the close of the conference, twelve members of ALA sailed to England to the International Conference of Librarians. One member of the party, Reuben Guild, tried to set the pattern for "ship togs" and frivolity. Unfortunately, before the ship got out of New York Harbor, he became sick and found it necessary to return to his room. Except during brief periods of good weather and smooth water, he remained there the rest of the journey. Arrangements abroad had been made by Dewey, and it was soon discovered that all of the hotels were temperance hotels. As a contemporary account points out, the librarians were "nowhere subjected to the allurements of the charms of the sociable and attractive barmaids of England. . . ."[14] After a quick tour of some of the libraries of Great Britain, the librarians went to London. There they met in conference on October 2 with two hundred delegates from other countries. More than half of the delegates were from the British Isles. All except four of the delegates to the conference were men.

John Winter Jones, librarian of the British Museum, was elected president of the conference. In his opening address, he paid tribute to American inspiration for holding the meeting.

> The idea of holding a Conference of Librarians originated in America—in that country of energy and activity which has set the world so many good examples, and of which a Conference of Librarians is not the least valuable, looking to the practical results which may be anticipated from it.[15]

As had been true of ALA's first conference, almost every library topic was discussed at this meeting. Two topics are worthy of note here. There was considerable discussion over the desirability of printing the catalog of the British Museum. Although there was not unanimous agreement that this project should be undertaken, the thorough airing of the possibility helped to lead to the catalog's eventual publication.

The lack of women librarians was noticed immediately by members of the American delegation, who were quick to point out the role females played in U.S. libraries. Justin Winsor introduced Annie Godfrey, the librarian of Wellesley College (and the future Mrs. Dewey), as prominent among those in administrative positions. But probably a more telling remark was Poole's assertion that "some of our most accomplished cataloguers are ladies."[16] Other librarians also commented that it was unfortunate that female librarians did not usually receive compensation equal to that of male librarians.

At the end of the conference, the members took steps to establish the

Library Association of the United Kingdom, with John Winter Jones as the first president. Its aims emphasized "promoting the best possible administration of libraries" and "the encouragement of bibliographic research."[17] In addition, the delegates passed the following resolution:

> That the *American Library Journal* be adopted as the official journal of the Association—it being understood that the word "American" in the title will be dropped, and that some English librarians be added to the board of editors.[18]

Although there were some complaints about having a foreign journal as the official publication, the changes were made as specified, and the tiny *Journal* assumed an international stature. Following the close of the meetings, most of the Americans visited libraries in Paris before returning home.

Enroute to the United States on the steamship *Alsatia,* the executive board of ALA decided to eliminate the annual conference in 1878. Instead, an international meeting would be held in Boston early in 1879. Meanwhile there was to be an emphasis on committee work and on cooperative effort within the organization. Committees had been very active already, and a number of proposals had been suggested. Firm progress had been made on several of the suggestions. By omitting a conference in 1878, further efforts might be realized in 1879, leaders believed, because committee members could concentrate on the work rather than on the meetings.

One of the problems receiving a great amount of attention at this time has remained to the present day. This was the proposal to have the books arrive at the library already cataloged, much as in the later project usually referred to as cataloging in publication. As *Library Journal* pointed out in 1879, "no other thing has served as cornerstone for so many library utopias.[19] A Committee on Publishers Title-Slips had been working on the problem for a period of time without coming up with a realistic solution. It was even suggested that advertising material be included with the title slips to help defray the cost of cataloging. Publishers, however, were unwilling to assume the additional financial burden of providing the cataloging information. For a short period, *Library Journal* included a Title Slip Registry that was similar in nature, but this, too, was unsuccessful and was soon discontinued.

In a related area, the Committee on Uniform Title Entries presented the "Condensed Rules for Cataloging" in March, 1878, according to *Library Journal.* ALA later accepted them as the basic cataloging rules and then presented them to the Library Association of the United Kingdom as a basis for establishing a common code of rules. However, the two library associations did not reach agreement on cataloging rules until 1908. In the

United States, too, many libraries with established collections refused to conform to the new rules because of the cost of catalog revision.

BOSTON CONFERENCE, 1879

On June 30, 1879, ALA convened a library conference in Boston that had been planned as an international event. Sir Anthony Panizzi of the British Museum and other leading foreign librarians had been invited, but did not attend; however, Panizzi's chair and table were sent to the conference and were used by the officers. Papers were presented on such topics as library legislation, theft problems in libraries, binding, cataloging and classification, ventilation of library buildings, and the spread of diseases by books. The major complaint heard at the conference was that so much time was consumed in presenting papers that there was little opportunity for discussion. Dewey, in a long and rambling report as secretary, began with this observation:

> Coincidences and surprises seem the order of the day, and I was lucky to have discovered a few hours ago that this first day of the Boston meeting is the thousandth since we met to organize. Our President shows his suspicion of the decimal character of my coincidence, but I plead innocent of any knowledge of the fact till last evening.[20]

He reported that during the three years, a total of 15,227 letters and cards had been sent out by the headquarters of the association. Membership stood at 365 in 1879.

During the previous year, ALA had undertaken the sponsorship of a major bibliographic project: the Cooperation Committee had announced the beginning of a "general cooperative catalogue," also called the "A.L.A. catalogue." This work was to serve as a buying guide for small libraries. It was to be a carefully selected list of several thousand volumes chosen by experienced librarians. The December, 1878, issue of *Library Journal* stated that the "A.L.A. catalogue is so far started that it may also be expected next year."[21] This was, however, an overly optimistic prediction. At the Boston conference, the membership was told that the cooperative venture had inadequate financial support. Not enough subscriptions had been received to guarantee financial success for the publisher. Dewey mentioned that 200 additional subscriptions were needed, and he said that he would be willing to be responsible for one-fifth of that total. Responses from the audience completed the required total, and publication of the "A.L.A. Catalogue" was thus assured. However, the catalog did not appear for another fifteen years.

During the Boston conference, Dewey suggested that ALA should be incorporated. The chief advantages, according to the secretary, were three: (1) the organization would gain a permanence and dignity that it presently lacked; (2) the actions of ALA could not in any way become liabilities to its members; and (3) the organization could receive large gifts and hold property legally without taxation.[22] The proposal was accepted by the organization; incorporation was obtained on December 10, 1879, but not announced until one year later. With tongue in cheek, the editor of *Library Journal* explained that the delay was in the futile hope that the "first considerable gift . . . could be announced at the same time."[23]

It was decided that it would be unnecessary to hold a conference the next year, and that the time required to arrange a meeting could be better spent in consolidating the gains already made. The next gathering was very poorly attended, even though it was held in Washington, D.C. The February meeting date probably accounted for the small response. A likely impetus for the selection of Washington was the repeated urging of the Librarian of Congress, Ainsworth Spofford. He, and librarians in general, were concerned about the lack of progress in the development of plans for the new Library of Congress building. Spofford wrote to President Winsor that the "Library of the Government needs the aid and influence of the assembled Librarians" in the struggle to get a new building approved by Congress.[24] Spofford thought that the publicity, and perhaps the criticism, might encourage Congress to act faster.

At this conference, excellent papers were presented on library training and the distribution of public documents, but the main emphasis was the proposed building. A feature of the program was the address given by J. L. Smithmeyer, one of the architects, who outlined his general plans and ideas. Poole also presented a paper entitled "The Construction of Library Buildings" which could only be regarded as an attack on the architectural philosophy of the new building. He rejected traditional library "monuments" as being more concerned with architectural effect than with the user. He called for library buildings constructed on a more functional approach, with the needs of the patron in mind. After the discussion, the association adopted the following resolution:

> In the opinion of this Association, the time has come for a radical modification of the prevailing typical style of library building and the adoption of a style of construction better suited to economy and practical utility.[25]

Melvil Dewey, in his report as secretary, sounded very discouraged. He felt that very little had been accomplished since the Boston conference in 1879. Many members had no involvement in the association except the annual conference; for the rest of the year they were totally inactive. According to Dewey, a great amount of work remained to be done, but no one seemed to have the time:

> I thought four years ago that our work was like a wheel which, once under powerful motion, would run itself for a long time. But it has proved itself to be like a pump-handle, and it is not in human power to pump so hard that a single stroke will go on by its own momentum.[26]

He suggested the association needed a full-time man "working the lever all the time" as its secretary. This suggestion was later introduced as a resolution but was defeated. Samuel S. Green commented that the missionary work of ALA would be better performed by the efforts of various individuals and through the *Library Journal* than through the efforts of one man. After the resolution was defeated by a parliamentary maneuver, Dr. H. A. Holmes of the New York State Library predicted that "the time would come when the Association would recognize the value and the expediency of the measure."[27] Holmes was correct, of course, but the association was not financially stable enough in 1881—or for many years thereafter—to successfully undertake such a project.

The perplexing problem of government publications had faced the association before without solution. At this conference, a resolution was passed that is worth noting, even though it failed to produce any immediate results. In this resolution ALA called for (1) the distribution to libraries of all documents through one central agency; (2) the sale of documents at a fixed proportion of actual cost; (3) the designation of a list of libraries to receive all public documents regularly; (4) the preparation of a catalog of all public documents to date, kept current by supplements; (5) the drafting of a scheme for arranging, cataloging, and indexing public documents to be submitted to the association.[28] All five goals were eventually accomplished, but not without major effort on the part of many individuals.

The year 1881 saw several developments in the library world outside ALA. First, there was the beginning of Andrew Carnegie's library endowment, with gifts to Pittsburgh and Braddock, Pennsylvania. Second, a number of local and regional library conferences were held. The Western Library Association was formed at Springfield, Illinois, as a result of one such meeting. This was the beginning of the proliferation of library organizations. The development was partly a result of the ALA leaders' 1877 visit to

London, where they noted that the newly formed Library Association of the United Kingdom had a larger membership and was far more active than ALA. It was felt that the success of the British organization was attributable to the close proximity of the libraries and to the frequency of the meetings. Many members of ALA felt that local and regional associations could meet frequently and thus reduce the necessity of having large annual meetings. Therefore, the "splintering" of the profession was actively encouraged as a partial solution to the problem.

Early conference attendance was greatly influenced by the distance from population centers. This effect was clearly shown in 1882, when the association met farther west than ever before, in Cincinnati. Because this city was so far from the center of library activity, the meetings attracted the smallest group thus far, only forty-six. A feature of the program was the emphasis on progress reports on the state of knowledge in various areas of librarianship. Reports were given on charging systems, classification, and library architecture. Plans for the new building of the Library of Congress were an important topic: the association unanimously condemned the plans of Congress as being faulty. ALA had taken the same stand at the Washington conference, only to have the chairman of the Joint Committee on the Library Building state that librarians "warmly approved" of the new plans. In a separate resolution, ALA informed Congress that this was not the case. The plans for the building were subsequently changed, but there is no evidence that the action of the association had any influence on the decision. As an editorial in *Library Journal* pointed out, Congress hardly seemed aware of the existence of librarians, let alone their national association.[29]

William F. Poole reported at this conference that the manuscript for the new edition of his *Index to Periodicals* was completed, and that printing had begun. Poole suggested that a "general index" to works other than periodicals should be the next cooperative effort of ALA. As envisioned by Poole, the work would analyze and index essays and miscellanies under specific headings. ALA later approved this project and published it in 1893 as the *ALA Index.*

LAKE GEORGE CONFERENCE, 1885

It had originally been intended to have the 1884 conference in Toronto. A meeting of British scientists was scheduled there in September, and it was believed that many members of the Library Association of the United Kingdom would be in attendance. When it was discovered that there would be no British librarians present, the 1884 meeting was cancelled. The executive board then decided to meet at Lake George, New York, in September, 1885. This action set a pattern of meeting at a resort in alternate years which was generally followed until ALA became too large to be accommodated by any resort.

An interesting highlight of the Lake George meeting was another clash between Poole and Dewey. This time it involved the question of transliteration. Dewey wanted the association to endorse the method of using letters rather than phonetic sounds. From the discussion it was obvious that few people really understood the principles of transliteration, and Poole therefore questioned the wisdom of a vote:

> What authority will any opinion have which we may express? We do too much voting. I have never asked the Association to endorse by vote any of my hobbies in methods of library work. . . . I will accept Mr. Dewey's opinions on some subjects [laughter]; but these opinions will not be strengthened by a vote of the Association.[30]

J. N. Larned commented that "Mr. Dewey is trying to get some opinion out of us who haven't any opinion."[31] Charles Cutter also joined in. He was chairman of the Transliteration Committee but admitted he knew very little about the subject:

> I do not think either that the Association knows anything about it. [Laughter] And I do not think that a definite vote at this time is desirable[32]

The opposition was too much for Dewey, and he withdrew his motion for endorsement.

At this meeting, the association completed its first decade of existence, and President Winsor announced that he would not be a candidate for re-election. He had written previously to Dewey that the association would be better off if it had a president who could "take a more active role in looking after the success of our meetings" and that Dewey should consider the letter his resignation.[33] He had served as president since 1876. Although there was no evidence of any dissension in the organization because of his long tenure, it was generally believed that the precedent should not be continued. If all offices of the association were open each year, there should be greater interest among the membership. The result was that only the secretary and the treasurer remained in office; even the committee memberships were changed as a result of this desire for wider participation. William Frederick Poole was elected ALA's second president.

During this initial period, the headquarters of the association was not the office of the president but that of the secretary, Melvil Dewey. Although the headquarters moved when he moved, it is perhaps a slight exaggeration to say that, for ALA's first fifteen years, its headquarters was one of Dewey's desk drawers.[34] The official designation was made in April, 1879, when the executive board agreed to call his Bibliothecal Museum the Office of the Association instead of Office of the Secretary. The museum was composed of two rooms at 32 Hawley Street in Boston, the center for Dewey's library supplies business and the Boston office of *Library Journal.* The museum prospectus clearly shows the visionary spirit of Dewey:

> There must be a library clearing-house for a score of different purposes—a librarian's Mecca, containing enough not to be found elsewhere, to repay something of a pilgrimage.[35]

Dewey had special display cases made to house the "library appliances" put on view for visiting librarians. In 1883 the office burned down, but Dewey reported that almost all the ALA materials were saved from destruction. The office or headquarters would move around as different men accepted the job as secretary. But it was the hope and dream of many members that the day would come when the association could afford its own offices.

SUMMARY

The end of Winsor's tenure as president of ALA may also be considered the end of the first segment of the association's history. During this period, the organization was firmly established, although its membership remained well under 500. Progress in the profession had been helped through the leadership of ALA members. A new edition of Poole's *Index* had been published, and work on the "General Index" had begun. Standardization had been promoted by general policy positions that ALA had taken. An excellent body of literature had already been established by the many papers presented at the conferences, as well as those published in *Library Journal,* the association's official publication.

If there were successes, there were also disappointments. The history of the association during the period was largely that of the conferences, for little was accomplished between meetings. As Charles Cutter remarked, the conferences were a "whip" to the members. Members noticed that the Library Association of the United Kingdom was more viable and were jealous of its activities. By comparison, ALA was thought by some to be "decaying"; certainly interest lagged between meetings. Support of the association by librarians in general was poor, if judged in terms of numbers. Support of its official publication was even worse. It was only through the charity of its publisher that *Library Journal* continued to exist during these lean years. Even in its activities, the association was led by its members rather than providing leadership itself. Its greatest accomplishment was the new edition of Poole's *Index,* and yet the association carefully avoided becoming financially involved in the venture. The *Index* was the work of cooperating librarians. Poole assumed full financial responsibility for it, but the association received most of the credit for the publication.

During this period, the chief concerns of librarians at conferences, as revealed in the papers and discussions, were technical matters. Attention to minute detail, such as the stamping of title pages, size of cards, length of shelves, and bibliographic description on cards, occupied their attention. This was understandable in view of the lack of library manuals and the inadequacy of library training; one might guess, however, that the topics must have been less than interesting to scholars such as Winsor who cared not for the technicalities or for attempts at standardization.

3

CONSOLIDATION AND EXPANSION

*T*he period following Winsor's resignation was one of both consolidation and expansion. The annual conferences of the association continued to be the focal points of the organization's activity. The emphasis at the conferences was almost always on the formal papers presented and the discussions they engendered. Very much in the tradition of the schoolmaster, the speaker expounded on the subject at hand and then answered questions from the audience. Older librarians in the audience offered their comments, and a protracted debate might very well follow. For example, the 1894 conference had an extended discussion on the place of newspapers in the reading rooms of public libraries. John Cotton Dana, then librarian of the Newark Free Public Library, questioned the wisdom of providing free newspapers (and free fiction) in public libraries. To the complaint that his policy would deprive some of the public of access to newspapers, he declared,

> Omitting newspapers from libraries is not "depriving" anybody of them, any more than omitting Sanscrit text is "depriving" any one of his due philological privileges.[1]

The attack was taken up by Frederick M. Crunden, librarian of the St. Louis Public Library, who maintained that anything covered in newspapers was described in better form in the weekly magazines, such as *Nation* and *Harper's Weekly*. And as for the people who did their newspaper reading in libraries:

> So far as I have observed, the people who come to the newspaper reading room only are the people who really do not count for

much anyway. They are the driftwood of society that has little influence one way or another. . . . The people whose opinions amount to anything get the papers somewhere else. . . .[2]

The typical conference covered many subjects in like fashion, thus affording the younger librarian a quick education in library techniques, or at least contact with the opinions of the elders. William C. Lane, president in 1899, looked back at the early conferences and wrote,

> For many years these meetings of the ALA were the only opportunity for librarians to come together and know one another and carry back to their individual work a quickened sense of responsibility and a new consciousness of power to grapple with difficulties.[3]

Attendance varied with the location of the conference, the time of the year, and the convenience of the transportation. A large attendance was not always a prime consideration, as it was generally recognized that the association could perform some "missionary" work simply by meeting in a city or an area with poorly developed library service. Conferences called attention to what other cities were doing and also acted as a stimulus to local librarians.

Library leaders were fond of saying that the conference was comparable to a vacation for librarians, and this seemed to be particularly true when the association began meeting in alternate years at resort areas. Conferences certainly were meant to be entertaining as well as educational. The evenings were always given over to social events, such as dinners, dancing, and humorous speeches. When possible, the conference included side excursions to local attractions. Postconference trips by boat or train were a common conclusion to the annual meetings.

Foremost among the leaders who enjoyed the social events and contributed to the humorous speeches was William Frederick Poole, ALA's second president. At the beginning of his first term, Poole was sixty-four years old; yet two years later, he left the Chicago Public Library and assumed the directorship of the Newberry Library. He was an imposing figure, about six feet tall and powerfully built. Poole wore a beard as well as side whiskers, and his eyes were apt to twinkle even when he was engaged in heated debate with Dewey. A contemporary described his platform presence in the following manner:

> Rising to his feet, and adjusting his eyeglasses, he gazes in a benignant manner upon the audience before proceeding to read from his notes. A slight impediment in his manner of speaking, and his

occasional departure from the written notes, to take the audience
into his confidence, so to speak, give him one of the most winning
expressions possible. He is plainly a man with whom the joy of
living will always count for more than mechanical routine. His
mellow view of life is something which imperceptibly communi-
cates itself to those who are brought into contact with him.[4]

He was a scholar-librarian, as can be attested by the fact that, like Winsor,
he was later elected president of the American Historical Society.

The 1886 conference was held in Milwaukee, and in spite of the fact that
the site was the westernmost yet chosen, the meeting attracted the largest
attendance up to that time. The most important outcome of this conference
was the establishment of a publishing section. Its stated purpose was to
further cooperation among libraries by preparing and publishing bibliographies, indexes, and special catalogs. The section began by assessing a membership fee of a dollar a year, which entitled members to receive all publications. This assessment policy was unsuccessful and was soon dropped because of lack of response. The section then turned to the more common
practice of charging individual prices on its publications. The establishment
of the publishing section is important for two reasons. It led to an increase
in the publishing of important library materials that might not be economi-
cally feasible for commercial publishers to undertake. It also indicated that
the association intended to take an active part in publishing. During its
first ten years ALA only endorsed publication of professional literature
undertaken by others. The establishment of the section, along with a firmer
basis for ALA itself, enabled the development of a concrete publishing
program.

In 1886, Poole was reelected president of the association. He was supposed to be the last president to serve two consecutive terms, as the organization had decided at its Buffalo meeting in 1883 that it would not again
reelect its president.[5] In the opinion of this writer, this extraconstitutional
decision was a significant change because it relegated the presidency to a
ceremonial position. No person elected would be able to gather personal
power during the one-year term of office. As a result, the power of leadership eventually devolved to an executive officer, not the president of ALA.
For as the organization grew larger, it required a permanency in its leadership that could not come from the president.

A number of topics occupied librarians, but possibly the most heated debate developed over the subject of classification. At this time, there were
several classification schemes, each with its very vocal adherents. In the
pages of *Library Journal* during 1886 there are many articles on the sub-

ject, especially concerned with the "Dui-Decimal Classification Scheme." The discussion was so protracted and became so personal that it was the subject of Poole's presidental address at Milwaukee. He urged an end to the debate and suggested that further efforts be directed toward making classification less complicated. According to Poole, a classification scheme should be such that a librarian "who has not the wisdom of Solomon and the ingenuity of a magician" would be able to understand it.[6]

As Poole had indicated earlier, he was not a candidate for a third term, so when the association met at Thousand Islands, New York, at the end of his second year, the position of president was available. An informal vote was taken and then the executive board chose Charles Cutter as the new president. Since the informal vote was not made public, there is now no way of positively knowing who the popular choice was in this election. But one can speculate that it might have been Ainsworth Spofford rather than Cutter. The only evidence is in a letter Charles Evans wrote to Poole on December 30, 1887:

> I think your successor should, naturally, have been Spofford, and not Cutter; and the manner in which the latter was put through seems to call for a reform in the manner of voting for officers.[7]

Evans was not at the conference and therefore would have had no first-hand information on the election results. He could have obtained the news from Poole, since the two were close allies and corresponded regularly. Furthermore, if the executive board had followed the wishes of the membership, Evans would presumably have had no cause for complaint. Whatever the basis for his belief, action was taken at the next conference that prevented the executive board from acting contrary to membership opinion in elections. Following a motion by Dewey, the board was restricted in its power to act as both nominator and elector. In 1893, direct election of the officers by membership was instituted.

Since the 1887 conference was at a resort, it was perhaps appropriate that the conference had many lighter moments. Dewey gave a report on the use of the electric light bulb in libraries and its suspected injurious effects. One result was said to be an increase in freckles. But Dewey pointed out that he had observed neither an increase in freckles nor a decrease in the number of ladies using the reading rooms. Many librarians suspected that a wealthy gas company was behind the rumor campaign, which was taken quite seriously by some people. Dewey also scheduled a baseball match between librarians and other vacationers at the resort. According to Dewey, since only two of the librarians knew "which end of the bat was for the hands," the opposition was chosen from those "equally efficient." On the team were Poole as the pitcher, Winsor as the catcher, and Dewey as the shortstop. Unfortunately, the proceedings of the conference do not report the result of this match.[8]

FIRST LIBRARY SCHOOL

The opening of the first library school, the School of Library Economy of Columbia College, in January, 1887, proved to be the major library event of the year.[9] At this point, it would be useful to trace the development of this school, which was Dewey's undertaking. The first written statement on library education to be made by Dewey appeared in May, 1879. It is interesting in view of his later ideas about professional education. He proposed a training school or "librarians' normal school," to be attached to a large library. The teaching would be done by experienced librarians as part of their job. Students would be exposed to a number of different teachers and therefore would receive a variety of viewpoints. Dewey seemed to have in mind a somewhat formalized apprenticeship program rather than a library school as it is known today. However, he also predicted that someday a central library school would be necessary for the profession.[10]

Four years later, Dewey demonstrated that he had changed his ideas about library education. At the Buffalo conference, he announced that he had proposed the establishment of a library school at Columbia. The proposed school was far different from those of today. Dewey saw the program as one primarily concerned with the technical aspects of librarianship."[11]

Although Dewey's announcement came as a surprise to the profession, it should not be assumed that the proposal was novel. The idea had been discussed a number of times previously. The first issue of *Library Journal* had carried a statement by Justin Winsor on the need for such training. The following year, the delegates to the international conference in London frequently debated the question on board ship. Samuel S. Green later recalled he had suggested to Winsor that Harvard offer courses for training librarians.[12] It remained, however, for Dewey to make the formal proposal to Columbia College. In his typical fashion, he then asked the association to approve his proposal. As was often the case, opposition came from Poole:

> I have entertained the idea that practical work in a library, based
> on previous education in the schools, was the only proper way to
> train good librarians. The information cannot be imparted by lec-
> tures; and who, that is competent, has the time to do the lecturing?

I do not precisely know what he intends to do, if anything, beyond what I have stated as desirable to be done, and what every large library ought to be doing.[13]

The reaction of Dewey to this statement was to remind librarians that Poole had also opposed the 1876 conference. Furthermore, according to Dewey, Poole had since invited Dewey to kick him in the seat of the pants for that opposition. A very angry Poole threatened to make public certain letters in his possession that disputed Dewey's claim to being the originator of the 1876 conference:

This sort of talk must stop, or I shall feel it necessary to say something in public which you won't like to hear. . . . I can give the public some extracts from these letters if it is necessary. I shall be sorry to do it, but I won't be attacked by you in this way.[14]

Poole further indicated that he was tired of being called an obstructionist every time he failed to support one of Dewey's projects. He asked for a public apology and a retraction. This Dewey refused to do, but he did promise not to repeat the statements.[15]

Other librarians also opposed any sanction of the proposal by ALA. In a compromise move, President Winsor then appointed a committee to decide what resolution might be appropriate. The result was a carefully worded statement in which the association expressed its "gratification" that the Columbia College regents were considering the possibility of giving instruction in library work. Further, the statement said it was hoped "the experiment may be tried."[16] This was not the wholehearted endorsement Dewey wanted from ALA. In view of the division on the question within the organization, however, it was the most satisfactory position that could be arranged.[17] In addition, a new committee was appointed to take into "consideration all projects and schemes for the education of librarians," and to report on its findings at the next conference. In this inauspicious way, ALA began its program of evaluation, which eventually developed into the accrediting of library science programs. Thus, even before the first formal course was offered, the organization had asserted its interest if not its complete support.

Dewey's School of Library Economy at Columbia opened in January, 1887. He had done some recruiting at women's colleges during the previous year, so that a group of seventeen women and three men formed the first class. The curriculum of the school followed the general pattern Dewey had outlined in 1883, and so assumed a rather technical nature. However, there is some evidence to indicate that Dewey himself was not strongly committed at this time to either a technical program or a more broadly based curriculum. He was perhaps more concerned with striking a balance between what ALA would accept and how far Columbia's regents would go. Although the new school had been in existence only a few months at the time of the Thousand Islands Conference in 1887, it was the subject of a committee report, which was enthusiastic and friendly. The only negative comments made suggested that there might be a danger of provincialism and that the atmosphere of the school was "slightly feverish."[18]

The relationship between Dewey and the regents of Columbia College was strained from the beginning. The primary cause of the trouble was the enrollment of women at what was then a men's school.[19] Therefore, it was not a surprise when it was announced in December, 1888, that Dewey had been appointed director of the State Library of New York. From January to April, 1889, the School of Library Economy remained at Columbia, but it was then transferred to the State Library at Albany, where it was again under Dewey's direction. The following portion of a letter is illustrative of the general understanding librarians had about the situation at Columbia:

> Columbia I understand does not regret parting with it. Your surmise that there must have been an inside history to Dewey's move is undoubtedly correct. . . . It seems to be generally conceded that there was considerable dissatisfaction at Columbia and Dewey had taken "time by the forelocks."[20]

CATSKILLS CONFERENCE, 1888

The association planned to meet in St. Louis in 1888, primarily because the city's new library was expected to be completed then, but the conference was cancelled when it became clear that the building would not be ready. It was too late to plan a regular conference; so an unofficial meeting was held in September, 1888. With only twenty-seven members present, informal sessions were held at Kaaterskill Falls (Catskill Mountains), New York. As was often the case, the librarians discussed library architecture and architects. Most of the statements were very uncomplimentary, with President Charles Cutter commenting that

> I think from our experience of architects' plans that we can safely say the architect is the natural enemy of the librarian.[21]

The *American Architect and Building News* responded in September with a very critical editorial. It said that the conference of librarians had "amused itself, as usual, by falling foul of the architects." The editor wondered how architects could help build libraries, since no two librarians ever agreed on building plans. What one librarian proposed, others laughed at, according to the editorial.[22] There was more than a germ of truth to this editorial, for there is a great deal of conflicting advice on architecture in the proceedings of ALA and in the articles of the *Library Journal* during this early period. A good example of this public disagreement is the statement of Poole on the St. Louis Public Library: "I never, in the course of all my experience, saw a building constructed on a poorer plan."[23]

Other topics at the Catskills meeting included a proposed portrait index and the concept of public access to shelves in libraries. On the latter subject, it was generally agreed that such access was not desirable. According to Cutter, "I should think that in a public library in a city all the books would finally disappear."[24] The need for a published portrait index was revealed by the fact that a large number of librarians had already begun to develop their own indexes. Such a project would obviously save librarians both time and money.

ST. LOUIS CONFERENCE, 1889

At the St. Louis meeting the following year, ALA began its first attempt at subdivision. This was the establishment of an association of state librarians as a section of ALA. Provision was also made for a section composed of college and university librarians, to be formed at the next conference in 1890. Another section devoted to the work of trustees was also formed at the 1890 conference.

As usual, one of the problems facing librarians was the distribution of government publications. A committee had been at work for some time trying to obtain desired changes in the government procedures but had not yet been successful. During the St. Louis conference, it was decided to try a different method. This was the appointment of a representative to go to Washington to lobby for changes. E. C. Hovey, a trustee of the Brookline (Massachusetts) Public Library, was chosen for this task. Although he did go to Washington, and was successful in seeing some congressmen, his efforts were not immediately fruitful. It took an additional six years before Congress enacted the legislation requested by librarians. This was the United States Printing Law of 1895, and it represented the first legislative victory for ALA. It was not a victory in the sense that it resulted from extensive lobbying on the part of the librarians, but it was the culmination of years of effort and many public statements on the problem. John G.

Ames, chief of the Documents Division of the Department of Interior, predicted that librarians would in general be satisfied with the new law:

> As I view the subject, nearly everything that was desired by the A.L.A. is embraced in the new law. . . . Taking everything into consideration, it seems to me that library interests have been largely sub-served by the passage of the new law. . . .[25]

Among other features, the 1895 law provided for the centralization of the distribution of documents, which was the chief concern of librarians because it expedited the acquisition of publications by libraries.

This conference at St. Louis displayed the most evidence of internal dissension yet seen in the organization. The division was primarily between the older members of ALA and Melvil Dewey. William I. Fletcher of Amherst College presented a paper called "Some Library Superstitions," in which he criticized the "worship of decimals." Since Dewey was the founder of the American Metric Association and had maneuvered ALA into adopting the metric system in describing book sizes, Fletcher's target seemed rather obvious. Dewey wasted no time in responding to the attack:

> A man who dares to stand up and argue against decimals today must be curiously unfamiliar with their recent wonderful growth in use. . . . Such conservatives will soon stand with poor old Ruskin bewailing the folly of the railroads.[26]

Although the debate on the decimal system then ended, it was resumed later when William Poole complained that the system had been endorsed by individuals and not by ALA. He pointedly commented, "I have my hobbies, but I don't want you to endorse them."[27] Spelling reform, another of Dewey's hobbies, was also criticized. It had entered into official reports of the association, a fact that was greatly resented by some members who felt it discredited ALA.

Poole had another complaint:

> Then we have colon names. You say that my name should be W colon, F colon. I almost faint when I see it printed. My name is William, not an F and a colon. N, with a colon turned down, means Nancy. I call any man who uses it a Miss Nancy.[28]

Dewey made no comment during this discussion aimed at his hobbies. Perhaps in a playful mood, Dewey as secretary reported the remarks were made by "Mr. W: F: Poole," as he had done in the past. However, the use of simplified spelling and the colon in personal names was almost completely dropped from association materials after this conference.

WHITE MOUNTAINS CONFERENCE, 1890

The 1890 conference, held in the White Mountains, was considered by many in attendance to be the best yet held. Excellent papers were presented in such areas as architecture, documents, and the role of the trustee. There had been a special effort made to get library trustees to attend, with the result that 25 of the 242 people attending were trustees and a special section for this group was formed during the conference. Led by E. C. Hovey, the association established what was hoped to be a permanent endowment fund. Although several thousand dollars were raised, the immediate goal of $20,000 was clearly unrealistic for the association at this point.

The debate between architects and librarians was continued at this conference and was enlivened by an after dinner speech by Poole. He criticized the plans of the new Boston Public Library and the fact that that institution's librarian had not even been consulted in regard to the plans. The attack was also an indirect indictment of trustees, since they were to blame for the lack of communication.[29] This speech brought Poole a letter from his friend Charles Evans, who was to have troubles with trustees throughout his career:

> I congratulate you upon the neatness and dispatch with which you have killed a trustee. They are the natural enemies of librarians. . . . This event overshadows the rest of the work of the convention.[30]

In an interesting development, Dewey refused to serve again as secretary. He had held the position since the organizational meeting in 1876 and had unsuccessfully tried to resign in 1885. An informal ballot for president was held, and Frederick Crunden received the largest number of votes. However, the executive board then elected Dewey. In an emotional speech at the final session of the conference, Dewey declined the presidency. The membership, however, refused to accept his decision. Instead, he was given a standing vote of approval, and Dewey then accepted the position.

Just before this conference, *Library Journal* had taken a look at the number of organizations for librarians and expressed alarm.

> The library profession can no longer be spoken of as an unorganized calling. It is, in fact, beginning to be difficult to remember how many Library Associations he belongs to. . . . The danger just now may be over-organization rather than the lack of it, and it is perhaps worthwhile to put in a word of caution.[31]

The caution had little effect, however. The New York Library Association had been formed the month before, with Dewey as president. Four more state organizations began in 1890, followed by another four in 1891. In addition, there were numerous city library clubs. Whether desirable or not, this fragmentation and specialization has been characteristic of librarianship to the present time.

SAN FRANCISCO CONFERENCE, 1891

Because of ill health, Dewey did not serve his full term as president. He resigned in July after his doctor refused to let him make the long trip to San Francisco, the site of the 1891 conference. Samuel S. Green was selected as Dewey's replacement and presided over the annual conference. The meetings were attended mostly by Westerners, and only forty members journeyed from the East Coast to California. Socially, the conference was very successful, but as a working conference it was not very productive. *Library Journal* called it the least effective of any of the annual meetings. The president said later that there was so much entertainment the members were not fit to do any work. He suggested that future conferences be held in quiet, "less seductive" places.[32]

During the succeeding two years, the energy of many librarians was consumed in the preparation of an exhibit planned for the Columbian Exposition in 1893. It was hoped to have an international congress of librarians at this meeting and to sponsor a major exhibit showing improvements in library methods in a practical manner, so as to be instructional for beginning librarians. The United States Bureau of Education donated space for the exhibit and also promised to underwrite the project. Chicago was chosen as the site of this exposition, or world's fair, and it was expected that the central location of that city would attract a record attendance.[33]

A PRESIDENT RESIGNS

In the interval before the celebration, ALA was caused embarrassment by the malfeasance of its chief elected official. The association had elected K. A. Linderfelt president at the San Francisco meeting in 1891. However, in May, 1892, the executive board met to accept his resignation. The board selected William I. Fletcher as president and instructed the secretary to record Fletcher as president for the entire term. The cause of this unusual action was the arrest of Linderfelt for embezzlement. He was the head librarian of the Milwaukee Public Library and was highly esteemed in the library profession. On April 28, he had been arrested for stealing public funds, and the news greatly shocked the membership. Samuel Green, who had preceded Linderfelt as president, said, "I should have as soon suspected myself as Linderfelt."[34] J. N. Larned admitted a "painful sort of inquisitiveness" about the circumstances surrounding the case. In a letter to Poole, he wondered,

> Has he fallen under slavery to some hidden vicious habit—gambling or wantoning with women?[35]

Dewey was perhaps the most understanding and sympathetic of the leaders. He urged Poole, as "the Nestor of us all," to go to Milwaukee to comfort Linderfelt. It was also Dewey who urged the action that was finally taken by the executive committee. This was the quiet resignation of Linderfelt and the appointment of Fletcher for the entire term. Dewey further suggested that absolutely no mention of the incident be made at the next conference, but it is not likely that the subject was avoided.[36]

LAKEWOOD CONFERENCE, 1892

The association met at Lakewood, New Jersey, in May, 1892, under Fletcher's leadership. The main topic was constitutional reform, for the organization was still operating under the original constitution, which was becoming outmoded. Two features of the new constitution, finally adopted in 1893, are worthy of note. Election of officers became the direct prerogative of the membership rather than that of the executive board. This change came in the form of an amendment to the revised constitution. It was narrowly defeated when introduced at Lakewood but was passed at the 1893 conference. The second important change was the addition of a council as an advisory board with very broad powers. Under the terms of the amendment, there could be no recommendation in regard to library policy of ALA without the approval of the council, and no new section within ALA could be established unless the council approved. The association membership would elect ten members to the council, who in turn would elect ten additional members. Commenting on the addition of the council, Dewey said,

> The design is to create a small body that can move easily and economically get together from time to time to discuss important questions, which can thus be more satisfactorily dealt with than in our large conferences. . . .[37]

It was not until 1896, however, that the council was completely organized, and it did not prove to be effective or active until years later.

The Lakewood conference was the largest meeting thus far in the association's history, with 260 in attendance. But in spite of that large number, it was considered neither a productive nor a successful conference. People had complained at previous conferences that there were too many papers presented; so as a result, no formal papers at all were read at Lakewood. An editorial in *Library Journal* commented that the new format was more like that of a library club than of ALA. It sarcastically added that the program committee had cut off "the patient's head to save him from hydrocephalus."[38] The unstructured format led to discussion of a wide variety of topics, including the association's poor financial condition. A deficit in the budget resulted in dues being raised from two dollars to five dollars a year, with Dewey protesting in vain that the increase would eliminate many potential members. He suggested that the proper course of action would be to run the organization in a businesslike manner instead of raising the dues.[39]

CHICAGO CONFERENCE, 1893

The scheduling of the 1893 ALA convention in conjunction with the world's fair in Chicago lent increased importance to the choice of president for that year. It was felt the nature of the fair would attract librarians from throughout the world. Therefore, the president should be the person considered to be the greatest librarian in the country. Following this line of reasoning, Dewey was chosen to preside over the conference, and Poole was extremely unhappy over the election. He thought Dewey was trying to establish himself as the "great bibliographer and librarian of the land."[40] If, however, we can accept the statement of the executive board on the matter, it does not seem fair to be critical of Dewey. The report on nominations makes it quite clear that Dewey resisted the attempts of the nominating committee (the executive board):

> The delay in the report of the Board has been caused by the obstinacy of one member, which the other four members have finally been able to overcome. . . . We were held off by the obstinacy and persuasive powers of one man, but four of us were unanimous from the beginning that the person who should preside at that meeting should be that ex-President who has never presided at a meeting. . . . The gentleman to whom I have referred indefinitely is well known to be a man who has great capacity for work. We

therefore present to you the name of Melvil Dewey for *President*.[41]

Poole was also upset with what he thought were overzealous activities of the library school people in obtaining Dewey's election. Since the executive board was still empowered with the final selection of officers, it is difficult to document Poole's belief. There was a large number of library school students and graduates at the conference, so it is possible that undue pressure was exerted. The executive board would probably have been well aware of, and responsive to, the opinion of a vocal majority. But Poole was not a member of the executive board, and thus any knowledge of such pressure would have had to come from another person.

The 1893 conference, with Dewey as president, was a success in the number of members present, but a failure as an international conference. In spite of the attraction of the world's fair, where most of the sessions were held, only six of the participants were foreign librarians. The chief feature for librarians was the "model library" of over 3,000 books, prepared by the New York State Library School. A catalog of this collection was published by the Bureau of Education as a buying guide, and the exhibit itself was later moved to the bureau's Washington offices. President Dewey in his inaugural address pointed out that much had been accomplished during the brief existence of the association. He said, however, it was really only the beginning because so much remained to be done.

Among the innovations of this year was the introduction of two printed cataloging services. The Rudolph Indexer Company announced "the end of library cataloging problems" at the world's fair conference. It proposed to supply catalog cards for all books in the ALA "model library" at the fair, and for all future books published in the United States. The company promised cataloging for a total of 100,000 books. Almost simultaneously, the Cooperation Committee announced that the Library Bureau, a private organization founded by Dewey, would begin a similar service. Subject cards would be included, and the books would be annotated in the Library Bureau service.[42] It seemed as if the struggle for centralized cataloging, urged at the first meeting of ALA, had been won.

The year also saw the realization of the long-awaited *ALA Index,* first proposed by Poole at the 1882 conference. A review of the index in *Library Journal* proclaimed that "its publication is glory enough for the publishing section of the A.L.A., even though it never do another thing. . . ."[43] Although many librarians aided in the effort, it was largely the work of William I. Fletcher, not ALA. The association still lacked the resources necessary to sponsor and execute a major publication project.

GROWTH OF LIBRARY EDUCATION

By this time the New York State Library School no longer enjoyed a monopoly on formal library education. In 1894 the Library School Committee reported on library classes at Pratt Institute in Brooklyn, begun in 1890, Drexel Institute in Philadelphia (1892), and Armour Institute in Chicago (1893). In addition, there were "training classes" at the Los Angeles Public Library (1891) and the Denver Public Library (1893). The training classes were intended primarily to train applicants for positions in the sponsoring libraries. In addition to these schools, Amherst College began offering summer courses in 1891.[44]

The appearance of the new library training programs was not taken lightly by the New York State Library School. Dewey regarded his school as *the* library school, and as the child of ALA. When the association's membership list indicated Pratt Institute as "Pratt Library School," Dewey protested to Frank P. Hill, ALA secretary:

> It seem to me wrong to record the members of the Pratt Institute as "Library School." They do not use that name and the understanding has been that there is only one Library School. . . .
> Of course, we have no copyright on the name Library School, but I have heard yourself earnestly make the point that we should use the name New York as little as possible because this was *the* Library School.[45]

Dewey went on to suggest that the membership list should include a mark by the names of those who had gone to the New York State Library School. This was "not for the purpose of glorifying the school," according to Dewey, but to show the extent to which graduates became members of the association. Hill complied with Dewey's request regarding the name of Pratt Institute but did not add the suggested mark to indicate Dewey's graduates.

The following year, the Albany school reported the demand for its graduates was so great that most of the senior class was assigned to field work. In addition, the number of applicants who were college graduates exceeded the number of available seats in the school. The ALA Committee on the Library School predicted that it would not be long before admission would be limited to those who held college diplomas. It was not until 1896 that the committee demonstrated an interest in comparing the training programs of the various schools. The purpose of such a study was to ascertain how the programs were similar and "to what extent they diverge in their purposes and places." Unfortunately, committee members found this to be such a difficult undertaking that they abandoned it. The committee report satisfied itself with one general comparison:

> The conspicuous difference is one well-understood as a general fact, namely that the training for library work given at Albany is more strictly technical than in any of the other schools.[46]

The committee also noted that typewriting was offered at three schools; several schools offered English composition and bookkeeping. Drexel alone had a course in children's reading.

CLEVELAND CONFERENCE, 1896

The association met in Cleveland in 1896 under the leadership of John Cotton Dana. His inaugural address was a radical departure from those previously given, for it had a distinctly pessimistic view. In his "Hear the Other Side," Dana complained about the mausoleumlike structures that so often housed libraries, the low caliber of much of the librarian's public, and the low repute of the library profession. *Library Journal* criticized Dana's approach because it did not set the tone of inspiration usually found in the presidential addresses. *Library Journal* also said that the press was apt to print the speech and thus present to the public an inaccurate picture of what librarians thought.[47]

Actually, Dana's gloomy statements, then and later, were misinterpreted. His purpose was usually to try to goad the profession into action. Unfortunately, he was instead often considered a crank and a soothsayer of gloom. Some people thought he disagreed just to disagree, as a sort of principle. But Dana had a deep commitment to the profession, and he wanted it to become better. He headed a public library, but he was also extremely interested in school libraries. To promote the latter interest, he encouraged a closer relationship with the National Education Association, and it was through his efforts that a library section of that association was formed in 1896. His thorough commitment to librarianship cannot be doubted.

A novel aspect of the 1896 conference was the discussion of literature of the previous five years. The purpose of this discussion was to help guide young and inexperienced librarians in book selection. *Library Journal* called it an "inquest," with Janet Cutler of the New York State Library School acting as "coroner." For three hours, the librarians debated the merits of current fiction, such as *A Lady of Quality* by Frances H. Burnett. Most of the books were relegated to "the darkest of library limbos," according to *Library Journal*.[48] While this discussion proved to be entertaining, its value was doubted by many members at the conference. To submit a novel to literary judgment by a show of hands hardly seemed dignified, intelligent, or fitting to some people. Even though this method awakened interest, it did not lead to well-considered judgment of books by librarians.

Another show of hands demonstrated a significant change in the attitude of librarians: the overwhelming approval of free access to shelves in public libraries. Only twelve of the three hundred delegates indicated they were opposed to public access and would not allow it in their libraries. This was in marked contrast to the sentiment shown at previous conferences. Indeed, as one member pointed out, such confidence in the public would not have been shown three years previously. But some librarians had been experimenting with free access, and the favorable results were soon well known.

Following the formal conference, about eighty people went on a boat excursion to Michigan. These post-conferences were a popular feature of most annual meetings and provided a welcome relief from the long hours of meetings. On this particular trip, it was reported that even those who "succumbed to the 'whitecaps' of Saginaw Bay were ready again by evening to go ashore at Alpena, Michigan, to 'do' the town." At the end of the trip, Dana's gloomy presidential address inspired a gift. He received a five-pound box of bonbons as a "gloom dispeller."[49]

Two months later, ALA held its first special session. The purpose was to consider reincorporation of the organization under an act of Congress. Chartered by Congress, ALA would become truly national, with headquarters in Washington. It would also act as a board of visitors in overseeing the Library of Congress. This movement was apparently started by Dewey and received the support of most of the officers.[50] But at the special session, held in New York, not enough support was demonstrated for the plan.[51] It was reintroduced at the general conference in 1897, but again there was not enough support. The question was then postponed indefinitely, which meant a quiet death for the idea.

INTERNATIONAL CONFERENCE, 1897

The 1897 conference, held in Philadelphia, was overshadowed by the second International Library Conference in London.[52] For forty-seven of the eighty Americans who attended the London meeting, the eastbound boat trip proved to be a harrowing experience. On the eighth day at sea, the passengers noted a "suspicious quiet aboard which boded little good." The problem was a bent shaft, and a northward drift was soon noted. The helpless drift continued for about twelve hours before a steamer appeared and towed the boat to the nearest port.[53] Once at the conference, the Americans could not help noting how different the meetings were from those of ALA. Here the emphasis was on scholarly research, there were no committee reports, and there was a noticeable lack of discussion of technical subjects.[54]

PHILADELPHIA CONFERENCE, 1897

The association met in Philadelphia in 1897 to commemorate its twenty-first year. In that sentimental spirit, the group once again elected its first president, Justin Winsor. However, on October 22, 1897, Winsor died. The matter of succession then became a problem for the first time in ALA's history. The constitution provided for three vice-presidents, without ranking them and without providing for the event of a succession. In the past, the vice-president receiving the most votes had been considered to be the first vice-president. Thus, when Linderfelt had withdrawn from the presidency in 1892, the executive board had elected the first vice-president as his successor. Although constitutionally unclear, the succession seemed to be logical.

With this background, on the death of Winsor, Rutherford P. Hayes had assumed the role of acting president. However, custom had also decreed that the president should be a librarian, and Hayes was not.[55] Because of these circumstances, Dewey sent a circular letter to members of the executive board stating that no one could succeed to the presidency. An expression of opinion was asked for by Dewey, and as a result two ballots were taken. The January, 1898, issue of *Library Journal* announced the selection of Herbert Putnam as president.

In a letter that appeared in the same issue, Hayes outlined the logic of his action. He concluded with this statement on the powers of the president:

> In my opinion, the present constitution and custom since its adoption give to the president full powers, and leave clerical duties only to the secretary.[56]

This position would seem to be based more on anger at Dewey than on any of the structure of ALA. Little power was held by either officer, but the presidency was almost completely ceremonial. Between conferences, at least, the secretary wielded more influence than the president. This was partly because of the fact that Dewey usually served as secretary, but also because the president was in office for just one year.

Whatever the constitutional validity of his appointment, Putnam served the remainder of the term. In his inaugural address, he asked the rhetorical question of whether he was de jure president or simply de facto. He suggested the question be settled by constitutional amendment.[57] The problem was partially solved in the revised constitution proposed in 1899, which designated the "ranking Vice-President" as the successor. However, the constitution did not state which of three vice-presidents should be considered "ranking," so the potential for conflict over succession to the presidency remained.[58]

CHAUTAUQUA CONFERENCE, 1898

The 1898 conference at Chautauqua, New York, was judged to be the most successful meeting held to that time. There was a remarkable attendance of five hundred out of eight hundred members. The chief topic of discussion was library education. Representatives of each school offering courses in library science were at the meetings to describe the distinguishing characteristics of the various programs. A central question asked whether the profession should have a few large schools with strong faculties or a large number of schools scattered throughout the country. Some speakers felt that the association was not yet in a position to judge or act in this matter. But it was generally agreed that the New York State Library School had the outstanding program that other schools tried to emulate. After this full discussion of library education, the ALA secretary wrote the president:

> Confidentially, there have been not infrequent expressions among members, in the past two years, to the effect that altogether too much is said and done in ALA about library schools. And that, to them, began to look as if the Association has worked more for that purpose than anything else.[59]

It was decided that the Chautauqua conference had more than adequately covered the topic and that library education would be omitted from conference programs for a time.

APPOINTMENT OF LIBRARIAN OF CONGRESS

During the first quarter of 1899, the association was involved with the appointment of a Librarian of Congress.[60] After serving as librarian less than two years, John R. Young died on January 17. Sensing a political plum, a swarm of would-be librarians pursued the vacancy. Among this group was Samuel G. Barrows, a former congressman who obtained the endorsement of Theodore Roosevelt, then governor of New York. On January 18, Barrows wrote to William C. Lane, president of ALA, asking for his support. This Lane refused on the grounds that the position needed a professional librarian. Several days later, Lane also wrote to Governor Roosevelt regarding the appointment. He stressed the need to have a trained qualified librarian at the head of the nation's greatest library.[61] In a similar memorandum to Roosevelt, the council of ALA on January 30 recommended the appointment of a professional librarian.

On February 3, Lane and R. R. Bowker had a personal talk with President McKinley at the White House. To their surprise, the president authorized Lane to offer the appointment to Herbert Putnam of the Boston Public Library. McKinley further volunteered the information that he would have preferred to have nominated either Putnam or Melvil Dewey in 1897. After both refused, he had appointed John Young as the third-best-qualified man.

After some hesitation over the salary and the problem of independence from Congress, Putnam informally agreed to accept the position. Meanwhile, however, Barrows had decided to press his own appointment. In embarrassment, Putnam withdrew his name. On February 15, McKinley sent Barrow's name to the United States Senate. Since Barrows had promised to withdraw his name if a prominent librarian were proposed, leaders of the association felt betrayed. An indignant librarian wrote to ALA secretary Henry J. Carr:

> I suppose you have heard how Barrows buncoed the A.L.A. and enraged the A.L.A.—after having won the game,—and apparently ensured the appointment and acceptance of Putnam. It was a pity to actually succeed but then be cheated out of the victory.[62]

However, the Senate failed to act on the appointment before adjournment. This was partly because of Barrow's activities on his own behalf and partly because of a desire for a prominent librarian to head the Library of Congress. McKinley, out of courtesy, then offered Barrows a recess appointment. Barrows refused in view of the attitude of the Senate. After considerable persuasion on the part of a number of librarians, Putnam agreed to again become a candidate. His decision was communicated to the President, and on March 13, McKinley sent the nomination of Putnam to the Senate. This was more than a personal victory for Bowker and Lane; it was also an achievement for ALA. Although it has been written that ALA "did not appear to sense the importance of immediate action," this does not seem to be an accurate assessment of the situation.[63] President Lane acted within a week of the incumbent's death. This would seem to be a desirable contrast to Congressman Barrows's activities the day after Young died. Furthermore, as president of the association and acting in its behalf, Lane pressed the issue to its successful conclusion.

ATLANTA CONFERENCE, 1899

The planning of the 1899 conference presented a problem. It was scheduled for Atlanta because of the need to do "missionary" work in the South. Annual conferences were often thought to have, and probably did have, some influence on the development of libraries and library interests. The publicity, activities, and zeal of librarians undoubtedly did create a climate favorable to libraries. One of the suggested topics, however, was "How to Make the Library Do Its Part in Negro Education." The proposed topic was to have been the first real presentation of its kind, and W. E. B. Du Bois, noted Negro educator, was slated as speaker. However, in a letter to the ALA secretary, Lane said:

> I am somewhat afraid to tackle [it] and sh'd not want to say anything about it at the present. . . . If we were meeting at the North I should not hesitate to ask him to give us a paper and we could be sure of something worth hearing.[64]

The final decision was to avoid the risk of angering the association's southern hosts. The topic was not discussed formally or informally at the Atlanta meeting.

APPEALS TO CARNEGIE

During the late 1800s and early 1900s, Andrew Carnegie was engaged in the distribution of his vast wealth. Between 1886 and 1898, he endowed fourteen libraries, and in 1899, he contributed $4,000,000 to thirty libraries in the United States.[65] The thought occurred to several people that Carnegie might also include ALA in his generosity. In March, 1900, two officers corresponded over the matter. Secretary Carr indicated he had already suggested the possibility to Dewey in February.[66] Charles Soule, member of the council, responded,

> I have already pushed out tentacles in various directions for getting at Mr. Carnegie, indirectly and socially.[67]

R. R. Bowker wrote to Soule that he would suggest to Carnegie a gift to the ALA endowment fund. Carr also wrote about the matter to Helen Haines, managing editor of the *Library Journal,* in July. He explained there was a "move on Carnegie" from Wisconsin and Indiana. If ALA also asked for funds, it might make it easier to obtain money:

> . . . he would have a trinity among which to choose; or he might endow all three if he pleased (as he probably will not); but which if any he would prefer I could not guess. In fact I doubt if he would deem anything of the kind as tending to prove such an effective apple of discord . . . or as tending to the glory of Andrew Carnegie.[68]

Miss Haines replied that she agreed ALA could do much that state organizations were desiring to do. The problem was to have the fact recognized. She wondered what Carnegie's attitude toward ALA was, and whether there was any chance of receiving a grant.

Apparently the careful and diplomatic approach to Carnegie was the proper method of handling the philanthropist. Two years later, he did contribute to the endowment fund, and through the years, he subsidized many other ALA projects that will be discussed later.

MONTREAL CONFERENCE, 1900

The Montreal conference in 1900 was the first ALA convention held outside the United States. The choice of this beautiful Canadian city was appropriate at this time, for the United States itself was engaged in some diplomatic fence mending. Having recently become a Caribbean power as a result of the Spanish-American War, the nation was very concerned about the need to establish strong friendships throughout the world, but especially in the Western Hemisphere. J. K. Hosmer built on this theme in his conference speech on the brotherhood of the English-speaking world. A contemporary source said of the conference,

> The 10 days of this Canadian conference will long stand out in the record of A.L.A. meetings, in their combination of beautiful surroundings, varied interests, large attendance, and the overflowing hospitality and kindliness of the welcome extended by friends and fellow workers in the Dominion.[69]

The association had always been open to Canadian librarians, and their membership was actively encouraged. Of a total of 452 librarians at the conference, 39 were from Canadian libraries. Although the program did not emphasize Canadian subjects exclusively, a number of papers were delivered on Canadian literature and libraries. A real interest in Canadian subjects and Canadian history was demonstrated by the visiting American librarians.

Perhaps the most important feature of this conference was the emphasis on cooperative cataloging. The assembled librarians recommended that a special committee be appointed to draw up a new set of cataloging rules to replace the brief list written up in 1883. A survey taken by the Cooperation Committee revealed that very few libraries used the authorized rules because they were inadequate. There was also renewed interest and hope in printed catalog cards. The committee recommended the establishment of a central bureau to catalog books and supply the information to libraries. Fifty libraries agreed to subscribe to this cataloging service. There was a general feeling at the conference that, by these efforts, ALA had taken a decisive step toward cooperation on a broad scale.[70]

It should be noted that there was already a limited amount of cooperative cataloging. The Library Bureau had started the service in October, 1892, under Nina Browne's direction. Financially it was not successful, and the service was transferred to the publishing section of ALA in 1897. The old problem of insufficient interest of librarians remained, however, and the enthusiasm shown at Montreal soon disappeared. In January, 1901, the publishing section (then called the publishing board) announced that it was transferring the service to the Library of Congress.[71] After several delays, the transfer was effected, and the publishing board gave up on its brief effort at cooperative cataloging.

The Montreal conference led to the establishment of a section for "library work with children." The section was actually formed by the executive board after the conference was over. There was also a "round table" for catalogers at Montreal to see if there was enough interest to warrant the formation of a permanent section. Finally, the 1900 meeting saw the abortive formation of a Canadian Library Association, with affiliation similar to the state library associations in ALA. Heretofore, Canadians had simply been included in the membership of ALA. As librarianship developed in Canada, however, some Canadians believed that it was not enough to be included in an all-American organization. It was hoped, of course, that Canadians would be members of both organizations. Soon after the conference, however, the organization became the Ontario Library Association instead of being a dominion-wide group.

As the 1901 conference approached, a novel event occurred that surprised and annoyed many members. *Public Libraries,* a journal started by

Dewey in 1896, announced that it was supporting Herbert Putnam for president. Prior to this time, there had been almost no campaign activity in the organization, and any suggestion of such activity had been regarded as unseemly. Helen Haines wrote to Henry Carr on June 8:

> I don't at all approve the announcement—it savors entirely too much of politics and influence and such dangerous currents. It is the *principle* of the thing I object to—not to the items of the ticket.[72]

The campaign was unsuccessful. At the Waukesha, Wisconsin, conference, John S. Billings of the New York Public Library was elected president of ALA. It is interesting to note that, one year earlier at the Montreal Conference, Billings had written to his wife,

> There are about four hundred librarians here and probably there were never so many people together so thoroughly satisfied with their own knowledge.[73]

There is no record of any similar judgment of the delegates to this conference. Although the meetings at Waukesha attracted a large number of members and the program was varied, it was not a productive conference. President Carr noted that, in this twenty-fifth year of the association, there were a thousand members. Twenty of the original sixty-nine charter members of 1876 were still members. The organization was growing and increasing in influence. But looking forward, the president was not optimistic. He doubted if anything new could be said, or that any old ideas could be placed in a new light.[74] It was an unusual address compared to the typical glowing report members were accustomed to. Fortunately, Carr was not correct in his prediction.

As previously mentioned, the Library of Congress took over the printing of catalog cards in late 1901. At the time of the 1902 conference, it was reported that 170 libraries were subscribing to the card service. Twenty had been designated as depository libraries to receive the complete set of cards. Although the subscribers formed only a small proportion of libraries in the country, the situation showed a considerable improvement over previous cooperative cataloging programs.[75] The publication of the revised ALA cataloging rules in 1902 furthered the cooperative movement. When these rules were accepted almost in toto by the Library of Congress, a great step forward was taken by the library profession. *Library Journal* noted this change in September when it called attention to the growing "progressive wing" of cataloging. The author saw less stress given to detail and minute rules by the progressives. The progressives were also more willing to accept the cataloging done by the Library of Congress.

The Magnolia conference of 1902 had the largest attendance yet recorded at an ALA conference. Over 1,000 of the 1,200 members attended the meetings at the Massachusetts resort. President Billings announced in his opening address that Andrew Carnegie had given the association $100,-000. The money was to be used for the preparation of bibliographies, indexes, reading lists, and other literary aids. The gift resulted from a letter Billings had written to Carnegie on March 14, 1902, suggesting a subsidy for the publishing board.[76] The idea was that such lists and aids would promote circulation of the best books—a goal consistent with Carnegie's philosophy of making reading materials more readily available to the public. The gift supported a publishing program that had been rather active almost since the establishment of the publishing section in 1886. Since the program made available to libraries small publications that might not otherwise be economically feasible to publish, it was very popular with the membership.

Within ten years of the establishment of the section, *Library Journal* was pointing out its many accomplishments in spite of adversity.

> There was some question . . . whether it were worth while to attempt to cultivate the somewhat difficult field outlined for it. Through the wise self-restraint of not attempting to publish for itself . . . it has avoided the rocks and quicksands of commercial enterprises, and yet has been able to obtain for the library public the benefit of many printed publications which, without its encouragement and direct aid, could not have seen the light.[77]

The successes up to that point, and later on, were not accomplished without difficulty. The problem was in getting the members of the Publishing Section and its authors to act promptly and to work cooperatively. There was also a conflict, at this early date, between public library and academic library interests. This was brought out in 1900, when a series of library tracts planned for publication by the section were delayed by arguments within the section. President Reuben G. Thwaites had written to Henry Carr about the delay, and Carr responded rather frankly:

> The "hitch" on those library tracts lies at the door of the Publishing Section, and more especially Mr. [William C.] Lane [Harvard librarian and a former president of ALA]. . . . Mr. Lane has declined to accept mainly because not so academic as he considers they should be in their diction. I think that Dr. [George] Wires is the chief offense in that respect, but even the others are not up to the *Harvard standard*.[78]

Carr informed the president that Lane also had a tendency to "disregard and belittle" anything done by women. Since most of the authors of the tracts were women, Carr thought this to be the main cause of the problem. Had they been written by men, or had there been a man at the head of the publishing committee, "they could have done almost as they pleased and not been upset by him."

Thwaites responded that something had to be done to "break the deadlock," because the tracts were too important to be delayed any longer. The president continued,

> Is the Publishing Section really supreme in these matters? Our obstructionist friend, whom I like very much, is of course one of the best college librarians; but I am afraid that he neither knows nor cares anything of what those sturdy folk are doing who carry the gospel of good books into the city slums, the small villages, and the isolated farmsteads.[79]

Thwaites concluded that Lane could hardly judge the merit of the tracts since he probably did not know the first principles upon which they should be built. After a series of diplomatic communications to Lane, Thwaites was successful in getting the program underway. Among these tracts, which proved to be very successful with librarians in small cities, was Charles C. Soule's *Library Rooms and Buildings,* published in 1902, which covered the principles and essentials of building a small library.

Carnegie's gift, which encouraged and expanded this type of publication, met with widespread comment and approval at the Magnolia conference. But another speech provoked the greatest amount of discussion: Charles Eliot, president of Harvard College, proposed the establishment of storage libraries. He had made a similar proposal one month earlier at the Massachusetts Library Club. Even with the advance notice of what was to be suggested, many members sat in stunned silence. The plan was simply to divide books into two categories: the living and the dead. Books still in use would receive the traditional care; unused books would be placed in storage libraries, but would still be available when needed. Eliot saw the immediate need for three storage libraries in the United States, and believed additional facilities should be built as needed.[80] The immediate reaction of many librarians was negative, but as time went on, library administrators saw the wisdom of the suggestion. However, the storage library concept developed slowly: the New England Deposit Library, opened in 1941, was the first one.

On the final day of the Magnolia conference, a constitutional question was raised concerning the power of the council. President Billings had ruled that no question could be discussed by the membership unless the council had considered it previously. This was a strict interpretation of the constitution and was immediately repudiated by the membership. However, the problem was not so easily solved. The ambiguous wording of the constitution prevented an understanding of the powers of the council, the executive board, and the membership. It would take a comprehensive revision of the constitution before the issue could be resolved.

NIAGARA CONFERENCE, 1903

The problem that had engendered the constitutional question was that of concern over library discounts from publishers. The American Publishers' Association, acting for the publishers, had turned down requests for larger discounts. This matter continued to annoy librarians during 1903. In spite of the action of an ad hoc committee on the subject, the publishers bluntly refused to reconsider the matter. The result was that discussion at the 1903 conference at Niagara Falls was concerned primarily with this issue. This development revealed how strongly librarians felt on the problem. Unfortunately, no degree of feeling on their part was sufficient to influence the publishers, and the problem remained.[81]

In the area of library education, the committee concerned issued the results of the most extensive survey yet taken of the field.[82] It found that there were a large number of institutions involved in library training. These were arranged in five categories: (1) nine schools giving winter courses; (2) ten summer schools; (3) thirty-three libraries conducting apprenticeship programs; (4) twelve state colleges or normal schools; and (5) four individuals conducting correspondence courses. The committee sent questionnaires to these schools and compiled the responses. It found much to criticize. There was a general lack of faculty competence as indicated by educational background. The curriculum was generally found to be in need of revision. As many as forty courses were taught in some schools. The committee did find, however, that entrance requirements ranged from "good intelligence" to a college degree. In summing up its findings, the committee recommended the formation of higher standards and work for greater uniformity in the programs. It also called for a standing committee on library training which would submit an annual report to the association.

Although this 1902 report could be criticized because the committee membership was composed entirely of representatives from established schools, it was a milestone in library education. It was, as *Library Journal* indicated, the "last word" on the subject, because it was so extensive.[83] Two years later the committee reported that, as a means of starting discussion, certain standards had been assumed to be desirable and had been submitted to the schools for their written response. The issues ranged from whether or not a library school applicant should already have a paid position in a library, to the desirability of offering correspondence courses. The responses of the library schools were so disparate that the committee felt unsure of its ground and could not offer unanimous recommendations. But it did offer the following tart statement:

> As the Association will see, there is unanimity on almost nothing, which shows two things: first, that the library schools are themselves somewhat uncertain as yet as to the necessary foundations of their work, and second, that it is time thought was being given to the subject.[84]

The two committee reports opened the way to the later formulation of library education standards by the association.

AN OFFICIAL JOURNAL

A growing sense of importance and ambition can be seen in an action taken in 1904. Meeting in Atlantic City, the publishing board discussed the possibility that the association might publish its own official periodical, to be sent free to all members of the association. The magazine was conceived as a reviewing periodical that would also include articles of general interest, occupying an intermediate position between *Public Libraries* and *Library Journal.*

Although several members stressed that the proposed periodical would not compete with *Library Journal,* it was clear from the discussion that it would actually be very competitive. Furthermore, *Library Journal* was criticized as being "tinged with commercialism." This charge seems to have been left over from the struggle with the American Publishers' Association over library discounts. At that time, many librarians felt that *Library Journal* was too close to the publishers to really press the librarians' viewpoint. John Cotton Dana had been the most outspoken opponent of the publishers' plans and was a leader in planning the new periodical. Dana had also been instrumental in the establishment of *Public Libraries* in 1896.

Talk of the new periodical upset R. R. Bowker, publisher of *Library Journal.* He resented the feeling that his publication had not totally supported librarians against the publishers. He believed the history of *Library Journal* showed its support of the library movement even before ALA was established. Bowker indicated in a letter that he felt the leaders of the association did not really appreciate all the sacrifices he had made in behalf of ALA.[85]

The threatened competition did not develop until 1907, when the *ALA Bulletin* was started. Although the *Bulletin* was given the "Proceedings" of the association to publish, it was not given the designation of "official organ." In a move designed to placate Bowker, *Library Journal* was continued in that capacity until Bowker resigned on May 13, 1907. However, the executive board then urged the council to reconsider its action. The result was that *Library Journal* continued as the official organ until the *ALA Bulletin* was so designated in 1908.

The change was not particularly advantageous to the membership, although the *Bulletin* was free. It was a rather pitiful publication in its early years, hardly deserving of its official designation. Poorly written, unattractive, and without financial support, it offered nothing that *Library Journal* did not already provide. But its existence did hurt *Library Journal* in terms of loss of subscribers for a number of years, an unfortunate result in view of that publication's long and dedicated relationship with ALA.

Another example of the publishing board's expanded activities was the birth of a new reviewing periodical, the *Booklist*. This began with a double issue in February, 1905, under the editorship of Caroline Garland. It was, as *Library Journal* pointed out, a "modest" little bulletin, only twenty-four pages in length, annotating recent books. Miss Garland had been a public librarian, and it was basically to the public library that the new periodical was geared. Its value was immediately seen by librarians and especially the various state library commissions. Largely because of multiple subscriptions by the commissions, the number of copies distributed quickly reached three thousand. While its value was apparent, it also had a readily discernible weakness: it was late in noting new books. This was acknowledged by the chairman of the publishing board several months after *Booklist* began publication:

> It has to be admitted that it is likely always to be disappointing in that it cannot, in the nature of the case, give well-digested criteria or even descriptive notes quite as early as they are wanted.[86]

Even with this major criticism, *Booklist* was a much needed and potentially valuable publication. It was also a further indication of the publishing board's responsiveness to the need of librarians.

While the work of the publishing board indicated what could be accomplished by working together towards common aims, the 1907 conference was the first real example of a political campaign. It had been the tradition since direct election of officers began to have a nominating committee prepare a slate of candidates, which was then elected by the membership. However, there was considerable opposition in 1907 to the list of candidates prepared by the nominating committee. A group of "radicals" headed by John Cotton Dana proposed a second slate of candidates, and the ensuing campaign was the most hectic of the association's brief history. The "scandalous" activities disturbed many members and brought a reprimanding editorial from *Library Journal,* which said that the polls were

> . . . a center for electioneering hitherto unprecedented in the annals of the Association. . . . While a general feeling of friendliness prevailed, there were cross currents of agreement and disagreement on the conduct of headquarters . . . and other vexed questions, and a regrettable amount of "corralling" of uninformed delegates.[87]

Arthur Bostwick, the rebels' presidential nominee, was their only successful candidate, and he found that he could do very little once he was in office. By his own account, he was a "rebel President with a conservative cabinet." The disruptive campaign necessitated a term of office concerned largely with healing political wounds, and the president could do little to satisfy the desires of his radical compatriots. Bostwick wrote that Dana was particularly insistent that the new president should make greater use of the powers of his position. This Bostwick refused to do, and the result was the gradual destruction of the friendship between the two men, according to Bostwick.[88]

ESTABLISHING A HEADQUARTERS

Before Bostwick took office, the association had for a short time been successful in establishing a headquarters and hiring an executive secretary. These accomplishments had been the culmination of long-held plans and dreams, but it was a speech given by George Iles that acted as the immediate spark to ignite interest once again. At the Niagara conference in 1903, he said:

> For years it had been plain that the work of this Association could be broadened and bettered if it had a headquarters at a leading center of library work. There might be gathered everything to inform the founder or the architect of a library, everything to aid a librarian in choosing books wisely, in making them attractive to his whole public.[89]

No action was taken immediately, but others took up his proposal.

Dewey was also rather visionary as to what a headquarters should be and what services it should perform.

> We must have a great central clearinghouse not alone for duplicate books but also for ideas and methods. . . . The system of library institutes now in its early but vigorous infancy will develop, and methods, conductors, and inspiration will be found in the new headquarters for this form of library training. Definite teaching by correspondence as well as desultory advice will center here. . . .[90]

Dewey was careful to stress that the ALA headquarters of the future should not undertake anything that could be done elsewhere, especially at the Library of Congress.[91] Arthur E. Bostwick, then of the New York Public Library, thought of the headquarters as a form of social club, with a librarians' library and a museum. He also believed that it should be a publication house.[92] In view of the financial condition of ALA, all of the ideas were quite visionary. Iles, for example, had in mind a plan that would appear to be entirely beyond the means of the small association:

> A million dollars would provide a suitable site, building and equipment, and would leave for endowment a sum which would greatly lift the efficiency of our libraries as a whole.[93]

As to the location of headquarters, there was some agreement on possible cities. Bostwick was willing to settle for a large city that was also a governmental center, such as Washington, or a geographic center, such as Chicago; but he preferred New York. Dewey was in favor of New York because of the number of large libraries there and because it was the center of the publishing industry. He opposed Washington because of its climate, keeping in mind the location of a library school at headquarters. A Committee on Permanent Headquarters met and approved an outline of activities for the new headquarters.

Unfortunately, the immediate result of all this discussion was failure because of lack of money. However, through continued discussion and planning, the committee was finally able to develop a workable solution. By combining the needs and resources of the publishing section and the association, it appeared as if a permanent headquarters might be possible. It will be recalled that Andrew Carnegie had given the association $100,000 for the development of indexes, bibliographies, and reading lists. Thus the publishing section was wealthy in comparison to its parent. But it was hoped that the association might be able to develop a considerable endowment fund that would cover its share of the expenses. In an effort to save money, it was decided to locate in Boston, where office space was cheaper than in New York, Washington, or Chicago. On September 1, 1906, the office, consisting of four large rooms, opened at 34 Newbury Street in Boston.[94]

At almost the same time as the association opened its "permanent" headquarters, it also employed an "executive officer," E. C. Hovey. Hovey was not a librarian, but ten years previously he had served as a trustee for the Brookline (Massachusetts) Public Library. He worked very hard in his new position, although the list of duties he had to perform make it clear that he was little more than a clerk. Unfortunately, both Hovey and the association's leadership had overestimated the possibilities of raising an endowment fund and underestimated the expense of running the office. The financial problems that soon developed indicated that the association had been premature in its expansion.

In May, 1907, the executive board met to determine the fate of the headquarters office.[95] It was decided to terminate the lease on December 31, 1907, and to inform Hovey that his services were no longer needed. Hovey resigned as of January 1, 1908, and the short-lived experiment with a paid officer was over. However, to a certain extent his duties were continued by the secretary of the publishing board, Nina E. Browne.

The termination of the lease meant that the location of headquarters was again up for discussion. The debate centered around the same cities—New York, Washington, and Chicago—as the most likely and appropriate for a national library association. However, the Carnegie Library of Pittsburgh was the first organization to offer free space, and this was tentatively accepted by the executive board. However, because of what was termed the "weight of dissenting opinion," the decision was then postponed until the annual conference in 1908. At that time, the executive board reversed its earlier decision and voted to move to free quarters offered in the John Crerar Library under construction in Chicago.[96] An embarrassing situation developed when legal complications forced a delay in the construction of the Crerar building. The A. C. McClurg Company of Chicago had also offered to allow the association to establish its offices in the McClurg Building free of charge, but this created a controversy. Many librarians felt that it would be inappropriate for the library organization to accept charity from a bookdealer. A resolution opposing the acceptance of the McClurg offer was passed at the Minnetonka, Minnesota, conference in 1908. *Public Libraries* commented sarcastically,

> The fact that there are five floors devoted to offices and various
> other classes of business between the space allotted to the ALA

and the book store did not seem to offer sufficient safety in the minds of some, to the morals of the unwary librarians who might wander into headquarters.[97]

The vote of the executive board to move to Chicago was still in effect, and several avenues were explored in that direction. The McClurg Building space was offered once again, but this time under the guise of the Chicago Association of Commerce; it was rejected by the committee charged with the responsibility to obtain headquarters in Chicago because the strength of the Minnetonka resolution vote left no doubt as to membership opinion. Even though the committee was chaired by C. W. Andrews of the John Crerar Library, no other library in Chicago could be persuaded to offer ALA space. One institution, the Field Museum of Natural History, did offer to provide the space, but it was rejected because of its location and because the offices in question were not desirable. These circumstances forced the organization to renew its lease in Boston.

The move to Chicago became a reality in 1909, after the Chicago Public Library, in a letter dated May 17, 1909, offered a large room and free utilities. The Chicago Library Club agreed to furnish the office and also to make arrangements for the move from Boston. The publishing board promised to contribute $1,500 annually so that an executive secretary could be hired. The executive board gratefully accepted these offers on June 28 and appointed Chalmers Hadley executive secretary. The new headquarters opened on September 1, 1909, and Hadley took over his position that same day.[98]

CONSTITUTIONAL REVISION

While the association was settling the problem of a permanent headquarters, it was also engaged in constitutional reform. At the 1908 and 1909 conferences, the primary thrust of the revision was in the strengthening of the executive board. The constitution of 1899 had failed to indicate clearly the division of power between the executive board and the council. Although the council was originally established as a deliberative body, it had never acted as such. The executive board, intended as a decision-making body, had had some of its power usurped by the council. To complicate the problem, the association had established the American Library Institute in 1905. The institute was intended to become a research and deliberating body such as the council had never been. Limited to 100 members, the institute was conceived as an organization of leaders and former officers of

ALA. However, it was never successful even as a deliberating body. It had inactive leaders, infrequent meetings, and poor attendance. Its similarity to the council confused members. As *Library Journal* pointed out, it was the fiifth wheel in the association.[99]

Under the constitution adopted in 1909, there could be no confusion as to authority. It stated, "The business affairs of the Association [are] to be entrusted to the executive board" unless otherwise specified. The board was to consist of the president, two vice-presidents, and six other members elected by the membership. The council was restricted to discussing library questions that involved policies of the association. No such questions could be voted by the membership without previous consideration by the council. The council was to consist of (1) the executive board ex-officio; (2) all ex-presidents of the association, and (3) fifty additional members, one-half chosen by the council and one-half chosen by the membership.

The autocratic nature of the council, as well as the self-perpetuating feature of membership, were both immediately apparent to some members. The power of debate was in the council, and the power of action was in the executive board.[100] Little was left to the membership except the power to offer votes of appreciation. One member called it "the most autocratic constitution I have ever heard of outside of Russia.[101] Nevertheless, the new constitution was approved in 1909.

SPECIAL LIBRARIES ASSOCIATION

The Bretton Woods conference in 1909 was the scene of the establishment of the Special Libraries Association. During the fourth session of the conference, John Cotton Dana took the floor to talk about the growing trend of special libraries and the need for an organization that would be more concerned about them. He asked interested librarians to meet after the session to discuss the matter further. This was done, and the Special Libraries Association (SLA) became a reality on July 2, 1909. Few of the twenty-six librarians at the first meeting were actually in special libraries. Seventeen were public librarians and two were not directly connected with libraries.[102] The purpose of the new organization was to promote effective cooperation among librarians doing special library work.

A problem at this time, and for some time to come, was in defining the term *special library*. When the term was first announced, Dana limited it to include municipal and legislative reference, commercial, technical, and public welfare libraries. In time, this definition was broadened and a unifying theme for special libraries was discovered, but during the formative years there was a noticeable lack of cohesiveness in the SLA. Dissatisfaction with ALA was perhaps the one common bond, as recalled by an early leader:

> The ties uniting special librarians at the outset were largely negative. They were dissatisfied with the American Library Association, but it must be admitted that they had little that was constructive to offer instead.[103]

It is interesting to note that, in spite of the dissatisfaction with ALA, there was at this time a strong desire to maintain a close relationship with the parent organization by becoming affiliated with ALA. The often extreme unhappiness between the two organizations was a later development and does not seem to have been present at this time.

INTERNATIONAL CONFERENCE, 1910

The international conference of 1910 at Brussels overshadowed the annual conference of ALA. There were four official delegates from the association in a group of thirty-seven librarians from the United States. Two congresses were actually held in Brussels during August. The first, a meeting for those interested in bibliography and documentation, took place on August 25–27. The second, on August 29–31, was for librarians and archivists.[104]

Several of the activities of the congresses are still worthy of note today. Following the lead of American libraries, the delegates went on record as favoring the least possible barrier between the reader and the book in libraries. While this recommendation might seem insignificant in the United States, the idea was a radical one in many other countries. The battle for public access to shelves had been won in American libraries, but advance notice was still necessary in many foreign libraries in order to obtain a book.

A second accomplishment was the acceptance on general principles of the Dewey Decimal System as the basis for an international classification system. It had been feared by some that there would be an attempt to make the acceptance of the decimal system universal, without significant change. The result was perhaps a compromise, since it was recognized that modification might be necessary, and that well-established libraries might want to continue to use their own system. In the area of international cataloging rules there was also general agreement. The Anglo-American rules were presented in French translation as a starting point for discussion. It was voted to adopt an international code, based largely on the Anglo-American code, but covering a minimum of points on which there could be general agreement.[105]

OTTAWA CONFERENCE, 1912

The ALA met in Canada for the second time when it convened in Ottawa in 1912. Although it was hoped this would be an international gathering, there were very few delegates from abroad. However, the large number of Canadian librarians present indicated once again the ALA was not limited to the United States. The conference was considered to be a pleasant event, but it produced little of significance. The theme was the importance of the librarian's personality. The result of this theme was a collection of vague and trite papers. However, in one area an important step was taken. After a number of years of fruitless pleading, the Committee on Library Training was granted $200 for the inspection of library schools. Although this amount was very small, the allocation represented an important move toward control over library education.[106] It is interesting to note that the committee was not able to spend all its money, and the same amount was carried over to the next budget.

Several social aspects of the Ottawa conference are also worth noting. Library school dinners had been increasing in number as schools grew in importance and in number of alumni. One conference goer noted the following:

> It is evident that the library schools are gathering traditions with age; and their alumni associations are growing in pardonable self-consciousness. A new feature was the exchange of rival "yells" ... One heard more or less at Ottawa of "the girls of our class," "dear old Pratt," "the way we do it at Albany," "the tradition of Wisconsin" (five years old!) and the like.[107]

Not all of the conference was friendly and pleasant, however. At one of the garden parties held during the week, the music was furnished by a Canadian regiment that was apparently unaware that some animosity still remained from the American Civil War. One of the songs played was "Marching through Georgia," which had an unpleasant effect on those who had been "marched through." Tempers flared for a time, but soon calmer dispositions prevailed. A second incident concerned the close relationship of the two nations. A delegate from the United States suggested in talking with a United Empire Loyalist that the countries should unite. Previously the president of the association, Theresa Elmendorf, had also made several comments that seemed to suggest the same thing. This was too much for the loyalist, who proceeded to give the librarian an unfavorable lecture on the revolutionary forefathers.[108]

During the annual conference of 1913, Mary W. Plummer, director of the Library School of New York Public Library, presented the principal paper to the professional training section. Miss Plummer defended the schools from the criticism of being followers rather than leaders. Although she stressed the need for experimentation, she said,

> It is not for the schools to practice or to teach library innovation—their business is to watch innovations and their results and report to their students.

Miss Plummer stated further that schools should not try to make every student a cataloger. Instead, efforts should be concentrated on those few people who would make good catalogers. Although the time was not yet ripe for change, she thought that within ten years cataloging would be offered as an elective in library schools.[109]

LEIPZIG EXHIBITION

The increase in tension in Europe in 1914 had eliminated the possibility of there being any international librarians' conference. However, the first International Exposition of the Book Industry and Graphic Arts was held in Leipzig, Germany, in May, and ALA participated. In an exhibit that was completed just fifteen minutes before the official opening of the exposition, library progress in the United States was graphically presented. There were separate sections devoted to the Library of Congress and to an exhibit of library work with children.

Within minutes after the opening, the ALA exhibit was visited by the king of Saxony, Frederick Augustus, under whose patronage the exposition was held. The king stopped and asked questions of Frederick P. Hill, chairman of the exhibit committee. Hill was so nervous, as he later recounted, that he forgot to include "your majesty" in his responses, but it was obvious to him that the exhibit had been singled out for special recognition. Later that evening, an official came to Hill to say that he hoped Hill appreciated the honor of having been presented to the king. He said the king intended to honor America in doing so, and wished Hill to tell his countrymen of the respect that had been paid.[110] The special treatment accorded Hill and the exhibit was apparently due to the growing hostility in Europe. The German government apparently hoped that the United States would either remain neutral or support Germany in the approaching war.

LIBRARY WAR SERVICE

Two months after the opening of the Leipzig Exposition, World War I broke out. A large number of librarians were in Europe and particularly in Germany, since the exposition was still in progress, and they found the conflict bewildering and frightening. At this point, war could not damage their respect and friendship for both German and French librarians. In September, it was still possible for *Library Journal* to state in an editorial,

> Our sympathy is with each and all of the contestants, our only
> hope an early return of peace.[111]

The effect of the war on libraries even before active American involvement was immediate and disastrous. Municipalities reduced their budgets and services, and public libraries everywhere had to make do with less income. The Los Angeles Public Library closed one of its branches for lack of funds.[112] Other large libraries faced similar situations. Activity within ALA likewise almost came to a halt. There was a large increase in membership in 1914 because of the record attendance at the Washington conference, but membership grew very slowly during the following four years of war. Even the important fortieth anniversary year of the association failed to produce much activity beyond a large conference attendance.

As part of the celebration of the association's anniversary, it was planned to invite the surviving charter members to attend. Among these was Melvil Dewey, who had retired from the library profession to his Lake Placid, New York, home. Even at this time, Dewey was capable of arousing strong emotions among librarians. One of those was Mary Plummer, president of the association. In a letter marked "confidential," she wrote about inviting Dewey:

> There is no demand on the part of librarians for M.D.'s presence
> at meetings, except in the case of Mr. Hill and one or two others,
> who have their personal reasons. Quite aside from the Scandal
> of some years ago, it seems strange to me that those who know
> the man's character as well as we do can wish him to figure again
> as a representative of the profession and exercise an influence over
> the younger and newer members that in the long run would be un-
> fortunate, since they too would finally come to know his essential
> falsity. I shall never, as long as I am a member of the profession,
> consent to meet him.[113]

Miss Plummer was spared the need to meet Dewey, since neither attended the 1916 Conference.[114] The membership sent a telegram to Dewey expressing its gratitude to "that one of its founders whose indomitable courage, energy and persistence assured the early and permanent success of the Association. . . ." Richard R. Bowker was presented a loving cup at the conference "commemorating forty years of service to American libraries."[115]

Soon after America's entry in the war, the executive board of ALA met to determine the role of libraries and librarians in the conflict. A preliminary committee was appointed by the board in April, 1917. Its duty was to determine from suggestions already made what would be most practical and helpful to the government. Among the members of the committee were Herbert Putnam, R. R. Bowker, and James I. Wyer.

In June, the committee suggested the following major activities for the profession: (1) the compilation of lists of books desirable as gifts for servicemen, (2) recruitment of more librarians, (3) a combined fund and book appeal for servicemen, (4) the appointment of a War Service Committee. After listing these activities, the committee cautioned the association about the need for coordination of ALA's war efforts with those of other organizations. It recognized that it might be possible for ALA to accomplish its war services independently. To do so would add immeasurably to the prestige and reputation of the organization.[116] However, it seemed clear that there were other groups with which ALA should endeavor to cooperate. Among these were the American Red Cross, the Young Men's Christian Association (YMCA) and the Commission on Training Camp Activities, an auxiliary of the United States War Department.

There had been some feeling on the part of members that a conference in 1917 would be inappropriate. However, there were decisions that needed to be made by the entire membership, and therefore a national meeting was thought to be necessary. As previously decided, Louisville, Kentucky, was the site. In spite of the emergency, the conference was not unlike previous meetings. The war occupied only a small part of the official program, although it undoubtedly was the primary topic of conversation. The president of the association, Walter L. Brown, did not once mention the war or its effects in his inaugural address. It seemed as if at this point librarians had not really grasped the situation. One speaker, in fact, felt the need to urge the membership not to continue "business as usual." This was the dean of the University of Chicago Divinity School, Shailer Mathews, who urged the assembled librarians to take an active role in the struggle with Germany. This role was accepted when ALA agreed to assume responsibility for furnishing library service to the American armed forces. This was a tremendous responsibility for ALA to take. It was to have a significant impact on the future expansion of the association, since it was ALA's first international effort.

The program to furnish library service to the armed forces was under the direction of Herbert Putnam, Librarian of Congress. As it was finally worked out, the program became a remarkable undertaking. There had been thirty-two cantonments established in this country for the training of soldiers. Each cantonment was to have a central library building. The buildings were of a uniform plan developed by Edward L. Tilton, an architect who had had considerable experience in planning libraries. Each library was constructed of wood, measured 120 by 40 feet, and cost $10,000.[117] In addition, the YMCA buildings in each cantonment were to be used as branch libraries. To stock the libraries and to provide them with librarians, it was agreed to have a fund-raising campaign, with the goal of $1,000,000 for 1,000,000 books for 1,000,000 men. Library War Fund Week was held September 24–29, 1917, for this purpose.[118] Although the effort took longer than one week, the fund was successful in raising far more than the original goal: $1,570,386. This amount included a Carnegie Corporation grant of $320,000 for the construction of the buildings in each cantonment, a gift announced after the success of the fund was assured. The cost of the campaign was slightly more than $44,000.[119]

The committee had hoped to man the libraries chiefly with volunteers, but problems of personnel soon became quite important. Many of the volunteers were on leave from local libraries, and their leaves were generally of a short duration. Librarians were then hired at salaries of $1,800 a year, financed by the Library War Fund. Prominent librarians were included in the list of people serving as camp librarians both here and abroad. Among these were Burton E. Stevenson, Carl B. Roden, Forrest P. Spaulding, and Carl H. Milam. The Library of Congress served as the headquarters for the service, providing space without charge.

In March, 1918, a national campaign was held to collect books for servicemen. This brought in 3,500,000 volumes, which were sent to camps here and abroad. Not all of the books were usable, but it was reported that a high percentage of the material was acceptable. To supplement the gift books, the ALA bought thousands of books with the funds collected earlier. Since there were in 1918 over 100,000 soldiers in the United States studying French, ALA bought thousands of manuals, texts, and dictionaries for beginning French students. Publishers performed an extremely valuable service by offering large discounts on books purchased by the association. Discounts of 50 percent were common, and some university presses offered their books free. Getting the books to the servicemen was a problem, both in this country and abroad. In order to get the books to European camps, the government granted ALA space for 50 tons of books per month on the transports. In addition, Gen. John J. Pershing, commander of the

American Expeditionary Force, allowed the association to have franking privileges on all mail parcels in France.

By June, 1918, it was reported that ALA, through its War Service Committee, could claim the following among its achievements: it had purchased 300,000 books, sent 1,349,000 gift books to camps and stations, and distributed 5,000,000 magazines. A total of 36 camp library buildings had been erected. Library service was available in 464 camps, stations, and vessels.[120] Truly this was already a remarkable achievement for an organization that had never even been able to raise $10,000 previous to 1917.

At the 1918 conference, Matthew Dudgeon reported on what the servicemen were reading. Dudgeon was the director of camp libraries, on leave from the Wisconsin Library Commission. He said that the serviceman's first interest was to win the war. Thus he was willing to read anything "that will help him lick the kaiser."[121] This accounted for the tremendous interest in materials on war, weapons, and military strategy. There was also a great demand for books on technical subjects. Dudgeon said that the recreational aspect of reading was overestimated by the public. He believed that there was usually a balance in reading between fiction and nonfiction.[122]

As might be expected in wartime, some people saw the possibility of dangerous propaganda in a few of the books. Camp libraries were ordered not to circulate *Deductions from the World War* by Freitag-Loringhoven. Soon after this order, it was also determined that *A German Deserter's War Experiences* was also unsuitable. All copies of this work were ordered to be returned to the War Service Committee's headquarters.[123] Additional lists of books were compiled later on for removal from camp libraries. At home, the danger of propaganda literature was also discussed. Many librarians felt that pro-German literature should be withdrawn from public libraries. As a result, the council voted on July 4, 1918, to appoint a committee to consider and act with power on the preparation of a list warning of books whose misuse should be guarded against. However, this committee never made an official report and apparently did not produce the suggested list of banned books. Presumably the end of the war removed the need to carry out the council's directives.

Pleased with the success of the first million-dollar campaign, ALA decided to conduct a second national fund-raising drive. This was to be in November, 1918, and had as its goal, $3,500,000. The funds would be used to supply every man in the armed forces with reading material he wanted.[124] Six other national organizations, including the Jewish Welfare Board and the Salvation Army, also decided to conduct fund-raising campaigns at the same time. During the month of October, there was also to be a Liberty Loan campaign. It soon became apparent to all organizations that it would be impossible to conduct the individual campaigns without a serious problem of duplication and conflict. At the suggestion of the secretary of war, Newton D. Baker, the heads of the individual war service units met and agreed, albeit somewhat reluctantly, to combine their money-raising efforts. The result was a campaign to raise $133,500,000 through public subscription.

Although rather unhappy with having its campaign combined with six larger drives, ALA was determined to be successful. With the smallest organization, association leaders were anxious to prove that it had the most capable membership. That determination helped to explain the selfish attitude the organization took towards the Special Libraries Association in the war effort. SLA had also formed a War Service Committee to direct its activities.[125] This committee attempted to coordinate efforts with those of ALA but was rebuffed by ALA committee members. They believed that camp library needs for technical materials could best be met by ordinary public library methods; so there simply was no need for SLA to become involved.

As a result of this attitude, the SLA War Service Committee was discontinued at the organization's 1918 annual conference. Although admiration for the ALA's war work was expressed at that time, there was an underlying feeling of unhappiness. C. C. Williamson, president of SLA, spoke at the conference on this problem and on the desirability of holding the SLA's annual meeting at a time and place other than that of the ALA conference.[126]

Several years later, this attitude of ALA was to bear bitter fruit. In 1922, its general session debate at Detroit was concerned with publications and how the association's publishing program could better meet the needs of various groups. When Adelaide Hasse, representing special libraries, was asked what the ALA could do in the way of publications for special libraries, the answer was a very abrupt "Nothing." She charged that, for too long, the association had had a public library point of view, and until that viewpoint changed, there was nothing it could do that would be of value to special libraries. Miss Hasse added,

> As a matter of fact I think it takes a good deal of nerve on the part of ALA at this late date to ask what it can do for special library work, when there is a well-organized association, much younger than the ALA, attempting to do it,—and doing what the ALA has not done. . . .[127]

Even at this point, it was thus becoming clear that an accumulation of affronts, neglect, carelessness, and selfishness was straining the once friendly relationship between the two sister organizations.

At the time of the first campaign for money, most librarians viewed the fund raising as a radical new step for the association, but as they looked back they realized that they had actually been quite conservative. The need for books and camp libraries had not yet been definitely established or proven. It was largely a matter of conjecture as to whether the armed forces would really use the facilities. Now that it had proven that the men needed such activities, it became easier to think in larger terms. The goal of $3,-500,000 represented a revised and enlarged concept of library service to the army and navy. The money was to be used as follows: (1) to purchase books for old and new camps; (2) to replace books worn out by use; (3) to furnish many trained librarians for service in selection, distribution, and use of books; (4) to provide library buildings in France and in the United States; and (5) to intensify the service then offered to the armed forces.

The joint campaign, which had seemed at first to be a disadvantage, proved to be helpful. The goal of $3,500,000 in pledges for ALA was easily reached in a campaign that produced pledges of $205,000,000.[128] The armistice of November 11, 1918, however, reduced the urgency of the situation in the minds of many people. Money so freely promised during the campaign became increasingly difficult to collect as people grew more concerned with their own needs. It was reported that many people and a few cities announced they would not pay their subscriptions to the united war work fund. The result was a restriction on spending of ALA funds well before there was a significant reduction of demands for its service to the military.[129]

As soon as the prospect of demobilization and discharge became apparent to the men, their thoughts immediately turned from military to civilian life. With little to do, they became restless. It was soon realized that it would not be possible for ALA to cease immediately the war service activities. There were still thousands of men stationed in Europe to be cared for. The ALA Library in Paris had just been opened on August 29, 1918, and it continued to service large numbers of men. Although the War Department announced that the troops would be brought home at once, it was soon apparent that the logistical problem of transporting them would prevent this from taking place. Five months after the armistice was signed, the majority of the men were still in Europe. For the bulk of them, disappointed over the turn of events, tedious waiting became the primary occupation. The single, negative desire was "to be out of it." The situation was well described in a letter from Florence A. Huxley of the American Red Cross at Le Mans:

> We could use a million books here in France right now if we
> could only get them, and I'm sure if the people at home only real-

ized the seriousness of the situation here as we realize it, we should have no trouble at all in getting the books. We don't want our boys to become lawless and destroy the good reputation they have made for themselves, but in a land where they do not speak the language and consequently do not understand the people, they are developing a recklessness and a lack of consideration of the rights of others, that frightens one. . . .[130]

Morale became such a problem that the military authorities were thoroughly alarmed. Part of the solution agreed to was the establishment of direct library service to every important post of the Allied Expeditionary Forces. The effect was an increase in ALA efforts although the war was officially over. Hospitals were overflowing with the war's casualties. At the request of the United States Surgeon General, ALA began to provide library service to these and to the new hospitals that were hurriedly built.

With the vast movements of men from France to America via the transports, a new phase of library service began. On the way over to France, reading material had been supplied the men by placing boxes of books on the decks of the transports. The boxes were opened and the books circulated to the men during the voyage. At the end of the voyage, the books were returned to the boxes and were then delivered to ALA in France. However, when the men began to return to America, books were too scarce in France to supply the transports. The result was the establishment of "permanent" library stations on each transport, supplied by the overseas dispatch offices. Books and magazines were supplied at first at a ratio of one publication for every four men. On most transports, however, this was inadequate because of the heavy reading demands of the men. Where possible, the ratio increased to one book and one magazine per man. At the end of the voyage, there were never any magazines and only a few "classics" left in the transport library.[131]

An interesting aspect of the postwar activities of ALA was the appointment of an "ALA Representative in Siberia" on December 3, 1918. American troops were stationed in Russia, and it was felt that effects of the bleak surroundings would be relieved somewhat by the addition of a small library. As a result, Harry Clemons was chosen to go to Vladivostok, Siberia, to develop library services for the American forces. Working with a small collection of about six thousand volumes for eighteen units of soldiers, Clemons was amazed by the popularity of the old, worn-out books. Shelves freshly filled with books were immediately emptied. Most of the reading done was of fiction, but Clemons did report that 26 percent was of nonfiction. Although Clemons did not attempt to assess the results of the program after his five-month tour of duty, others were not so hesitant. Several company commanders reported that, whenever new books arrived in the library, there was a reduction in the number of requests for leave of absence. They also noted letters back home were distinctly more cheerful for a while.[132] When Clemons left the post on May 18, his place was taken by an army chaplain, and the library was thereafter maintained by the War Department.

Instead of declining, then, with the end of the war the service work of ALA increased. The peak of activity was not reached until April, 1919. During the first part of May, there was a leveling off of activities and expenditures, but it was not until the end of May that there was a noticeable decrease in ALA participation. It was generally accepted that the government should now take over the job for the association, but everyone concerned felt strongly the need for an orderly transition. This meant that, in some situations, there was a mixed administration. For example, at Pensacola, Florida, the navy bought the library's collection for one dollar because it could not accept it as a gift. But the navy had no funds to employ the civilian librarian who was left in charge. Therefore, ALA paid the salary of the librarian, but the library was owned and operated by the navy.[133] Similar situations occurred elsewhere as the nation attempted to return to a peacetime basis.

SUMMARY

Although the war service efforts were not completely terminated by the summer of 1919, librarians could look back on their work with a great sense of accomplishment. During the war, an almost phenomenal amount of work had been accomplished through the organizational efforts of ALA. Almost $6,000,000 had been pledged as a result of strenuous campaigns. Over 4,000,000 books had been donated for the use of servicemen, and over 700 librarians served in the war service work. The effect of ALA on the war effort was indeed significant.

But the war service work also had a profound effect on the association. For over forty years, ALA had been a small professional organization with little activity other than an annual meeting. By the act of accepting a role in the war work, its character changed completely. Almost overnight, the organization became a public service organization. While it is true that this service was of an emergency nature, at least part of the change was to become permanent.

It is difficult to assess any change in public attitude that might have taken place towards the library profession as the result of the war. However, hundreds of thousands of young men had contact with libraries for the first time, and for most this was probably a pleasant contact. Therefore, it would seem logical to assume that the war experience would have a positive effect on attitudes towards libraries and librarians. Whether or not this would be translated into greater public support, as so many librarians believed might happen, remained to be seen. Undoubtedly the work's greatest effect was on the members' faith in the association as an active organization. Although the members had always seemed to have a missionary spirit about their organization, the war work was the first proof that ALA was capable of being welfare oriented, rather than being strictly a professional organization.[134]

The two financial campaigns had been heady experiences for ALA. A sizable element in the organization wanted to ensure that ALA continued its more active role in American life. The time seemed appropriate for this expansionist activity, since the public had so willingly contributed to the war services program. Furthermore, millions of men who had benefited from the library service were at home and could presumably be counted on for support. Therefore, in 1919 the association embarked on what became known as the "Enlarged Program," which will be described in the following chapter.

On the other hand, problems raised during this period continued to face ALA throughout its history. As it grew in size, the association experimented with its own internal structure, unsure of where to delegate authority and power. The single term of the president prevented that officer from achieving a significant measure of effective leadership. The rapid development of library schools, essentially unregulated by the profession, became a serious problem. The establishment of the Special Libraries Association marked the beginning of competition for loyalty within librarianship. No longer could the structure of the profession be thought of as a pyramid, with ALA alone at the top. The success in influencing the selection of the Librarian of Congress in 1899 was a major accomplishment, yet it set a standard that would be difficult to match in later years. Finally, the atypical demands and opportunities brought to ALA by World War I created an atmosphere of success that was misleading. This atmosphere led to a program of action that the nation and the profession were not ready to accept.

4

DEFEAT OF THE ENLARGED PROGRAM

*T*he movement for what was called an Enlarged Program of activities officially began on January 11, 1919. On that date, at a meeting of executive board, President William Warner Bishop appointed a Committee of Five to survey the whole field of library service. Bishop had in mind a survey similar to the famous Reports on Secondary Education and Primary Education made by the Committee of Eleven and Committee of Fifteen of the National Education Association. The survey by this Committee of Five would point out to what extent American libraries were meeting or failing to meet their opportunities. It would also establish a plan of action to meet the needs seen in the survey. Part of the result would be a group of standards for libraries. These standards would deal with equipment, buildings, services, salaries, and other areas where guidelines needed to be established.[1] The committee members were as follows: Arthur E. Bostwick, Linda G. Eastman of the Cleveland Public Library, Carl H. Milam of the Library War Service, Azariah S. Root of the Oberlin College Library, and Charles C. Williamson of the New York Public Library. The committee was instructed to make a preliminary report at the Asbury Park, New Jersey, conference in June, 1919.

At this conference, the first general meeting of ALA after the war, there was reminiscing as well as looking into the future. Many of the problems discussed were the same ones as before the war. But as President Bishop said in his address, "We are none of us quite the same as we were in 1916 or 1917." Even the trivial or routine work could no longer be done in the same way because of the war experience. "We have dreamed dreams and seen visions and we are turning to the future," he wrote.[2] Librarians could

72

not go back to 1917 and continue where they had left off. The momentum must be continued. Standing at the crossroads, the association had to decide to press on "to greater and nobler service," according to Bishop. Another speaker pointed out that, although the days of easy public contributions were over, it was still imperative for librarians to build a constructive program for future action. No longer could activities of the membership be limited to the "best reading for the largest number at the least cost," as the motto stated. Instead, it should be the greatest possible public service through books and materials, whatever the cost."[3]

PLANNING THE PROGRAM

The Committee of Five that President Bishop had appointed in January issued its preliminary report at the Asbury Park conference. The report described the proposed plan of action and organizational structure for its work, making the assumption that the survey itself would have to be done by a volunteer staff. The committtee estimated expenses for travel, clerical assistance, and publication of the final report would be about $80,000.[4] Four principal areas of library work were designated, and each was assigned to a committee member for overall investigation. Azariah R. Root was to cover the acquisition and processing of books. Linda Eastman was to be concerned with the use and distribution of books. Carl H. Milam was assigned the area of library public relations. Charles C. Williamson was asked to cover library staff and its training. The primary method of investigation was to be the questionnaire, with other methods supplementing the information thereby gained.

At this conference, Williamson presented a paper on library training that is worthy of note, although he made it clear that he was not speaking for the committee. The paper discussed the state of library training in an unusually frank manner. It was also critical of the library profession and ALA.

> We cherish the delusion that library work is a profession. At best
> it is only semi-professional. What real profession is recruited
> largely from untrained persons?[5]

It was clearly the duty of ALA to provide the leadership necessary for librarians. But Williamson said that, in order for ALA to do so, it had to become more than a debating society or social club. He thought ALA should perform two main functions in library training. It should organize all training activities under a training board with a permanent staff headed by an expert in library education. According to Williamson, there was a multiplicity of training agencies but no system and no recognized standards. The Association of American Library Schools had made some progress in raising standards. However, it was "ineffectual to produce any real cooperation." The proposed training board, similar in function to the publishing board, would establish a method of grading library positions, set minimum qualifications for such positions, issue certificates to graduates, and accredit all library training agencies. Details would be worked out by the board, with the approval of the association.

In the council meeting that considered the Enlarged Program, there was general agreement over the need to press forward. The one exception to the accord was John Cotton Dana. He hesitated, Dana said, to speak his mind because he was so often misunderstood. However, after that introduction, he showed little hesitation in speaking out. The library was likened to the human appendix: an organ that had largely outlived its usefulness. Changes were necessary if it were to be retained by society. Instead of spending $80,000 for a survey of library conditions, Dana suggested there should be a study of the library phenomenon in a print-using society. He also suggested that a study of association headquarters should be made. The organization had had an endowment of $100,000 for seventeen years, by which publishing had been supported. Over $5,000 each year was needed to subsidize this program, yet according to Dana, it would be extremely difficult to prove that "we had extended knowledge of ourselves to an extent worth mentioning." In his view, the main problem was the quality of librarians:

> The thing that stands in the way of efficient work by the American Library Association is primarily the lack of brains on the part of its members: there is no use blinking the fact.[6]

Part of the problem, he charged, was also the antiquated constitution, which was burdened with tradition. Dana proposed that a one-page document replace the old constitution, and that authority to conduct the business of the association be placed in the hands of three to five people. Whatever others may have thought of Dana's remarks, there was no public response during the council meeting, and none of his proposals were accepted.

Certainly other members shared his views on the constitution, as was made clear in President William Warner Bishop's presidential address in 1919. He called the structure "a most clumsy organization" and pointed out some of the "obstacles and anomalies" that resulted from the constitution. The executive board was allowed to take votes by mail, but the results had to be unanimous in order to pass. And the treasurer served the association without being on either the executive board or on the Finance Committee, thus depriving those two groups of his expert advice on financial matters. Bishop also had a number of suggested changes, even going so far as drafting a model constitution. But when the association drafted its new constitution in 1920, most of Bishop's ideas were rejected. Apparently as a result of what he considered this personal slight, the sensitive Bishop then withdrew for a period of time from the active affairs of the association.[7]

On June 27, 1919, the executive board approved a resolution accepting the responsibility to "encourage and promote the development of library service" for all Americans. A Committee on an Enlarged Program for American Library Service was appointed. It was to study various suggestions and prepare an expanded program for the association. Members were Caroline F. Webster, Walter L. Brown, George B. Utley, John Cotton Dana, Carl H. Milam, and Frank P. Hill. On September 9, the executive board named Milam as director of the Expanded Program. During that meeting, the board also approved the calling of two special meetings of the association. These meetings were for the purpose of considering constitutional revision and the Enlarged Program.

Constitutional reform was considered to be an integral part of the Enlarged Program. Indeed, much of the revision was done by the Committee on the Enlarged Program. In November, 1919, the proposed constitution was made public. Its most salient feature was its "democratic" emphasis, a reaction to the council-centered constitution then in effect.[8] The council was stripped of most of its powers, to the benefit of the executive board. The board was to become the governing agency of ALA. All questions of policy were to be referred to it first. All committees and boards would be appointed by the executive board. All that remained for the council to do was to discuss library questions and adopt resolutions regarding library practice or policy. The effect, then, of this constitution was to substitute the executive board for the council as the most powerful agency within ALA.[9] This change in the centralization of authority was viewed with suspicion and hostility by a large segment of the membership.

Resentment was also aroused by an attempt to move the headquarters from Chicago to New York. To many people, especially in the Midwest, the proposed move appeared to be an essential feature of the proposed Enlarged Program. It seemed to them that the leadership was trying "to put something over on its members," as President Chalmers Hadley stated.[10] He was undoubtedly correct in saying that the two proposals were unrelated and that no official plan was underway to move from Chicago. The accusation, however, was not entirely false. Certainly there had been proposals to move elsewhere. Hadley admitted that the Committee on an Enlarged Program had discussed the issue in September, and it was, in fact, at his urging that the issue was not included in the committee's report. *Library Journal* in November had carried an editorial denying that any discusion of a move had taken place. This contradiction undoubtedly added to the belief that a move was contemplated and was actually a part of the Enlarged Program, in spite of what the leaders said. Additional evidence seemed to turn up in December, 1919. At that time, the committee announced that it had established "financial headquarters" for the Enlarged Program in New York.[11] The wording seemed to be unfortunate and inaccurate. This additional staff consisted of a group of nine librarians who temporarily assisted Carl H. Milam in developing publicity for magazines. It was hoped that, through these efforts, enough interest would be generated to ensure the success of the campaign. But the announcement added fuel to the controversy and probably weakened support for the program.

DETAILS OF THE PROGRAM

As for the Enlarged Program itself, the committee had developed an extensive project for involvement on the part of the association. Part of this program included the continuation of work under the limited United War Work Fund. It was also proposed that books and periodicals should be supplied by ALA to the 2,788 men located at the nation's 273 Coast Guard stations. The appropriation would be $15,000 for this service. An equal amount was suggested for supplying books to lighthouses and lightships until such time as the federal government was prepared to take over the responsibility.[12] A similar plan was proposed for the hospitals under the control of the U.S. Public Health Service and the U.S. War Risk Bureau. These hospitals were established in 1918 for the purpose of caring for veterans and certain other government employees. Although Congress had appropriated large sums of money for the hospitals, no provisions had been made for libraries. The U.S. surgeon general assured representatives of the Enlarged Program Committee that, if first class library service was demonstrated through this program, provision would be made to carry on the work. The result was an appropriation of $100,000 in the Enlarged Program budget.[13]

The American merchant marine, consisting of 2,000 vessels, was to be given library service through an appropriation of $150,000. This would average out to less than 100 books per ship, but many of the ships had been supplied with libraries by the War Service Committee. In this case, it was more a question of providing adequate library service than a simple problem of obtaining 100 books for each ship.[14]

In addition to continuing and expanding some of the services begun during the war, the Enlarged Program Committee sought the expansion of activities through the various state library commissions or associations. This was to be encouraged through an appropriation of $85,000 from ALA, to be used in aiding underdeveloped areas of the country where library service was inadequate or not of sufficient quality. A hypothetical example was given of a large Southern city without a public library. The aid of ALA would be primarily used for public education to favorably influence public action toward libraries throughout the nation.[15]

A definite proposal was also made for the national certification of librarians. A National Library Examining Board was suggested. The board would make up an examination and establish three levels of librarians. Graduates of approved library schools would be certified without taking the examination. A tentative budget of $10,000 was included for the preliminary work of this board. The controversial library survey was also included in the suggested expansion of services. The influence of Dana's earlier criticism seemed to be indicated in an added area of study for the survey: a review of the role of the library in the social and educational life of the country.[16]

The Enlarged Program strongly emphasized information and education. A budget of $75,000 was allocated for the promulgation of the "library idea," as it was called. This meant publicity, magazine articles, library exhibits, leaflets, and a general program of promoting better library income and higher library salaries.

One other proposal resulted at least partly from Dana's criticism. He had charged that there had been no significant result from ALA's Publishing Board, and the report suggested a general review of ALA publishing, including the work of the *Booklist*. This review was to be done by someone with extensive publishing experience. Provision was also made for the future publication of bibliographic aids that might not be commercially feasible because of small demand. In particular, it was proposed that an International Bibliography of Humanistic Literature be established. This publication would attempt to cover the whole field of the humanities, and would be in the English language.

Another large expenditure in the proposed budget was $25,000 to promote closer cooperation with affiliated and nonaffiliated organizations. Although no money was suggested for improving relations with the National Education Association, this idea was also emphasized. Improvement of relations, it was hoped, would lead to a greater appreciation by teachers for the value of library service as a necessary adjunct to classroom instruction. It might also lead to the endorsement of the Enlarged Program by this important organization. Such an endorsement could have considerable impact on the public appeal for funds. As for the other organizations, such as the League of Library Commissions and the Special Libraries Association, the committee called for closer cooperation with ALA. However, there were no specific suggestions as to how the appropriated money would be expended. Finally, the largest appropriation was $105,000 for the purpose of underwriting the financial campaign. This campaign, it was hoped, would raise $2,000,000. In addition, the committee believed that the War Service Committee would release some of its unexpended funds for this purpose.[17]

The first special membership meeting called by the executive board to consider the Enlarged Program took place January 1–3, 1920. A frigid Chicago served as the site for this gathering of about two hundred members. Discussion centered largely on the program and constitutional revision. There was also a strong undercurrent of feeling about the threat of a move to New York. Of this latter problem, *Library Journal* commented that it was

> a proposal of which New York had heard almost nothing and which existed chiefly in the fearsome imagining of its critics.[18]

In view of the statements often expressed on the subject, this editorial comment was not only inaccurate but ridiculous as well.

The first day of the special session was devoted to a discussion of constitutional revision. In general, the proposed changes were approved by the membership. A major unresolved problem centered around the role of the affiliated organizations. A federation seemed undesirable to many people, yet it was not clear how the various groups could be integrated into a comprehensive organization. The membership was unable to solve this problem satisfactorily, and so a committee was appointed to effect a compromise.

The Enlarged Program actually engendered little discussion or opposition. In what seemed to be a carefully orchestrated performance, the issue was presented by a select group of respected leaders, questions were quietly laid to rest, and the Enlarged Program was approved. There were only three difficulties encountered by the leadership. First was the fact that a publicity man had already been hired to promote the Enlarged Program and to develop a plan to raise the necessary funds. Since the program had yet to be approved by the membership, this premature action caused some resentment. In answer to a question, it was explained that the executive board had already appropriated $50,000 for the program; the money had been borrowed from the United War Work Fund. R. R. Bowker apparently expressed the conviction of many that this act, unintentional as it may have been, prematurely committed the Association.[19]

The second problem involved the method of raising the money needed, estimated to be $2,000,000. The Enlarged Program Committee was very indefinite on financing. As was pointed out, the committee had first of all said that there would be no fund drive, and then it had described how the drive would be carried out. Discussion brought out the fact that the committee hoped to raise the $2,000,000 through corporations, individuals, foundations, and through a quota system for each state. Exact methodology would be determined later, following regional meetings throughout the country.

The third problem concerned the issue that *Library Journal* said did not exist. This was the threat of a move to New York or at least the establishment of a second office in that city for the activities of the Enlarged Program Committee. In a surprise move, Arthur Bostwick offered a resolution that would solve the problem completely:

> Resolved, That it is the sentiment of this meeting that whatever enlarged activities are engaged in . . . should be operated from the headquarters in Chicago, so far as possible, and under the supervision of the executive officer at those headquarters.[20]

President Chalmers Hadley ruled that this was a question of policy and would therefore have to go before the council. Bostwick appealed the decision, and the membership overruled the president. Herbert Putnam criticized Bostwick for raising the question and asked if Bostwick knew of any proposal to remove headquarters from Chicago to New York. Bostwick replied that it was common knowledge the intent of the executive board was to operate the Enlarged Program from New York. He said he was not opposed to the move itself, but to the duplication that would result from the move. The effect of this resolution was to put a stop to the suspected move to New York. It also prevented the further use of the public relations firm to head the Enlarged Program, since the resolution specified that the campaign should be under the executive officer of the association. However, the resolution notwithstanding, the work of the Enlarged Program Committee continued at its New York office for some time. The reason given was that its director, Carl Milam, was also director of the Library War Service, which was still located in New York.[21]

The second special membership meeting, scheduled for Atlantic City, New Jersey, on April 29–May 1, was cancelled because of the necessity for scheduling an earlier annual conference than had been planned. Colorado

Springs had been chosen as the site of the 1920 conference, but it had proved to be impossible to get accommodations there later than the first week in June. Rather than schedule two membership meetings within one month, the executive board cancelled the special meeting. Development of the Enlarged Program, however, went on as planned. Regional directors were appointed to spearhead the fund drives throughout the country. Meetings were held with local library groups to solicit funds and the personal support of librarians. On March 3, 1920, it was reported that loans in the amount of $202,340 had been negotiated from the War Service Fund for the Enlarged Program.[22]

In spite of the fact that ALA had at its special meeting approved the Enlarged Program, considerable criticism began to develop at this time. The focal point of the problem was the expenditure of such a large sum of money over a short period of time. The Enlarged Program had been budgeted for three years. A commonly expressed complaint was that it would be better to raise an endowment fund of $1,000,000 to support the association's activities. In this way, a substantial amount of work could be undertaken, and its management would be more efficient.

This criticism led to the publication in April, 1920, of a circular letter addressed to the members of ALA and signed by thirteen librarians. The letter pointed out that a substantial proportion of the membership was opposed to the Enlarged Program as it was then constituted. A still larger percentage believed that more definite limits must be placed on the executive board in carrying out the Enlarged Program activities. Therefore, the librarians who signed the letter suggested several guidelines to define the extent of the campaign: (1) an end to free service by ALA to government departments as soon as current funds were exhausted; (2) placing service to these departments on a self-sustaining basis, the same as service to other organizations; (3) limiting the campaign to obtaining funds for professional goals suitable for the association; and (4) requiring that adequate information be given by officials to members of the association. Among the librarians who signed the letter were such prominent leaders as Edwin H. Anderson of the New York Public Library, Arthur E. Bostwick, and Everett R. Perry of the Los Angeles Public Library.[23] A postcard indicating agreement with the letter was included for the purpose of registering dissent with the executive board.

The group later asserted they were not opposed to an enlarged program of activities. They simply wanted a clearly defined program and the establishment of limitations as to the methods used. It is difficult to say how damaging the circular letter was, but it clearly did not help the Enlarged Program. Criticism had only been hinted at in print before this. With the letter, there was a clear indication of dissension in the profession and among the most distinguished leaders. The extent of the problem became apparent later when over a thousand postcards indicating agreement with the circular letter were received by the executive board.[24]

A compromise was worked out at an unofficial meeting held April 30– May 1 in Atlantic City. As had happened occasionally in the past, ALA found that problems could be resolved through discussions held wherever members gathered. This occasion was the annual Bi-State Meeting of the New Jersey and Pennsylvania Library Associations. Critics and advocates of the Enlarged Program were present, and the discussions cleared the air of some of the differences. The main result was the decision that half of the amount raised would be set aside for the endowment fund. In addition, both sides agreed not to postpone or hinder the appeal for money.

While this compromise served to patch over the split in the organization, the end result might also have been to hurt the fund drive. As an editorial in May *Library Journal* pointed out, people are more interested in giving money towards specific activities. An endowment fund seems less urgent and thus has less appeal in a fund campaign. Nevertheless, the compromise at least ended the visible internal trouble in ALA. One month later, the association met in Colorado Springs for its annual conference. The Enlarged Program, restated to include the endowment feature, was approved unanimously. It was approved also by several sections of ALA and several affiliated organizations meeting at the same time in Colorado Springs. However, the apparent unanimity at the conference was deceiving. Some known dissidents refused to take part in discussions—although others made up for their hesitancy. The final vote was not taken until the last session, after a number of members had left. Thus the stage was set for the embarrassment that was to follow.

June 30, 1920, was originally set as the end of the financial campaign. However, this was said to be inconvenient for some librarians, and the appeal was extended. By September 1, *Library Journal* was blaming the "heat of discussion" and "the heat of the summer" for the slow progress. One month later a *Library Journal* editorial recounted the mistakes that had been made and decided that the campaign was a total loss. On September 25, the executive board issued a report on the results of the Enlarged Program, which it called "peculiarily perplexing."[25] In spite of a state-by-state account that was optimistic for the future, only $68,000 had been raised or promised. On October 11, the executive board decided to terminate the campaign for funds by November 30. When the receipts and expenditures were balanced, it was reported that approximately $80,000 had been realized by a campaign that had had a goal of $2,000,000.[26] The failure of the drive was so complete and so humiliating that the subject was almost immediately dropped from the columns of both *Library Journal* and the *ALA Bulletin*.

SUMMARY

The probable causes for the failure of the Enlarged Program are noted. Enthusiasm and the rise in organizational self-esteem, results of the two very successful war campaigns, undoubtedly played a large part in the headlong rush to disaster. An organization that had done little to attract national attention during most of its existence became heady over optimistic plans for the future. In this regard, it must be stated that the leadership was probably too far ahead of its members. It not only planned the program too quickly, but it also made the mistake of committing the organization to action before such action had been approved. The hiring of a publicity man to direct a fund drive that had not been sanctioned particularly annoyed many members. This gave rise to the feeling that the leadership was trying to "put something over" on its members. This feeling was heightened by the unfortunate attempt to move the headquarters to New York. Denials that any such relocation had been proposed, when in fact it had been, increased the credibility gap, particularly in the Midwest.

Important, too, was the failure to assess accurately the country's general reaction to the war. The American people had given a great deal in the various drives that had been held during the war. They were tired of giving—a fact that had been demonstrated by the failure of other drives. Similarly, there was an unrealistic view of the attitudes of the foundations. The leadership had apparently assumed that philanthropic foundations would be willing to support increased library service. This was, of course, incorrect. There were no large grants from any of the foundations.

Part of the blame also lies with the internal structure of the organization. It was a professional organization attempting to be a welfare organization, and its structure would have been ill equipped at this time to handle the program if it had been successful. As some members had often pointed out, ALA was undemocratic and unresponsive to change. Yet at the same time, the nature of its meetings was such that action could be, and sometimes was, stymied by the propensity to endlessly discuss minor details. The membership often refused to delegate responsibility, even though it knew from experience the problems connected with open and long debate of every issue. Finally, there was the feeling among many members that the association was trying to undertake work that was really the responsibility of the federal government. Providing library service to lighthouses, the merchant marine, and war-related activities during peacetime seemed to some members to be beyond the realm of a professional organization.

Thus, the "noble experiment" as a welfare organization was short-lived for ALA. In the process it had suffered a humiliation that would be remembered by members for many years. The experience also led to a reappraisal of the organizational structure. The dissension had pointed out the sharp differences within the organization, which needed to be dealt with if the association were to remain a viable organization. Finally, the experience brought home the painful reminder that ALA desperately needed more members. There followed a series of projects designed to boost membership and the influence of the organization.

5

INTERNAL CRITICISM

*D*uring the Enlarged Program campaign, in April, 1920, George B. Utley resigned as executive secretary of ALA. He had held the position since 1911, the longest any man had been secretary since Melvil Dewey. While the war was in progress, Utley had also served as the secretary to the War Service Committee. In both positions, he had earned a reputation for being unusually skilled as an administrator. He resigned his position at ALA headquarters to become librarian of the Newberry Library in Chicago.[1] To take his place, the executive board chose Carl H. Milam at its March 13, 1920, meeting.

Milam graduated from the New York State Library School shortly after Dewey resigned as its director. His first professional employment was at Purdue University. In 1909, at the age of twenty-five, Milam was appointed secretary to the Indiana Public Library Commission. During his term of office, he became well known throughout the country for his leadership capabilities. He was active in writing library legislation, in the formation of the Indiana Library Trustees Association, and in the extension of library services to rural areas. In 1913 Milam was appointed head librarian of the Birmingham (Alabama) Public Library. At this time, the city was small and the library was mediocre. By actively promoting the library and its potential services, Milam was able to increase its budget considerably. He had also added six branch libraries to the system. When the war began, Milam helped to marshal library service for servicemen at both the local and the state levels. He acted as state director of ALA's first book campaign and then assisted Herbert Putnam when the latter was chairman of Library War Service.[2] During this national work, Milam's administrative talents were recognized by library leaders and library periodicals. He seemed a natural choice when ALA needed a new executive secretary.[3]

PROPOSALS FOR CHANGE

The defeat of the Enlarged Program caused an intensive study within the association. Constitutional revision was not new to the membership, for it had been under consideration for some time. The need for significant change was evident to most members. Few seemed to desire continuance of the organizational structure as it had been. The problem was to agree on what changes should be made. A stronger organization was needed, but there was no consensus on the method of achieving that goal.[4]

In addition to the old problem of whether the executive board or the council should provide the avenue for leadership, other proposals were considered. A suggestion for a two-year presidential term received wide support at this time. The effect of this change would be to strengthen what had become a largely ceremonial position. A term of two years, it was felt by some, would enable the president to gain a better understanding of the organization. It would also allow him to develop a program and carry it through. Perhaps with two years in which to act, the president could provide more effective leadership to the organization.

Other members suggested that biennial conferences might be preferable to annual conferences. Under this plan the off-year would provide opportunity for regional conferences and for meetings of sections and affiliated organizations. The ALA conferences could then be occupied chiefly with general meetings for the entire membership. The assumption was that the encouragement of local participation would lead to greater participation on the national level. The need to develop a sense of unity within the profession had been shown clearly in the failure of the Enlarged Program. Biennial conferences seemed to some people to be a partial answer to this need.

Another suggestion was to organize a number of local chapters throughout the country to be affiliated with ALA. Bostwick originally suggested this idea, and he established the first such group. His St. Louis local was open to all librarians in the area. The local's function was to act as a feeder to ALA, as well as to provide unity in the profession at the local level. The obvious problem was that the local attracted many librarians who were not members of ALA.[5] This incongruity prevented any extensive development of Bostwick's proposal, although on the surface it seemed to have considerable merit.

Constitutional revision, as it was finally accepted, was inadequate. It was a compromise that satisfied few people. As *Library Journal* predicted soon after its enactment, further changes seemed to be needed immediately.[6] The major change made at this time was in the procedure for nominating officers. Under the previous constitution, a nominating committee provided the membership with one name for each office, and it was obvious that the election itself was perfunctory. The new constitution called for three nominations for each important position. The membership would thus be guaranteed a choice for each office.

In spite of the generally recognized need for a more democratic election process, the editors of *Library Journal* repeatedly attacked this new provision. In April, 1922, before the system had been tried for the first time, an editorial commented that it "does not seem to be working well." The arrangement was compared with civil service examinations for chief librarians, in which it had been found that eminent librarians refused to enter into any competition. The following month, *Library Journal* again criticized the provision. The editorial pointed out that problems with the new arrangement had already been encountered by the nominating committee. The editorial ended on this sour note:

> It is hoped that this triple method of nomination, which is less in favor now that its defects are being shown, will not leave any misunderstandings behind it as the result of choice of one out of three.[7]

The Detroit conference of 1922 demonstrated the popularity of the new method of election. Of the 5,307 eligible members, 2,950 cast ballots. This total was far more than had been cast under the previous constitution. The same editorial admitted the new plan had been worth trying, since previous elections had been so perfunctory. But, according to the editors, the interest would not continue after the novelty had worn off. Members could not be expected to remain interested when there was no real difference of principle among the various candidates.

In spite of the defeat of the Enlarged Program and the cessation of war in Europe, some of the war work activities continued. One example was the service supplied by ALA to servicemen and their families in occupied Germany. The ALA library at Coblenz served the fifteen thousand soldiers in the area, plus their families. It was housed in a former German officers' club and functioned more as a public library than as a camp library. Its branches were YMCA huts, hospitals, and deposit stations. Unfortunately, the United States Army refused to allow the German people to make use of the library and its services. This led to the employment of many subterfuges by Germans who could read English and wished to be eligible. A commonly used reason was, "My wife is English." One man used the more original story that he was "an American by principle."[8]

At this time, another event grew out of the wartime activities: the launching of the *Ala,* a cargo ship, on December 18, 1920. The Emergency Fleet Corporation was engaged in rebuilding the merchant fleet, which had been depleted and damaged during the war. The corporation had invited each of the major organizations that had participated in war service work to name a ship then being built. When it was ALA's turn, a contest was held to pick a name. The result of this contest was the choice of the unimaginative name *Ala* for the 9,000-ton cargo ship. It was christened by Shirley Putnam, the daughter of the Librarian of Congress.[9]

The business depression of 1921 caused economic problems for libraries in both 1921 and 1922. Appropriations to public libraries in general were directly affected by the depression. At best, city administrators simply kept the appropriations at the same level as in previous years. More often, however, librarians found their budgets drastically reduced. Many services were, as a result, limited or completely curtailed.[10] In numerous cases, salaries of librarians were also reduced. These problems were reflected in a slowdown in the growth of ALA. In 1921, before the full effects of the depression were felt, the membership showed an increase of 806. One year later, the net increase was 377, for a total membership of 5,684.[11]

In view of the financial problems plaguing libraries, it is interesting to note that it was at this time that ALA chose to establish a basic standard of support for public libraries. At its midwinter meeting in 1922, the council accepted the minimum standard of one dollar per capita. This was the least amount necessary for communities desiring to maintain a good modern public library with trained librarians. A per capita expenditure of two dollars was suggested "for the highest grade of service."[12] It is understandable that the minimum standard did not meet with complete approval. A number of librarians, including Clement Andrews of the John Crerar Library in Chicago, believed one dollar per capita would be an unnecessarily heavy burden on taxpayers in the larger cities. Small towns, others pointed out, needed a considerably larger basis of support than the minimum. Outside the profession, reaction to the standard was generally negative. Some newspapers took the statement to mean ALA was proposing what they called a "head tax." Others simply declared that the time was hardly propitious for advocating heavier taxation.[13]

THE NEWBERY AWARD

Aside from the acceptance of the minimum standard of financial support, the greatest' interest shown by the membership was in a new award in children's literature. The Newbery Medal had its genesis in a proposal by

Frederick G. Melcher at the 1921 annual conference of ALA. He had been the chairman of the Children's Book Week Committee for two years. It occurred to him that the association might give added impetus to the writing of children's books by rewarding creative ability. This would be in the form of a medal given to the author of the most distinguished book for children published during the preceding year. Melcher suggested that the medal be called the "John Newbery Medal" in honor of the eighteenth-century bookseller. Newbery was the first publisher to realize that children have reading interests of their own, distinct from those of adults, and he produced books to meet those interests.

After ALA approved the idea of the medal, Melcher provided the funds for its design. The medal was the work of a young American, René Paul Chambellan. He was a modeling instructor at the Allied Expeditionary Forces Art Center and had previously completed sculpturing projects for a large number of public buildings.[14] The first recipient of the new award was Hendrik Van Loon for his *Story of Mankind*.

This conference of 1921 also saw a group of librarians meeting as a round table to discuss the needs of Negroes in libraries, the types of books to supply them, and the services to be provided. This was followed the next year at Detroit with similar papers and discussions, including a paper that pointed out the happy news that materials for Negro branches of public libraries could be purchased more cheaply because they would be at a more elementary level. Not until the association met in a southern city did the work of the round table engender acrimonious debate. This was at the Hot Springs, Arkansas, conference in 1923, when, according to *Library Journal,* the "only untoward episode of the conference" occurred at the round table's meeting. Although this "episode" did not go beyond the stage of very angry debate, the *Journal's* editorial suggested that the subject was really too delicate for national discussion, and that it should be left for regional meetings.[15] This implied that the problem was a local matter and should be discussed by those who were involved. As a result of the unpleasant experience at Hot Springs and the publicity that followed it, the round table for librarians working with Negroes became inactive.

LIBRARY EDUCATION

While the usual calm atmosphere of an ALA conference could be occasionally disturbed by "untoward incidents," the major problem of the library profession at this time was the education of librarians. There had been a tremendous growth in the number of institutions engaged in the training of librarians. The profession had initially viewed this development with immense pride but now perceived it as a serious problem. With no overall guidance from the association, training schools had multiplied in number and variety. Public libraries, normal schools, colleges, and universities were engaged in library education. Only very limited supervision over the programs was exercised by the Association of American Library Schools, formed in 1915, and the ALA's Committee on Library Training, founded in 1902. There was frequent criticism of the quality of instruction even in the accredited library schools. Practitioners often declared library education to be irrelevant. All schools shared the common problems of inadequate financing and the difficulty in finding qualified personnel to teach. Schools also complained about the quality of students who attended, especially during summer sessions. Summer students were often of a much lower quality than the regular students. This was brought out in council debates in 1922 over proposed changes in library education.

The Committee on Library Training had recommended that (1) regular library schools offer summer school courses for equivalent credit, (2) some library schools should offer correspondence courses in certain subjects, and (3) the library schools should adopt a uniform system of credits.

W. E. Henry of the University of Washington Library School led the opposition to this report. Amid much laughter, he described the quality of students who had attended his school's summer sessions:

> Some of them were ex-teachers and some were ex-almost everything else. Some of them had been worn out in the service of the Lord or somewhere else, in other lines, I don't know just where.[16]

As for the idea of teaching library science by correspondence, to many people the idea was totally ridiculous. There had been a few attempts at it, and the idea of extension was very popular. However, Henry's ascerbic wit again rallied the opposition. He caustically commented, "I should just as soon take to teaching swimming by the same process."

On April 23, 1923, the chairman of the Committee on Library Training reported to the ALA council on the shortcomings of library education. Malcolm G. Wyer pointed out that, although the association had always been keenly interested in library training, it had never been able to formulate any definite policy. According to Wyer, the committee could no longer meet the growing problems connected with library education. He asked ALA to "move forward to take a more direct influence over all library training agencies." He also suggested the desirability of making a very careful study of the whole field.[17]

The following day, the council voted to establish a Temporary Library Training Board to replace the Committee on Library Training. The board was ordered to survey the entire field of library education, to formulate tentative standards for all types of library training agencies, and to establish a program for the accreditation of such agencies. The board began its activities on May 24, 1923.[18] The following year it was replaced by the Board of Education for Librarianship.

It was with this background of criticism, dissent, and concern that the Carnegie Corporation, with ALA's approval, commissioned Charles C. Williamson to prepare a detailed study of library education. Other professions had had similar investigations financed by the corporation. Dr. Abraham Flexner had written a report on medical education that brought many changes in the medical schools. Joseph Redlich's investigation of legal education led to significant changes in some of the nation's law schools. Education and engineering had also been studied and reports made public under subsidies from Carnegie. These investigations, plus the corporation's long interest in libraries, made it natural for a like study to be suggested for library education. Although the ALA enthusiastically agreed to the proposal, it does not seem to have originated within the profession. It came originally in a 1916 report to the corporation by an economics professor; it was revived and accepted by the corporation in 1918.[19] Although he had yet to be appointed to head the survey, Williamson acted as the corporation's emissary to ALA's 1918 conference at Saratoga Springs to make preliminary plans. For a number of reasons, the actual fieldwork done by Williamson and his staff did not take place until 1920 and 1921. It reached its final published form in 1923 under the title of *Training in Library Service*.

The Williamson report was factual and very critical. Too critical, in the view of some people. Frank K. Walter of the University of Minnesota said the reaction of library school faculty there could be expressed in the following verse:

> Perhaps it was right to dissemble your love
> But why did you kick me downstairs?

Walter thought of the report as primarily a review of "matters of open record or common knowledge."[20] Reaction among library educators was generally favorable, in spite of Walter's verse. Most saw a few shortcomings, however. For example, Walter himself thought the study had been too concerned with large libraries and large communities. He also viewed its recommendations as too impractical to put into effect. Alice Tyler, director of the Western Reserve Library School, criticized Williamson for his suggestion that her school, and others, increase enrollments. As she pointed out, the governing factor in determining enrollment was the budget. Most schools were simply too poor to become larger. Objections of other library school directors were also mostly to specific points rather than to general statements. The most laudatory comment about the report came from Anne Wallace Howland, director of the Drexel Institute Library School. In her opinion, only the establishment of the first library school was more significant in the history of library education.[21]

Walter's assessment of the report as essentially a review of what everyone knew to be true is basically correct. Although Williamson's work did stir up considerable debate, this was not because any startling items were uncovered. The discussion centered on the recommendations, not the findings. As Sarah Vann has written, the report was "factual but lacking in originality." Most of the ideas that formed the basis of the report, according to Vann, had been widely accepted since the "beginning of formal library education. The importance lies in the role the report played in the eventual enactment of most of its major recommendations."[22] The basic recommendations made by Williamson were as follows:

1. Library schools ought to be connected with colleges or universities, not with public libraries.
2. The first year of library education should be devoted to professional education.
3. The second year of library education should consist of specialized library science courses.
4. Library schools should have strengths and specializations in the second year program.
5. Correspondence study should be allowed and encouraged.
6. The first year of the program should be open to college graduates. Second year students should also have some library experience.[23]

The report was also significant because it stimulated a serious self-study within library education. Although the ideas were not new, it was the first time they had been collected together to give a comprehensive picture to educators. This was demonstrated by the statement of Adam Strohm, chairman of the Temporary Library Training Board. In a harsh report to the ALA council, Strohm said:

> We needed such a challenge, such an implied request to take account of ourselves. It is timely. During recent years we have been dangerously infected by the toxins of sentimental tributes for services rendered during war days, leading even to self-laudation. . . . It is well that someone has called a halt.[24]

When plans for the 1924 annual conference were being formulated, it was announced that Williamson would speak before the Professional Training Section. According to the *ALA Bulletin,* the topic was to be, "What I would have said had my report been written today." Since his report had been based on the lean postwar years of 1921–22, the topic seemed to some library educators to be very appropriate. They had criticized the report in part because they felt the years covered were not representative. However, in May, 1924, the *ALA Bulletin* retracted the statement about the forthcoming speech. Dr. Williamson had never agreed to speak to the group, and he objected strongly to the implications of the proposed topic.

> I have not changed my mind in any essential respect. Some of the detailed facts and figures would necessarily be different, but the conclusions and recommendations still seem to me to hold.[25]

Two years later, the Board of Education for Librarianship issued its first annual report. This document established the first minimum standards for programs of library education. In doing so, it provided guidelines that made possible the accreditation of library schools. In a plan approved by the council, the board proposed to study the schools during the forthcoming year. The second annual report was to include a list of schools meeting the minimum requirements.[26] The board also announced that a school for the training of Negro librarians had been established: Hampton Institute, in Virginia, under the direction of Florence Rising Curtis. The school had the support of the board and the financial backing of the Carnegie Corporation.

The Board of Education for Librarianship also pointed out in its first report that there was a serious deficiency in library education: there was no advanced graduate library school that could offer "instruction adequate to important developments in library work." The board expressed the hope such schools would be developed as the profession expanded its needs. Later in 1925, the board provided a more definite plan. It suggested that a National School of Library Science be established. This would be an advanced school, requiring a college degree for admission. Its main point of difference from existing library schools would be its provision for greater specialization by students.

When word spread about the proposal, there was an immediate debate over the location of such a school. As with the location of ALA headquarters, partisans expressed their preference for New York, Chicago, or Washington. At this point, however, the Carnegie Corporation intervened by proposing a large grant to the association, part of which would help to found a graduate library school. In 1926 it was announced that the University of Chicago had been selected to receive a grant of $1,385,000 for the new library school.[27] While the main thrust of the program there would be towards the master's degree, the university would also develop a doctoral program in library science, the first in the United States.

Two years later, the Graduate Library School of the University of Chicago began what became a distinguished program, under the direction of George A. Works. His tenure was short, however, and his resignation the following year brought many questions but not many clear answers. It seemed likely that among the early problems besetting the new school, however, was the strong proprietary feeling of the profession. This was reflected in the literature of the period, which included numerous articles questioning the relevance of the Chicago program, with its emphasis on research and scholarship. It took the leadership of Louis Round Wilson, who became dean in 1932, to fulfill the promise held out by the originators and, at the same time, satisfy the profession. He did it by building an exceptionally fine faculty, attracting outstanding students, and broadening the curriculum. In ten years' time, the school was, in the words of Jesse Shera, the "greatest single force of its generation in American librarianship and American library education."[28] That much of this was accomplished in the face of rather determined opposition within the profession was beside the point. Chicago had proven that library education could go beyond what it had been satisfied with doing for decades.

AMERICAN LIBRARY IN PARIS

While the association was largely concerned with library education during this period, there came now a reminder that an obligation established during the World War remained to be settled. By 1924 one of the last remnants of ALA's war service involvement was the American Library in Paris. Founded in 1918 for the use of American soldiers stationed in Paris, it had been funded by the association for two years. After the withdrawal of the soldiers, the library's clientele became American civilians living in the city. Control of the library remained for some time with ALA. A board of trustees, composed of fifteen members, directed the immediate operations. One-third of the trustees were appointed by the executive board of ALA. The remainder were elected by a controlling group called the American Library in Paris, Inc. This was a Delaware corporation composed largely of American citizens. The librarian was nominated by ALA but had to be approved by the board of trustees.[29]

There were repeated assertions that the relationship between ALA and the library was strictly a cooperative one, yet the association found it impossible to break away entirely. Financial support was still needed in order for the library to survive. In addition to the annual ALA grant of $2,000 in effect at this time, the Carnegie Corporation made a two-year grant of $25,000 in 1923 to the library. But it was more than just a financial obligation that ALA felt. As the association's 1923 president, George B. Utley, said,

> For a long time to come our Association . . . must recognize peculiar obligations to this offspring, and do whatever lies within its power to help that institution to a position of strength and to an assured future.[30]

As a parent, the association could and did complain about the behavior of its offspring. At the executive board meeting on July 5, 1924, dissatisfaction with the library's operation reached its peak. The most vocal member was Sarah Bogle, the assistant secretary of ALA. She had spent the previous summer at the Paris library and presumably spoke with authority and knowledge of the situation. According to her, the library was not fulfilling its function. Part of the problem was, of course, a lack of funds, which hampered operations. But Miss Bogle said the primary problem was the poor administration of funds available.[31] Carl Milam added that he was afraid both the Carnegie Corporation and the library's board of trustees would soon decide that a librarian simply could not administer the library. Based on the experience of the previous four years, his conclusion would seem to be justified. According to Milam, none of the men sent by ALA to administer the library had been a success. The executive board then decided to make a thorough investigation of the library.

Although encountering problems and in constant financial straits, the American Library in Paris had made some progress. It had developed a representative collection and seemed to have built a strong bond with Paris residents. It had also expanded its program to include the education of librarians. Since France had no training of librarians in American methods, it was decided to offer a modest beginning. The program got underway in the summer of 1923. Its director was Sarah Bogle, and its sponsor was the American Committee for Devastated France, which granted funds to ALA in order to support the school for its first two years. It was expected that the school be self-supporting after that time. The need for such a school was apparently great. Even before it began operations, it had received over three hundred applications for admission.[32]

Within a short time, a serious problem developed with the funding of the Paris Library School *(Ecole de Bibliothécaires),* and with it the question of what organization should assume responsibility. The financial situation was so serious that it soon became obvious that the future of the school was in doubt. President George H. Locke, in reviewing the dilemma, told the executive board:

> We have an obligation we have to see through, we can't see it fail. . . . Let us get out with all our dignity and still carry on the school that is worthwhile. . . . How can we close up this matter satisfactorily, how can we get out of this Library School and save our dignity? We have to get out of it.[33]

The association used the war fund money to subsidize the school, realizing that it would fail without the assistance. Yet this could only be a temporary measure, as had been the case with the American Library in Paris. The original period for which the association was responsible was extended to five years in order to secure new funding. Various appeals for aid were successful in continuing the school's precarious existence. The Carnegie Endowment for International Peace, the Rockefeller Foundation, and personal contributions through the ALA kept the school alive until the five-year period was completed. On June 12, 1929, ALA signed an agreement with the school that concluded the relationship and relieved the association of its responsibility. By that time, the school had already suspended operations.[34]

SARATOGA SPRINGS CONFERENCE, 1924

The 1924 conference, held in Saratoga Springs, New York, was noted as a particularly pleasant and successful gathering. In the rural resort setting, the meetings lacked the hustle and bustle usually associated with the annual conferences. The twin discussion topics of adult education and education for librarianship attracted about fourteen hundred participants. At the end of the first general session, there was an unscheduled sentimental event: a loving cup was presented to Mr. and Mrs. Henry J. Carr. Carr had attended thirty-nine conferences, and Mrs. Carr had attended thirty-five. At various times, Carr had served as president, vice-president, secretary, and treasurer of ALA.[35]

During the conference, there was also a second unscheduled, but less pleasant, event. This was an attempt on the part of some members to dissolve SLA and absorb it into ALA as a business section. The question of a merger had always been attractive to some members of both organizations. The lack of growth and vitality of SLA had probably heightened interest in merging the two groups. The disunity in the profession, demonstrated by the failure of the Enlarged Program, may have added some incentive. The following plan was quietly developed by a small group of librarians. The nominees for offices in SLA would, upon election, form a committee to negotiate a merger with ALA. This would be accomplished by combining the similar groups of the two organizations. The business librarians would become a new business section in ALA. Other parts of SLA would similarly become sections of ALA. To forestall any further activity within SLA, the newly elected officials were to copyright the name *Special Libraries*. The old organization's official publication would therefore no longer be available for use by any dissident group. The SLA would cease to exist.[36]

Unfortunately for the planners of this coup, the activities became public knowledge at Saratoga Springs, where SLA was also meeting. Reaction was immediate. SLA elected new officials pledged to continue the organization. Since the action rallied support to the smaller organization, the result of the merger attempt was to strengthen SLA. In its failure, the attempt also hurt relations between the two organizations and ended any possibility of a future merger.[37]

THE ALL-AMERICAN CONFERENCE

During the spring of 1924, the association became involved in a propaganda conference that brought unfavorable publicity to the organization. The participation was innocent and without knowledge of the real purpose of the meeting. The conference was initiated by the American Legion, which invited many organizations to "discuss a constructive Americanism and citizenship program."[38] The executive board authorized the president to appoint a delegate to attend the meetings in Washington. President-elect H. H. B. Meyer was chosen to attend what was hailed by its sponsors as the "All-American Conference."

The meetings soon showed that the real purpose was to provide a demonstration against what was called "revolutionary and destructive radicalism."[39] The conferees passed resolutions censuring the British ambassador, denouncing the Soviet Union, and protesting against any speeches made in Congress that might place the United States in an unfavorable light. The group also demanded

> . . . unadulterated and undiluted American history in American schools, as opposed to the emasculated history which has been introduced so generally, robbing Americanism of much of its elemental significance, and robbing democracy of its most precious heritage.[40]

Newspapers noted that ALA was among the thirty groups that participated. It was an embarrassing incident for an organization that had so carefully chartered a course of nonpartisanship throughout its history.

CARNEGIE ENDOWMENT

During the midwinter meeting of the association in 1925, President Charles Belden told the executive board he had received the most important and far-reaching proposition ever laid before the association. Frederick Keppel of the Carnegie Corporation had informed Carl Milam that he was working on a long-range plan for the corporation. There might be available about two million dollars, which they wanted to divide up in advance. For ALA it could mean as much as half a million dollars a year, Keppel said. He added,

> Make that sum capitalize all the things we are now doing and all the things that ought to be done, in so far as it will cover.[41]

Inherent in the proposal at this point was the stipulation that ALA must demonstrate its ability to raise money from other sources besides the Carnegie Corporation. A figure of $1,000,000 was suggested as a "matching" amount for ALA. Board members then discussed the possibilities for raising such a large sum. Bishop commented ruefully, "One might strike a philanthropist unawares, but I think most of them are pretty well buried." There was a general agreement among the executive board members that it would be very difficult for the association to raise the required amount of matching money.

When finally made public in 1926, the grant from the Carnegie Corporation was quite different from the one originally proposed. A grant of $1,385,000 was made to the University of Chicago for the establishment of the first advanced library school. The endowment fund of the association was increased by $1,000,000. An equal amount was given to support the general activities of the association. Library education was also supported by a grant of $1,000,000, to be used to subsidize schools and students.[42] However, the grants were to be made in the form of successive installments over a ten-year period. They were to replace the annual miscellaneous grants given to support various activities of the association. The net result of this large gift, then, was a reduction in Carnegie Corporation support for general ALA activities. Under the old system, total Carnegie support in 1926 was $190,000. Under the new grant, support was $125,000 in 1926–27, $60,000 in 1928–29, and diminishing amounts each year thereafter.[43] The new program of support did at least keep the appropriations on a definite continuing basis. Although there was less money than before, there was the advantage of knowing how much money would be forthcoming in subsequent years.

FIFTIETH ANNIVERSARY CONFERENCE

The Carnegie Corporation gift came at a particularly appropriate time, since the association was preparing to celebrate its fiftieth anniversary in 1926. A drive to reach a membership of 10,000 had already been started. Funds were being collected to support an elaborate celebration. The United States would also be celebrating its anniversary in 1926 in Philadelphia. This celebration was not to be of the magnitude of the 1876 centennial exposition, but it was a good time for ALA to point out the progress made in its fifty years. In addition, there was some hope that this might be made an international library conference. As there had not been one since 1904, it was believed that library progress in the intervening years would be shown to be remarkable. The many foreign libraries, library schools, and library associations were invited to take part in the celebration. In a sentimental gesture, the executive board also moved to honor its past. The board elected as honorary vice-presidents of the association the surviving members of the 1876 and 1877 conferences. Members from the 1876 conference were R. R. Bowker, Florence M. Cushing, Melvil Dewey, Charles Evans, William E. Foster, and E. Fannie Whitney. Members from 1877 were Walter Biscoe, Walter Harden, and Caroline M. Hewins.[44]

The fiftieth anniversary exhibit at the Philadelphia Sesquicentennial of the American Revolution was housed in the exhibition's Education Hall. Earlier elaborate plans calling for an exhibit costing $25,000 were replaced with a more modest exhibit costing $8,500. The main feature was an eighty-foot map showing the Cleveland Public Library's system, which was meant to show how a library serves its public. Another display was a printing press such as was used by large public libraries for publicity work. The press poured forth a steady stream of book lists and brochures which were very popular with the public during the conference. There was also a small model library set up for demonstration purposes. The collection consisted of 2,000 adult books, 500 juvenile books, and 100 of the most important reference works.[45]

The emphasis at the anniversary conference was on the general sessions. The registration of 2,300 was the largest ever at an ALA conference. Of that total, 1,200 traveled to Philadelphia for the commemorative sessions; the main sessions were held at Atlantic City, New Jersey. The sessions in Atlantic City were on the theme of international cooperation, and most of the speeches were made by foreign librarians. With this emphasis, it seemed particularly appropriate when the association elected George H. Locke of the Toronto Public Library as its new president. This was the first and only time a Canadian has ever been elected president of ALA. The anniversary sessions were held at Drexel Institute in Philadelphia.

Richard R. Bowker and Melvil Dewey were the main speakers for the occasion. Bowker spoke on the development of ALA during its first fifty years. Dewey talked of the need to meet the challenge of what he saw as the enemies of reading. He also called for an educating process for the public so it would give complete acceptance to the work and value of libraries. The presence of both Dewey and Bowker, as well as Charles Evans, contributed greatly to the success of the conference.[46]

The anniversary meeting provided a time for evaluation of the progress made during ALA's half century of existence. President Charles Belden spoke of the accomplishments in his address to the conference. Both Dewey and Bowker spoke of the association's role in the development of librarianship. But all three were less concerned with the past than with what the future held in store for the organization. Bowker spoke of the "problems of bigness" that confronted the library world. He wondered if the field of library work, as it seemed to be developing, would not in time outreach the possibilities of ALA. Belden placed great emphasis on the association doing tests and experiments to improve library service throughout the country. He believed that, if ALA provided better methods, directed the training of personnel, and delineated more carefully defined aims, the public library would be doing in fifty years what had hardly even been dreamed of in 1926.

Dewey was particularly modern sounding in his prophecy for future years. Noting the tendency of librarians to think of books as being sacred, he cautioned instead to regard them as tools to be used. According to Dewey, the future library might not have books at all, and librarians should be prepared for that possibility. The association, too, would have to be changing constantly if it were to remain a viable, relevant organization. The next fifty years would be far more important than the first fifty in terms of challenges and opportunities. Much work remained to be done, and Dewey was convinced that it was within the province of ALA to do it. Otherwise, less capable but more aggressive agencies would attempt to do the same work. It was a valedictory message in its call for action. Dewey's final words to the conference were, "What will you do with these stupendous fifty years ahead?"[47] In reading these speeches, one is struck by how modern sounding and prophetic these pioneers were.

ALA HEADQUARTERS

Throughout most of this period, there were frequent discussions about the need for additional space at headquarters, and the desirability of moving to another city. The annual conference provided the forum for such debate, as illustrated by the Hot Springs meeting in 1923. At that time, the council requested the executive board to prepare a list of cities suitable for the headquarters. Frank P. Hill noted that voting on a new location was probably a waste of time. As Hill said,

> The trouble with this association is that it votes today in favor of one thing and tomorrow or next week or at the latest next year we take an exactly opposite stand on the same question.[48]

On the day following the council's request, the executive board presented the following list of cities as possible sites for headquarters: Boston, Chicago, New York, Philadelphia, and St. Louis. It also recommended that no further action be taken on the question until sufficient funds had been accumulated to indicate that a building would be possible. The suggestion was made that there should be no vote on the city because some people would not contribute to a building fund if they knew where the building would be located.

In 1924, after fifteen years in quarters provided free of charge by the Chicago Public Library, ALA moved to the John Crerar Library in Chicago. This move was made possible by a grant of $7,500 from the Carnegie Corporation, which helped to defray the cost of moving and to subsidize the rent.[49] It was hoped that the successful completion of the endowment fund would enable the association to afford the rent at some time in the future. The new offices were on the ninth floor of the Crerar Library, and they were never adequate. The headquarters staff had grown to fifty by 1924, and several activities, including publishing, had to be continued at the Chicago Public Library. The new quarters were an improvement over the old, but they became less satisfactory as time went on. Although no new building was possible at this time, it was becoming evident that something had to be done about the office accommodations.

By 1928, according to *Library Journal,* ALA had the "most extensive, expensive and effective" staff of any of the "learned societies."[50] The size of the staff and the extent of the activities inevitably led to space problems. Forrest B. Spaulding visited headquarters at the John Crerar Library and wrote of the situation. He compared it to the black hole of Calcutta and to the filled sardine can.[51] The problem had worsened because, between 1917 and 1928, the ALA staff had increased eightfold and the office space had only doubled. New quarters were desperately needed. The obvious answer to many people was to purchase or construct a building. However, in 1929 the building fund amounted to only $600. It was therefore necessary to secure a lease on larger office quarters rather than to build or buy a building.

A selection committee from the staff narrowed the choice to three sites: the Chicago Evening Post building on Wacker Drive; the DePaul University building on Lake Street; and the McGraw-Hill building on Michigan Avenue. The Evening Post building was eliminated because of the undesirable physical quarters. The DePaul building was eliminated because of staff objections to the nature of the school. Carl Milam called it a

> Catholic school of mostly sundown character and rather low grade, if one may judge from the general impression he gets of the students who come there.

The staff, according to Milam, was depressed by the low ceilings of the rooms and the presence of the students. Milam also disliked

> the atmosphere that was created by the students who were using the lobbies for a campus, as well as the sidewalks.[52]

The result was an unanimous vote for the McGraw-Hill building, and the move to it was made on May 1, 1929. There the association stayed until it was able to purchase the McCormick mansion in 1945.

SUMMARY

Although ALA went through a period of retrenchment following the defeat of the Enlarged Program, some of the expanded activities of World War I continued. Chief among these was the American Library in Paris, which held the special affections of librarians in the United States. Almost all other activities having their origin in World War I were gradually phased out or taken over by other organizations.

The selection of Carl Milam as executive secretary was a particularly fortunate choice for the association. Fresh from his work with the Library War Service, Milam was young, ambitious, and international in his attitude. He assumed the leadership when such qualities were particularly necessary because of the disastrous defeat of the Enlarged Program.

The large grants of money from the Carnegie Corporation also came at an opportune time. The grants placed the finances of the association on a firm foundation and also ensured the establishment of the first graduate library school. The Carnegie Corporation grant to underwrite the Williamson report was also fortunate, although the report was critical of what had been done in library education. The report synthesized information about training for librarianship and helped lead to changes in library education. Finally, during this period the question of relocation of headquarters again came up for discussion, and it was decided to remain in Chicago. Rented quarters, however, were still a necessity, for the association did not as yet have the resources to acquire its own building.

6

DEPRESSION YEARS AND INTERNAL STRIFE

*A*s ALA began its second fifty years, its members found business conditions were changing radically. In 1926, there was an abnormal business "high" followed by a brief recession that affected libraries sharply. Incomes were reduced as all areas of the economy except the stock market suffered a setback. In spite of this recession, however, the growth of ALA continued unabated. The goal of 10,000 members, which had been set for the anniversary year, was reached in 1927.[1]

CENSORSHIP ATTEMPTS

ALA was innocently drawn into a verbal war the mayor of Chicago was waging on Great Britain during 1927. It was a one-sided and for the most part ridiculous, war. The affair began with Mayor William H. Thompson's attempt to prove that the public schools were disseminating pro-British propaganda. A committee appointed by the mayor reported the use of books that contained "sinister alterations" from the truth. To the committee, this seemed to reflect fruition of the seeds planted by Rhodes scholarships, the Carnegie Foundation, and the English-Speaking Union.

Following the mayor's attack on the school system, a member of Chicago's Public Library Board took up the attack. Urbin J. Herrmann threatened to withdraw all pro-British books from the library and burn them on the lake front. Only a court injunction prevented this from taking place. Herrmann contented himself with buying himself a copy of Arthur Schlesinger's *New Viewpoints in American History* and having a small private bonfire. Mayor Thompson then attacked a bibliography published by ALA and distributed by the Chicago Public Library. This was in the "Reading with a Purpose" series which the association had provided to libraries to encourage reading. The specific list that the mayor attacked was *The Europe of Our Day,* compiled by Herbert Adams Gibbons. According to Thompson, the list contained books that were biased and unfair. He called the books insulting in their comments on America and American policies.[2]

There was no response from ALA to this criticism. Carl Roden, librarian of the Chicago Public Library, said he would not resist any attempt to remove the offending books. Fortunately it did not come to that point. The resulting unfavorable publicity convinced the mayor that further attack would be unwise. He then settled for a ban on the use of the lion in school architecture. The country followed the farce with a mixture of amusement and outrage. Newspapers gleefully chronicled each new episode, but editorials tended to take a more serious view of the affair. Apparently Thompson's attack had little effect on Anglo-American relations, and British newspapers generally ignored Thompson. The only serious reaction came from a group of British children. They burned the mayor in effigy.

TORONTO CONFERENCE, 1927

The association met in Canada for the third time in its history when it convened in Toronto in June, 1927. Attendance almost set a record, being second only to that of the anniversary conference the previous year. With the conference in Canada, it was appropriate that the formation of the Canadian Library Association was again announced.[3] The new organization was not thought of as a rival to ALA. It was hoped most members of the Canadian group would remain affiliated with the older organization. This, of course, had always been true to some extent with other national library associations, even the SLA. All began with the initial blessing of the older organization, and with no outward show of antagonism on the part of either membership.

President George A. Locke, in his presidential address at this conference, raised anew two proposals aimed at strengthening the inner structure of ALA. The first was to increase the president's term of office to two years. According to Locke, if this were not done the power of the president would steadily decrease, and the power of the headquarters organization would increase proportionately. The continuity of policy could be taken care of by the permanent officials, while the more theoretical outlook could be provided by the elected officials. Locke pointed out that "unfettered Idealism" and strong leadership could not be expected of a president who holds office for only one year. Instead, the president might become a figurehead whose main function would be to approve the actions of the permanent staff.

It is significant that Locke offered this advice at the end of his term rather than at the beginning. He had already had a year in which to learn the power structure of the organization. Yet in truth, what Locke predicted might take place had already occurred. The traditional dislike of a second term for the president had developed in the early years of the association. By default, the actual direction of ALA went to the executive secretary and the developing headquarters organization. The bureaucracy Locke warned about was already in existence and in effective control. This was only natural, since the elected officials were too far removed from the day-to-day operations. It is entirely possible that, even with a two-year term, a president might have had difficulty in exerting any meaningful personal power at this point in the organization's history.

Locke's second proposal was an effort to encourage greater personal involvement. He renewed the idea of biennial conferences. Regional conferences were suggested for the intervening years. Locke predicted greater attendance and interest at the local meetings than had been true of most of the annual conferences. Concurrently there would be increased interest in the national conferences because they would be less frequent.[4] However, in spite of the editorial support of *Library Journal*, neither of Locke's proposals received serious consideration.

JOHN COTTON DANA

Later in 1927, John Cotton Dana resumed his letter writing after a period of inactivity. The subject was library education, and he tried the Board of Education for Librarianship first. A member of the board, Harrison Craver, commented to Sarah Bogle on the letter:

> Dana's letter is interesting and will lead to a spicy controversy, probably. He has been quiet a long time, and that is never an agreeable permanent state to him.

Any answer, according to Craver, would have to be done carefully, as Dana "is a slippery antagonist."[5] Dana found much to condemn in the association, and he did not hesitate to make his views known to the leadership. His communications were apt to be received with a resigned air, acknowledged, referred to a committee, and then forgotten. Dana's later letter of December 20, 1927, to members of the council is a typical example of his criticism. It was an attack on the activities of certain ALA boards and committees. He charged that the Board of Education for Librarianship had, through its standards, introduced the "goose-step into a flourishing private enterprise." He saw not a "single spark of originality" in its minimum requirements. Library schools, according to Dana, had changed little under the board's direction, except possibly to become more timid toward new ideas.

The association's work in adult education received similar treatment. Dana resented the use of the new term *adult education* as implying a new work or new emphasis on the part of librarians. Librarians had been doing such work for many years. Yet the Adult Education Committee had spent $50,000 without any indication that the results and the efforts were at all meaningful.

Dana was also critical of the books published as a result of a curriculum study done by the association. The study had simply surveyed what the current practice was in libraries. Prominent librarians were then paid to write textbooks based on the results of the study. Dana sarcastically commented the books would have been precisely the same even if the authors had never heard of the $30,000 worth of answers acquired by the curriculum study. Looking back, Dana said he had often made himself a burden like the Biblical grasshopper. After seeing the work of ALA in these areas, he expressed a wish that he had made himself even more burdensome.[6]

Within several days, Dana then wrote to the executive board asking that his previous letter be read at a council meeting. There were objections to the board doing what Dana asked, but as Frank K. Walter pointed out,

> If any attempt is made to suppress it, Mr. Dana has many avenues to publish it. . . . If we attempt to suppress it, it will be looked upon as persecution, and the fact of the matter is there is some truth to it.[7]

Matthew Dudgeon of the Milwaukee Public Library added the brief comment, "A lot of truth in it." Walter then said he believed the only way to deal with Dana was to use Dana's own weapon. That, according to Walter, was "pitiless publicity." In the past, Dana had written to the executive board to express his dissatisfaction with what ALA was doing. He had, in fact, suggested the association employ himself to make a study of its activities. Dana undoubtedly was not serious in his suggestion, since he disliked studies very much. Furthermore, he surely realized the executive board would hardly employ a known critic. It would appear that the suggestion was made with puckish humor, for which Dana was also well known.

Some members of the council recognized the accuracy in Dana's latest letter, or the spirit in which it was written. Henry Van Hoesen said one might have to look closely to find the constructive criticism, but it was there. Others agreed with the basic ideas, although they objected to the bluntness with which Dana wrote. The suggestion was made that the boards and committees involved should answer the charges if they desired. Arthur Bostwick was strongly opposed to this plan. He said this would place the different agencies in the position of accused persons, with Dana acting as the prosecutor:

> It would, of course, please Mr. Dana to death. He would get back at the different boards, and Mr. Dana can act as public prosecutor very much more effectively than anybody connected with the board or anybody connected with the ALA can act as defenders.[8]

It was decided not to suppress the letter. The complete text was printed in both the *ALA Bulletin* and the *Library Journal*. Less forthrightly, the council avoided the issue by forming a special committee to investigate the charges. Six months later, this special committee made its report to the council. It was primarily a defense of what the association had done, rather than the unbiased, thorough investigation Dana apparently had in mind. A significant change was recommended, however. Dana had noted the association published the salaries of hundreds of librarians; yet it did not publish the salaries of its own staff. The committee suggested that this information ought to be included in an early issue of the *ALA Bulletin*.[9] The recommendation was accepted, and the published budget included the salaries of the officers of the association, but not their names.

Dana wrote another critical letter to the executive board in December, 1928. This was a ten-page critique of the association's activities. He again asked to have the letter read aloud at the meeting. Executive Secretary Milam angrily commented,

> If we are going to still further to prolong that [the meeting] by reading a harangue from Dana in which there are certainly two or three remarks which would be considered as discourteous if made on the floor in person, it may be doubtful wisdom, though I recognize exactly the danger of doing anything else.[10]

Milam later agreed to read the letter at the end of the session, but the minutes do not indicate that this was done. The *ALA Bulletin* reported the receipt of another stimulating letter from Dana but declined to print it. The editor declared the letter was too long to print and it did not lend itself to being abstracted. However, to avoid criticism, mimeographed copies were available to those interested.

This was the last of the Dana letters designed to disturb the serenity of

ALA headquarters. In early July, 1929, librarians learned that Dana was seriously ill and beyond hope of recovery. His death came on July 21. Dana was one of the best-known librarians in the country, and his death was widely mourned. The *New York Times* noted that Dana's colleagues often thought of his comments as destructive. He certainly had a penchant for stirring things up, and he enjoyed being the center of controversy. The *Times* concluded:

> He was like a gadfly to stodgy conservatism. He was always calling for a reassessment of old traditions and standards in library work. . . . Mere red tape in administration was abhorrent to him. . . . The library world will not soon look upon his like again.[11]

Within the profession, there were many librarians who were not sure of Dana's motives or were convinced that he was simply a very argumentative individual. Representing the latter point of view was Arthur Bostwick, who had been associated with Dana in the 1907 "rebellion" of liberals that had led to Bostwick's election as president. Bostwick said of Dana,

> I came to the conclusion, which I still regard as justified, that Dana was one of those persons who love an argument and prefer to take an unpopular, or even an impossible side; and that one could without difficulty come to any conclusion about his real opinions from what he then said.[12]

However, Bostwick and Dana ceased to be close friends following that election, according to Bostwick's own account, and this may have colored his opinion of Dana.

It is difficult to determine to what extent Dana was speaking for the membership, or any large segment of it, in his criticism of the activities of the headquarters staff. Occasional letters to the editors of the professional journals, and a few letters in existence in the association's archives, support the obvious point that he was not alone in his dissatisfaction. Furthermore, it seems likely that a good many people enjoyed his sharp tongue and perhaps recognized his basic motivation as good. But there is no evidence to indicate that he spoke for any large percentage of the membership.

BUSINESS LIBRARIES SECTION

At the same midwinter meeting of ALA, the council took a step that formerly would have caused considerable trouble but at this time only caused resentment. The action was the approval of the formation of a Business Libraries Section, an apparent encroachment on the Special Libraries Association. Interested members had attempted to establish such a section in 1925 and again in 1927 but had failed. In his 1925 presidential address, Frances Cady of SLA had reported on the negotiations with ALA over a business library group. He had conveyed to ALA leaders the sentiment within SLA that there was no need for the new group to be formed. SLA already amply covered the field of special libraries and was hampered only by the lack of funds from doing all that needed to be done. President Cady continued:

> I have felt that if the A.L.A. really wishes to aid in the develop-ment of special library activities, another way lies open to it. It can discourage defections from our association to its utmost ca-pacity. I can see nothing to be gained by setting up within A.L.A. a small group drawn from an affiliated body, to do with the full backing of the A.L.A. what that body is already undertaking to do with such backing withheld.[13]

The section's adherents failed to show in their request how SLA had failed to meet their needs or how affiliation with ALA would be more de-sirable. It was apparently a matter of desiring a relationship with ALA, regardless of the effect such an action might have on the already tenuous bonds between the two organizations. The request for the section was re-ferred to a committee, which reported to the council on December 29, 1927. The committee recommended that a Business Library Section be formed, although it recognized the section's goals could be achieved through a better understanding between ALA and SLA. Furthermore, the commit-tee admitted that SLA's affiliation with ALA would be nullified by the sec-tion's formation.[14]

After considerable discussion, the council voted to lay the petition on the table. This action came after one member commented that approval of the section would "bear the aspect of a direct slap by the ALA in the face of the SLA."[15] The organ of SLA, *Special Libraries,* reprinted the council proceedings verbatim with the added statement, "We reserve comment un-til a later issue."[16]

No comment was made, however, until the problem came up again. This was on December 29, 1928, when the council voted to reconsider the ques-tion. This action was taken in spite of warnings from the *Library Journal* and members of SLA.[17] President Frances Cady of SLA spoke of the danger of a breakdown in the affiliation with ALA if the new section were allowed to be established. Cady further pointed out that a majority in both organiza-tions had indicated in a mail vote their opposition to the proposed section.

In spite of the strong feeling shown at the meeting, the council created a Business Libraries Section by a standing vote.

The new section then sparked additional interest at the 1929 conference by holding a secret, unannounced session. Attended only by the original signers of the petition to establish the section, it elected officers and announced bylaws. An editor of *Special Libraries* called the unusual session "unprecedented" and "unconstitutional."[18] There was considerable discussion over this matter, since ALA and SLA were meeting concurrently in Washington at the time. It was clearly a defeat for SLA and something of an embarrassment for ALA. However, the SLA president emphasized conciliation. In his address to SLA, he pointed out that that organization "attached great importance to those cordial relations with the greater sister Association. . . ."[19] ALA unofficially also tried to smooth over the troubled areas. Two prominent members of the association addressed SLA at its first general session. R. R. Bowker expressed the hope that there would be no rift between the organizations. Frank P. Hill endorsed Bowker's remarks and also told SLA it should not let ALA hinder its programs. Fortunately, the conciliatory attitude of SLA's leadership helped to prevent any open breach between the two groups. However, the council's action in establishing a section in direct competition with SLA was unfortunate. It helped foster the growing impression within SLA that its sister organization was more interested in gaining members than in coexisting peacefully and without rivalry.

A WORLD CONGRESS

Immediately following the 1929 ALA conference in Washington, a group of fifteen delegates sailed to Rome for the World Congress of Libraries and Bibliography. Among the representatives were Carl H. Milam, Herbert Putnam, Arthur Bostwick, and Andrew Keogh. The congress, held June 13–19, attracted twelve hundred people from eighteen countries. Although there had been a number of international library meetings before, this was considered to be the first official meeting of its kind. By means of sixteen sections, the congress tried to consider all international aspects of library and bibliographical work. One of the most significant addresses was by Herbert Putnam; he called for establishment of international systems of libraries for the sharing of library resources. Benito Mussolini, premier of Italy, gave a welcoming address that *Library Journal* called admirable in scope. A further highlight was the visit of Pope Pius XI, who "left his throne and his pontifical aloofness to mingle with his fellow librarians."[20]

Before the close of the congress, the International Federation of Library Associations (IFLA) was formed. The general hope was that the new organization would be another bond in the interest of world peace and that it would help to accomplish Putnam's goal of the international sharing of library resources.

PROBLEMS IN LIBRARY EDUCATION

The year 1929 also saw the surfacing of tension between two of the major organizations concerned with library education—the Board of Education for Librarianship and the Association of American Library Schools (AALS). AALS had been formed in 1915 as an organization of professional people directly concerned with library education. It had met with immediate criticism because there were already a Professional Training Section and a Library School Round Table in existence to discuss the issues and problems of library education. However, these groups were open to all members of ALA, and so questions might be decided by people not directly connected with the training of librarians. Therefore, AALS limited its membership to people having positions in library schools. The actions of AALS thus obviously expressed self-interest and perhaps, at this time of poor economic conditions, were based somewhat on self-preservation. Just as in its beginning AALS did not want people outside of library education in its organization, so it now did not want supervision from people not immediately connected with such education.

The Board of Education for Librarianship, on the other hand, was formed in 1924 (replacing the temporary board) and, acting as the agent of ALA, began with some hesitancy to exercise control over the schools. The control, to be sure, was not firm in the beginning, but it came at a time when AALS was relatively inactive. When AALS started to exert itself, it found that the board was at least in an advantageous position, if not a position of power. And, of course, the board as the agent of the association represented the profession, not the schools. It was soon evident that philosophically the two organizations were far apart, and the philosophical difference in time developed into open enmity. An apparent example of this is a bylaw of the 1928 AALS constitution, which prohibited anyone connected with the board from attending AALS meetings.

Antagonism, then, between the two organizations was not new, but the criticism of the board by AALS members in 1929 was especially strong. At AALS's meeting in May, Phineas L. Windsor presented some of the objections to the board:

1. The lack of background in library education on the part of the board's members prevented their understanding the problems of the library schools.
2. Decisions were made by the Board of Education without any prior consultation with the library schools.
3. Library schools were not given enough time to discuss major recommendations before the board referred them to the ALA Council for approval.
4. The board advised the council on the granting of funds for library education. This gave the board an unfair advantage, since the schools felt they could not disagree and still obtain funds. According to the schools, the result was a standardization and regimentation that left no room for experimentation.
5. In spite of the expenditure of large sums of money, the board had accomplished little for the benefit of teaching. The preparation of a few textbooks had been the sole activity in this area.[21]

For its part, the board recognized some of its weaknesses. The Fifth Annual Report of the board declared a need to establish and maintain a close relationship with the library schools. The report also pointed out the need to revise the minimum standards used in evaluating the schools. As library education was improved, new goals had to be established in order to prevent stagnation in the profession, according to the board.

Problems between the board and AALS continued into 1930. The Activities Committee of ALA, established after criticism by Dana to review all aspects of the association, commented on the strained relationship in a 1930 report:

> Anyone who has attended a meeting of the AALS cannot fail to be impressed by its evident antagonism towards the board.[22]

Conditions deteriorated to the point where a special committee was appointed to improve relations between the two groups. At a meeting of this committee on June 24, 1930, there was a very frank discussion of the library schools' attitudes towards the board. Arthur Bostwick was particularly outspoken. He said the board's connection with the Carnegie Corporation in the granting of subsidies to library schools was unfortunate. Since the board then held the purse strings, at least as far as grants from the Carnegie Corporation were concerned, it was impossible for the schools to oppose board policies and activities. Bostwick said the board was "held in awe by the schools which fear they will incur loss of subsidy" if they criticized any of the board's actions. Bostwick's comments were echoed by other leaders in library education and in the profession. Before his death, Dana had attacked the board through the council. Dana was particularly critical of the board's attempts at establishing standards, which he saw as standardizing, or requiring uniformity in all library training institutions. He concluded,

> Of twenty-five standardizing agencies operating in the last twenty years, our association is shown to be the most active, and so far as its powers extend, the most injurious.[23]

At the end of the year, the Activities Committee again referred to the problem. During the midwinter meeting, Louis R. Wilson of the University of North Carolina spoke for the Activities Committee when he criticized both groups. He said there was "too great an air of secrecy" over library education. Nothing could be gained by this, according to Wilson, except continued misunderstanding.[24]

In its survey, the first Activities Committee found that more membership criticism was directed towards library education than towards any other activity of ALA. Since the Board of Education for Librarianship was the agency responsible for library education, it naturally bore the brunt of the blame. The committee decided that there was no need to limit the powers of the board, but it did conclude that there was a basis for the many complaints.

Not long after these exchanges took place, there was a noticeable change for the better in the relationship between the board and AALS. It seems likely that both the public airing of the dispute and the continuing economic depression were major factors in the change. But the death of Sarah Bogle, secretary of the board, might also have contributed to the improvement, since some of the criticism was clearly aimed at her. One year before her death, former AALS president Windsor wrote to Charles Williamson, "I am coming to think that if there was someone else in Miss Bogle's shoes, the Board of Education might become a very responsible body."[25] The combination of her strong views on education and her position as assistant executive secretary of ALA was perhaps too much for some people.[26]

Library education was facing an economic problem as well as internal strife. The profession had been used to an ever increasing demand for the graduates of its schools. The rapid growth in public libraries had meant increases in the library staffs as well. The raising of educational standards had resulted in huge demands for school and academic librarians. But as with other professions, such as teaching, the situation changed drastically early in 1929. The economic law of supply and demand caught up with librarians, and many graduates were without positions.

Louis Shores, librarian of Fisk University, saw the problem before it had reached full bloom. He suggested a course of action similar to that taken by the trade guilds of the Middle Ages. This was to limit the number of people who could enter a profession. The number would be based on probable need. The limit protected the people already in the profession, but it also prevented training people for jobs that did not exist. Shores wrote that the profession was not justified in allowing young people to prepare for positions they could probably never fill. He called on the library profession to establish the necessary machinery to maintain a balance before it was too late. Maximum enrollment in each accredited library school would be fixed by a committee of ALA. The result would be to raise the standards, as well as to level off the supply of librarians. The library profession, according to Shores, should "establish a precedent for the entire economic world."[27] However, the profession did not respond to Shore's suggestion. The Board of Education for Librarianship did discourage the establishment of some new library schools, but this policy was in effect before Shore's article was published.[28]

The oversupply of librarians during this period led to the frequent suggestion, and occasional demand, that limits be placed on the output of the accredited library schools. To make matters worse, it was reported in California that there was a new threat to the already dark employment picture. Although by 1929 the situation was already so bad that many graduates of library schools had no jobs, in 1931 it was reported that the junior colleges of the state were beginning to offer courses in librarianship.[29] For the hard-pressed professional looking for a position, this was a serious threat for the future even after the effects of the depression were eliminated. A statement in 1932 by the chairman of the Board of Education for Librarianship also reminded the profession that it could not place all of the blame on the economic upheaval:

> Two contributing factors are the rapid expansion of training agencies, particularly summer courses, and increased enrollment in most library schools.

This statement urged library schools to reduce their enrollments by " a more rigid scrutiny of applicants."[30] Charles Williamson, dean of the library school at Columbia University, saw the eventual need for compulsory enrollment curbs if the economic problems continued. He proposed a "selective draft" of highly qualified students from which the library schools could choose, a system apparently based on that of the armed forces. A general examining board would determine the most qualified students but would not assign students to particular schools. Students would be free to select the school they wished to attend, and schools would be allowed to add more qualifications for entrance should they desire.[31] Although widely discussed, these recommendations were not formally considered by the Board of Education for Librarianship, apparently for lack of support.

The director of the University of California School of Librarianship, Sydney B. Mitchell, also offered suggestions for limiting the output of library schools. He pointed out that there were a number of schools that probably should never have been born, "but being in existence, they share the human dislike of committing suicide." He suggested the Board of Education for Librarianship consider paying subsidies to schools willing to limit their enrollment. This probably would be necessary since the natural desire of the schools was to raise income by increasing enrollment. He also suggested that the board discourage the existence of summer schools, since the quality of the people attending was not usually very good.[32]

Other suggestions followed a series of conferences held during the spring of 1931 at the request of the Carnegie Corporation. The meetings brought out the fact that the board was continuing to discourage the establishment of new library schools. It had refused to accredit the School of Library Science at the University of Buffalo and had withheld approval of the school at Syracuse University until academic and administrative conditions were improved there. The board had placed certain restrictions on the operations of the Chautauqua School of Librarianship. When there was a proposal for another library school in New York City, the board argued that the area was already too well supplied with librarians. The participants of the conferences, however, generally saw the need for further curbs in order to achieve a balance between the supply and the demand for librarians.

Even though the board discouraged new library schools, an opposite course was pursued on the West Coast. The Los Angeles Public Library Training School had closed its doors when the 1932 class graduated. This action left only one library school in southern California, the unaccredited Riverside Library School. The employment picture at the time indicated that one school was probably sufficient to supply the demand for librarians for the immediate future. Led primarily by the alumni of the Los Angeles Public Library Training School, however, a determined effort was made to establish a new school in the area. This effort culminated in a confrontation at a meeting of the Southern California Library Association on November 19, 1932. After what *Library Journal* called a "battle royal," this association voted in favor of establishing another library school.[33]

Charles F. Woods of the Riverside Library School led the opposition on the basis of the oversupply of librarians. He reminded those present that the California Library Association had already gone on record as being opposed to another library school in southern California. But the majority view was that once the depression was over there would be a strong need for another school in the area. In response to this expression, and in opposition to Board of Education for Librarianship policy, the University of Southern California began offering library science courses during its summer sessions.[34]

PUBLISHING ACTIVITIES

The Board of Education for Librarians was not the only arm of the association to receive criticism from the first Activities Committee. The publishing program was also castigated for not becoming more involved in sponsoring and publishing scholarly and bibliographical work, in spite of the apparent need for this type of material by the profession. The committee commented that this neglect by ALA had been so extensive and prominent "as to threaten at times actual withdrawal of the College and Reference Section" from the organization.[35] It suggested immediate action be taken to correct this important deficiency and to forestall any such threat in the future. The program of the association must be responsive to all areas of membership, not just a few areas.

In general, however, the first Activities Committee found little to criticize in the publishing program. For the most part, publishing was popular with the profession because the program helped to make commercially unfeasible publications available to libraries. At this time, all publishing activities were under the direction of an Editorial Committee, which was charged with the responsibility for providing the overall direction for the program. As the Activities Committee pointed out, publishing was somewhat haphazard and lacked comprehensive planning. But with the exception of a few unsuccessful textbooks and general tracts, the books and materials were generally well received.

The publishing of the association's periodicals remained a problem, however. The *Booklist* was still not self-sustaining, although it had been published since 1905. A more important criticism related to its role as a book-selection tool. Librarians felt that its main weakness was its time lag in reviewing new books. In answer to this criticism, the staff of *Booklist* saw the weakness as inherent in this type of publication. They were forced to wait until publishers supplied them with the books. Furthermore, the periodical depended on the Library of Congress to supply the cataloging information included with the review. This meant a further delay for most books. The committee's view, however, was that these problems were not insurmountable. Changes were recommended to reduce the length of delay.[36]

The Editorial Committee also initiated two projects that were rather ambitious in view of the depressed economic conditions. The first was a new periodical devoted to the reviewing of major reference works. This publication, the *Subscription Books Bulletin,* first appeared in January, 1930. Although it shared the *Booklist*'s tendency to review books later than librarians would have preferred, it was well received. The second venture was the successful culmination of almost five years of effort to found a journal of research and discussion. In 1926 the librarian of Johns Hopkins University, M. Llewellyn Raney, had proposed an expansion of the *ALA Bulletin* beyond its role as the official publication of the association. He wanted to see it become a journal of discussion that would welcome the serious papers of scholars.[37] The Editorial Committee investigated the practices of various learned societies and found that their news publications were almost always completely divorced from their scholarly journals. It therefore seemed unwise to enlarge the scope of the *ALA Bulletin* to include the type of material Raney had in mind. The Editorial Committee requested the appointment of another committee to determine the feasibility of publishing a separate scholarly periodical. This was done, and a Committee on the Journal of Discussion reported at least initial success. A survey had indicated enough interest among members of the profession to make the journal potentially successful.[38]

As plans developed, it appeared to be very desirable to committee members to have the journal connected with a prominent library school. The Graduate Library School of the University of Chicago seemed to be the most logical choice, and so university officials were approached. They indicated a tentative willingness to accept the responsibility but asked for assurance of financial support. This support was beyond the ability of ALA to provide. In March, 1930, Frederick Keppel of the Carnegie Corporation was contacted for financial assistance. Keppel supported the plan, and a grant of $25,000 was provided by the corporation.[39] In January, 1931, the journal of discussion, under the name *Library Quarterly,* made its first appearance. "Rather disappointing" was the sour comment of a *Library Journal* editorial; it added that the new periodical carried articles that "would be welcome in any of the existing periodicals." In summary, *Library Quarterly* was "just another library periodical of the common, ordinary, or garden sort," according to the pioneer in the field.[40] In time, however, this journal was to live up to the expectations of the early planners.

FINANCIAL PROBLEMS

The effects of the Depression were very visible in 1931. Libraries throughout the country reported drastic cuts in service, personnel, and appropriations. For example, employees of the Chicago Public Library were given a two-week vacation without pay. In addition, the library halted the purchasing of books on the order of its library board.[41] Public libraries in other cities, such as Toledo, Cincinnati, and Pasadena, tried to meet their reduced budgets by cutting library hours or eliminating clerical positions.

ALA itself encountered the economic problems suffered by most libraries. Income dropped because of the failure of members to pay their dues. By March 1, over 2,200 members were in arrears. Yet at the same time, discussions were held in regard to raising the dues to improve the quality of the *ALA Bulletin*.[42] It appeared as if the leadership at headquarters was very much out of touch with the membership. An earlier statement by a member seemed especially appropriate now: the organization had a "Tiffany attitude" when it really should have a "Macy attitude."[43] Asa Don Dickinson of the University of Pennsylvania wrote of ALA's "expensive pursuit of what appears to us as rather unsubstantial moonbeams." He suggested it might be appropriate to change the association's motto to "Busy Being Bigger."[44]

In January, 1931, the executive board announced that $20,000 had to be raised immediately in order to continue some of the most important activities. The areas affected by the deficit were library extension, education for librarianship, personnel service, and adult education.[45] Part of the problem could be traced to the nature of the Carnegie Corporation gift of 1926. At that time, the corporation stated it would decrease and eventually discontinue its grants to the association. In 1931 the grant was only $15,000, and Carnegie support was to cease almost completely after October 1.[46] The association had not been able to replace the Carnegie grants with gifts from other sources. Therefore, income from internal and external sources was decreasing while expenditures were steadily rising.

Ironically, while ALA was feeling the economic strain quite severely, it was at the same time nearing the completion of its endowment fund drive. When the Carnegie Corporation gave the association $1,000,000 for the endowment fund in 1926, there had been an assurance of more money in the future—if the association could match it. ALA then announced that, if the association could raise $1,000,000 on its own, an "educational foundation" would add an equal amount. Everyone knew this promise came from the Carnegie Corporation, but the corporation did not want its offer stated publicly. In figuring the matching money, the corporation allowed the association to count new memberships at a capitalized value of twenty to one. This meant that dues from new members were worth twenty times their dollar value in meeting the goal. Thus, in January, 1931, when the executive board stated $20,000 was needed immediately, the endowment fund was lacking $450,000. However, at the capitalized value allowed, the deficit was actually only $22,500.[47] So the money asked for by the executive board would serve the double purpose of meeting current needs and also help to reach the goal of the endowment fund.

Success was achieved at the New Haven, Connecticut, conference of ALA in June, 1931. There it was announced the fund needed only $3,300 to complete the $1,000,000. The result was an oversubscription from the floor of the convention—a remarkable achievement for any organization during the depression, even considering the generous capitalization feature offered by the Carnegie Corporation.[48]

It is necessary to add that the corporation did not respond quite as expected by the association. When notified of the completion of the fund drive, the corporation's answer was alarmingly nonchalant. It would, as a first step,

> . . . be glad to receive from the association a statement of a program upon which the corporation may base its consideration of further grants for the general purposes of the association.[49]

This resulted in a hurried reevaluation by the association of all current and proposed activities. Fortunately, the resulting statement satisfied the Carnegie Corporation. The second grant of $1,000,000 was announced to the membership in April, 1932.

In spite of this large grant, there were already indications that the association's major benefactor was in the process of questioning and perhaps reevaluating its support. The Carnegie Corporation's *Annual Report* for 1930–31 included the following statement which suggested that its subsidization of ALA may have been a mistake:

> Organizations, like men and trees, grow best if they develop according to natural laws. The present activities and development of the American Library Association may well have surpassed the limits of prudence, and may perhaps have overlooked important and even vital aspects of its necessary work. If so, the present achievement may possibly be paid for in retarded future growth.

This was the first instance of public criticism of the activities of the association by the corporation. It was indeed a serious threat to the funding of special programs, for which ALA could often count on the corporation to provide the financing. The report implied the need for a careful, mature program of development if any future aid were to be forthcoming. As indicated by the granting of the $1,000,000 in 1932, the subsidization did not end immediately. But in time, the funds did become more difficult to obtain, were usually less than asked, and were often in the form of emergency assistance, with the association simply acting as the disburser of monies.

Keppel remained a staunch friend of libraries and the association, but at the same time he did not hesitate to take exception to some of the activities and priorities of librarians. He often attended ALA conferences, and his pithy statements came to be expected, if not particularly welcomed. His comments, in the form of a private memo, on the 1936 midwinter meeting are perhaps illustrative of his frankness:

> Objection to metamorphosis of librarians into social service workers, YMCA gladhander rotarian goodfellow type, or hostess. . . .
> The librarians haven't realized yet that they may become overorganized. They seem always to wish (1) a grant; (2) a committee.[50]

But in spite of the criticism, occasional support of ALA activities continued; furthermore, the corporation's officers were often very useful in contacting other foundations that might be potential donors.

NEW HAVEN CONFERENCE, 1931

The New Haven conference of 1931 was noteworthy for reasons other than reaching the endowment goal. The meetings attracted a total of 3,225 registrants, by far the largest attendance in ALA history. Considering the economic conditions throughout the country, such a response was outstanding. The main attraction for librarians at the conference was the new Sterling Library at Yale University, considered to be a landmark in library architecture.

The conference was the first in which federal aid to libraries was proposed in concrete form. The council asked Congress to appropriate $100,000,000 for libraries over a ten-year period. The money was to be distributed to the states in proportion to their rural population. A federal library commission would be established to supervise the state work. The fund's purpose would be to equalize and stimulate funding for rural public library service.[51] Given the economic circumstances of the country, it seemed to many people to be a very inappropriate time to introduce the subject. The August *Library Journal* noted that such huge government commitments could not be expected in view of the economic crisis. More careful plans were drawn up during September but abruptly postponed in December. At that time, President Roosevelt made a plea to delay all such broad and expensive plans until much later.[52] Although this initial action met with an early defeat, it is interesting to note that later, successful programs embodied the proposal's two major principles: a library agency and federal aid based on rural population.

DEATHS OF DEWEY AND BOWKER

On December 26, 1931, members of the library profession were saddened to learn of the death of Melvil Dewey. Even though he had ceased to be active in the profession many years previously, the many legends associated with him kept the memories of his accomplishments fresh in the minds of librarians. One year previous to his death his fertile mind had conceived a new plan involving librarians and his Lake Placid Club. He announced his desire to build a retirement home for librarians in the Adirondacks of New York. The "library colony" would also serve as a vacation area for librarians. Although *Library Journal* commented rather disparagingly, Dewey still had hopes for its eventual construction.[53]

Some of the opposition to the plan probably lingered from the problems that had developed over the Lake Placid Club. Since it had been developed as a club and not a hotel, Dewey could apply his own stringent rules as to admission of guests. His practices gave rise to the belief that he was anti-Semitic, a belief that was probably accurate. It is certainly true that the Lake Placid Club, of which Dewey was the founder and leader, was anti-Semitic in its restrictions.[54] This problem, in addition to the doubt as to whether librarians really should vacation together, resulted in the permanent postponement of the plans for a librarian's colony.

In the past, Dewey had been well known for his ability to succeed in ventures in spite of considerable resistance. In July, 1931, an old friend had written Dewey to recall how things had once been in the association:

> I often think over with renewed courage how often you put over matters in the old days despite the opposition—when you held the cards, as you usually did.[55]

Dewey was, of course, tremendously important and influential during the early days of ALA. He was often viewed with something approaching worship by some people, as illustrated by the following incident related by Arthur Bostwick. At one of the conferences, a young librarian was at the table of Mr. and Mrs. Bostwick when Dewey stopped to chat. After Dewey left, the librarian said, "Oh, Doctor Bostwick! You can't imagine how I feel! Why, it's just as if I had been talking to Moses or Elijah or one of the prophets!"[56]

Dewey was a man of great ability and personal drive. He was also capable of using a variety of techniques in achieving his goals. The methods used sometimes led to personal antagonism between Dewey and his colleagues. His ambition and gigantic ego often caused others to dislike him intensely. Some people undoubtedly saw him as devious and unscrupulous, and there are numerous veiled references to his immorality and womanizing.

Never one to hide his own accomplishments, Dewey was particularly possessive towards ALA and *Library Journal*. As the years passed, he became' even less inclined to share with others credit for founding both of them. Thus he could write quite sincerely just two weeks before his death that he had in 1876 established the ALA, the American Metric Bureau, the Spelling Reform Association, three periodicals, and the Library Bureau. As for ALA, according to Dewey, it was his own "burning faith and optimism [that] kept the treadmill turning." Similarly, *Library Journal* owed its continued existence to Dewey:

> Our monthli Librari Journal to which was given 5 strenuus years, twys in anser to its SOS when the publisher anounst its suspension, was kept alive by great personal sacrifys, til it has gone on to 56 stout volumes.[57]

Such inaccurate and immodest claims might tend to reduce one's opinion of Dewey, but the fact remains that Dewey was extremely influential throughout his active association with ALA. Whether in committees or in official capacity, his hands were very much at the helm. If he did not accomplish as much as he thought in his later years, he at least accomplished more than any other man during the early history of the association.[58] Even in retirement, his influence was considerable. His presence at a meeting almost guaranteed a capacity crowd. His speaking ability was well known, and he was justly famous for his ability to persuade others to his way of thinking. This is perhaps best illustrated in a statement made by St. Clair McKelway, who had been a member of the Board of Regents of New York at the time when Dewey was its secretary. McKelway said Dewey could introduce a subject to the board and have it adopted unanimously. One month later, Dewey might ask to have the matter reconsidered, present the opposite point of view, convince the board that that was the only possible policy, and have the new view adopted unanimously. According to McKelway, this happened many times.[59]

In November, 1933, Richard R. Bowker died at Salem, Massachusetts. He was a publisher rather than a librarian, but he had been one of the most stabilizing influences within ALA since its establishment. He was proud of the part he played in the formation of the organization, although he was less inclined to talk and write about it than was Dewey. It was only when anyone suggested that *Library Journal* was a child of ALA that Bowker became incensed. The result invariably would be an editorial in *Library Journal,* setting the record straight on the correct genesis. He seemed less concerned with Dewey's version of who first thought of the idea of a national association of librarians. Perhaps he remained quiet because there was no way of proving who was the first to suggest ALA, or possibly, he did not really care who got the credit. His role in ALA was essentially behind the scenes, because he never allowed himself to be nominated for any of the offices. Yet through the council and through committees, he was able to exert considerable influence in the association and in the library world. Librarians benefited from his political work, too. He was actively concerned with postal reform, copyright, and tariff reform.[60] Thus the death of Bowker was a serious blow to librarianship, and to ALA in particular.

DEPRESSION AND RECOVERY

Meanwhile, the continuing depression caused increasing financial problems for the association. In October, 1932, President Harry M. Lydenberg reported that over 3,000 members had failed to pay their dues.[61] In addition, many of the sustaining members who had pledged support in the endowment fund campaign failed to make their payments. A $15,000 deficit resulted, although there was some hope the financial picture might improve later in the year. The immediate result of the loss of income was a budget cut at headquarters. The staff took a 10 percent cut for the last six months of 1932—in addition to a previous 3 percent cut effected by closing the offices on Saturdays.[62]

The repudiation of the administration of Herbert Hoover in the landslide victory of Franklin Roosevelt in 1932 showed also in the change of public attitude. Within a month of Roosevelt's inaugural address, *Library Journal* noted a new atmosphere of confidence in the country, replacing the fear and uneasiness so evident before. This new feeling was in response to the sense of vigor and confidence that seemed to permeate the new administration. It was also a result of the rapid enactment of recovery legislation aimed at stimulating business and putting men back to work. While the Hoover administration had not really had a laissez faire attitude towards the depression, to many people it had seemed to have. This contributed to the feeling of hopelessness so prevalent throughout the nation in 1932.

Yet the new spirit evident in April, 1933, was based largely on expected results and changes. It was still too early for libraries to be affected directly. For example, the problem of placing graduate librarians was still acute. Almost 1,200 unemployed librarians were looking for positions during the spring. The 1933 graduating classes added 1,200 more.[63] At the same time, some libraries were still cutting budgets, reducing services, and generally retrenching. ALA income continued the downward plunge that had been evident since 1930. The predepression budget of 1926 had almost reached $400,000; in 1933, the expenditures had been pared to $232,000.[64] Thus the improvement in morale alluded to by *Library Journal* was based more on the promise of the future than on actual changes in economic conditions.

The relief work for which the first part of Roosevelt's administration is famous began in 1933. It was not, however, until 1934 that the real thrust of the activity developed. As the so-called alphabet agencies started to function, federal assistance in its many forms trickled down to the local level. These agencies, including the Federal Emergency Relief Administration, the Civil Works Administration, the Civil Works Service, and the Emergency Education Program, channeled money into areas especially hard hit by poverty and unemployment. Projects of many types were begun in an effort to raise the level of employment. In a number of states, studies of library service and educational opportunities were financed for this purpose. Special library collections were established; for example, art and music collections were put together with the assistance of artists and musicians. During the year, hundreds of libraries were cleaned, painted, repaired, and in some cases enlarged. Unskilled workers repaired books to an extent never before possible. Unemployed journalists prepared library publicity. Altogether, thousands of persons were given at least temporary positions in libraries. Several hundred unemployed librarians found professional work.[65]

Nevertheless, the financial condition of libraries in general remained extremely poor. Book budgets were still being reduced, and in some communities the public library received no book budget at all. Salary cuts of 50 percent were not unusual. In view of the wholesale dismissal of employees, the remaining librarians felt that even half a salary was better than no salary at all. Budget cuts meant reduced hours of service for most libraries. Some branches, stations, and school libraries were closed in an effort to reduce expenditures. These were all sharp indications that prosperity had not yet arrived for most libraries.

In spite of considerable resistance in the profession, the ALA leadership persistently worked toward greater federal involvement in libraries and library service. Milam, in particular, played an important role in persuading the federal government to include libraries in the massive projects being planned. An early example of this is a 1934 meeting between Milam, ALA president Charles A. Compton, and the secretary of agriculture, Henry A. Wallace. The thrust of the librarians' arguments was the need for federal aid to develop library service in rural areas. Wallace was not convinced that this was one of his areas of responsibility, but he promised his support if the matter ever came up. In his record of the meeting, Milam wrote that Wallace was "tired, defensive at first, obviously interested, but not at all sure that it was his funeral."

Later, as some of the relief programs got underway, many librarians protested that nonprofessionals were doing library work while hundreds of librarians remained unemployed. Commercial binderies complained that they often had nothing to do because the federal government paid untrained workers in libraries to repair books. Although Milam was outspoken in his advocacy of such projects when properly planned, the association also produced critical reports and articles on the federal programs. The Works Projects Administration (WPA) in particular was the target for much criticism. At a meeting of the executive board in October, 1940, one member, Carleton Joeckel, complained:

> . . . I have been reading some of the voluminous mimeographed material which comes out from the A.L.A. and I rise in protest. It has seemed that about 50% of it is sniping at the W.P.A. In other words, they are trying to find as much fault with things that have gone on as they can, instead of looking at it in a constructive way.

But other members criticized WPA's methods and lack of planning. If the results were going to be unsatisfactory, then perhaps it would be best not to get involved. One such viewpoint was expressed by Ralph Munn:

> Pennsylvania is, you know, one of the most backward states in the Union. We are getting no place fast. Here is the W.P.A. standing right on the border, ready to come in with a million dollars. They would do more in the way of actually peddling books than we will do without them in the next one hundred years.[66]

Munn was convinced that, from the long-range viewpoint, it would be better to do without the books and the libraries than to let the WPA come into the state with the methods then in use. Part of the problem, according to librarians, was the failure of the WPA to include librarians in planning the projects and in the supervision of them once they got underway.

To a certain extent, Munn's opinion was validated when, in December, 1941, a WPA official appeared before the executive board to ask for an advisory committee from the ALA to help avoid future problems:

One thing that I have observed is this. If we get the support of local librarians more, there wouldn't be so much deficiency in program operation. The mere existence of the committee would have a good effect.[67]

As a result of his request, a National Advisory Committee on WPA Library Projects was chosen. Unfortunately, since the WPA went out of existence in 1943, the committee probably had very little influence.

The long-awaited improvement in conditions for libraries and librarians began in 1935. The relief and recovery previously mentioned helped to remove many librarians from the ranks of the unemployed. In March, 1935, an estimate by the ALA Subcommittee on Unemployment showed that from 1,300 to 1,700 librarians were looking for professional positions. By comparison, in July, 1933, there were almost 2,500 unemployed, so the improvement was substantial.[68] In addition, the financial condition of libraries in general began to improve enough so that the salary situation was not as bleak as it had been. By 1935, 70 libraries reported that they had partially or fully restored salaries to their previous levels, and this favorable trend continued unabated.[69]

The improved economic conditions affected ALA's financial situation. Income was still far below that of predepression years, of course, but there were some indications that the downward trend of income had ceased. The treasurer reported 1935 income at $220,500, compared to $250,000 in 1931. His report optimistically predicted that some revenues would be increased during 1935, resulting in a balanced budget.[70]

QUESTIONS OF ALLEGIANCE

It was perhaps fitting that, at a time when the association was facing financial problems, it was also enduring a crisis in internal allegiance. Reduced library budgets had forced librarians to review their priorities, to take stock of what was on hand, and to formulate new goals. This process also seemed to be applied to the profession and its major organization. Discontent within ALA was definitely on the increase for negative expressions over the directions taken by the association were frequent and harsh. The question of federal aid to libraries was a particularly divisive one, and many members found the organization's open courting of this money especially galling. Opposition stemmed not only from concern over federal control, but also from dislike of a professional organization's becoming involved in politics. Polarization of the membership over this issue promoted discontent. This in turn encouraged the idea of independent groups within the profession. At least one regional organization openly discussed withdrawing from ALA and charting a course of its own. Other such organizations joined in with expressions of independence that demonstrated the dissatisfaction within ALA.

The warnings of Ralph Shaw helped to restore a sense of calm, if not a renewal of allegiance to the association. Shaw cautioned that the profession would only be weakened further by what he called a "multiplicity of impotent, non-representative societies."[71] His solution to the problem was to suggest two structural changes: (1) to decentralize the association by building strong local and regional subdivisions, and (2) to provide for a professional classification of membership based on ability and achievement. Although seeming to be of considerable merit, Shaw's proposal failed to receive any substantial support in the profession.

The problem within the association went beyond a concern over the structure. There was also a growing disenchantment with the organization itself. Perhaps this was in part the natural result of the general unhappiness and dissatisfaction of the times. But it would also appear that the self-examination that followed the failure of the Enlarged Program had opened the doors to extensive criticism. Members then were unhappy primarily because they believed the leadership was going beyond the wishes of its constituency. This problem had surfaced again on the issue of federal aid. While the majority of the membership was probably behind the leadership's request, a sizable and vocal minority protested strongly.[72]

Another issue that caused dissension was the failure to restrict the output of the library schools. During a time when hundreds of qualified librarians could not obtain jobs, every graduation ceremony added to the oversupply. The revelation that at least 20 percent of the graduates had physical or personality difficulties that would make them difficult to place even in normal times contributed to the strong feeling that library schools could not be expected to exert the needed self-control.[73] The Board of Education for Librarianship, which had some authority over library education, could probably have affected the output if it had chosen to do so. This it did not do. Instead, it continued its policy of discouraging the establishment of new schools. This policy did little to alleviate the immediate problem of the oversupply of librarians, although it probably had a long-range effect. It did nothing towards satisfying the immediate demands of unemployed librarians.

Finally, one must take into consideration the long-felt estrangement between the headquarters bureaucracy and a sizable proportion of the membership. This was not so much a matter of hostility as simply a feeling that the two had very little in common. The first Activities Committee had noted an almost total lack of rapport between headquarters and members, and it had criticized the headquarters staff for failing to try to understand the problems of librarians.[74] Five years later, the situation seemed perhaps to be even worse, according to some librarians. Ralph Shaw had noted the disturbing lack of allegiance to the professional organization. Others wrote to the editors of library periodicals to voice their complaints. But there seemed to be no response to this insistent call for a change, even though it seemed to come from a sizable segment of the profession.

To a certain extent, this criticism was brought out in the report of the second Activities Committee. This committee, under the chairmanship of Paul North Rice, began work in 1933 and reported its findings the following year. Its report was not as comprehensive as that of its predecessor, for three main reasons: (1) criticism was not quite as widespread or as acute as it had been in 1928; (2) the first Activities Committee's report had been extremely wide ranging, and some of its recommendations had not as yet been put into effect; and (3) some of the matters under consideration by the second committee were taken care of by the executive board.

The committee criticized the organization in three main areas. First, it took note of the employment situation and the failure of the Board of Education for Librarianship to take any significant steps toward reducing enrollments. It pointed out that some unaccredited schools had actually increased enrollments, while very few of the accredited schools had reported a decrease. Other professions, such as medicine, had already restricted enrollment in order to try to achieve a balance between supply and demand. The committee suggested that ALA, its boards and committees, and AALS "attack the problems of the present crisis with greatly increased vigor. Second, the report criticized the ever expanding staff and activities of headquarters. After commenting on the increase in staff size, it asked, "Is there not a limit to the number of activities which should be added to headquarters organization?" Finally, the report suggested that the membership choose its presidents more carefully; selection should be based on leadership and not on the wish to honor someone. It concluded that longevity of service should not be the chief reason to select a president.[75]

In addition to the Activities Committee report, the membership considered a proposal for federal aid to libraries. The idea had been discussed on many occasions and approved by several groups at various times. The Committee on Library Extension was the first ALA group to advocate such aid.[76] It passed a resolution in 1929 calling for federal assistance to libraries. The council approved the principle of federal aid in December, 1930; June, 1931; June, 1934; and December, 1934. Opposition on these occasions had been minimal or nonexistent.[77] As finally approved by the council, the 1934 resolution included two important features that involved the federal government. First, it proposed the establishment of a national library agency. This was a basic part of the *National Plan for Libraries* that had been approved in 1934. The *National Plan* called for the following improvements in library service:

1. Federation and coordination of public libraries into systems encompassing a fairly large geographical area
2. Provision for total state library service by each state government
3. State allocations to local units in order to provide at least a minimum level of library services to everyone
4. Coordination of library activity through the establishment of a federal library agency
5. Certification of librarians by individual state agencies
6. Provision for federal aid to equalize library facilities throughout the country.[78]

The proposed national library agency was to be part of the Office of Education. There had been some early sentiment for its association with the Library of Congress, but this was not supported by the library. Herbert Putnam said,

> We should not welcome them, and I believe that they would tend to confuse and impede the service to learning, which should be the primary duty of our National Library.[79]

The second proposed feature of federal participation was federal aid to libraries. The resolution passed by the council was worded so as to limit the amount of governmental interference. Programs for library development would be submitted by each state to the library agency. These programs would carefully outline the need for money and the plans for allocating the funds once received. Half the federal aid would be distributed according to need, as set forth in these programs, and the other half would be distributed to the states on the basis of population. Council members voted to ask for federal support in the amount of $50,000,000 to $100,000,-000.[80] These figures were arrived at by using the recommended $1 per capita minimum expenditure, and the calculations took into consideration local and state support. It was recognized by the council members that such federal support would not be immediately forthcoming. Rather, the figures were to be used as a basis for discussion in Congress, and a lower amount would eventually be accepted as a compromise. At the same time, the council authorized the officers of the association to request additional amounts of money from the public works fund.[81] This money was to be used for the acquisition of building sites for public libraries and for the improvement of existing library buildings.

In general, the proposal was far reaching, well developed, and carefully constructed. It was in part a response to the unpleasant problem of federal controls attached to federal money. The resolution carefully confined any participation by the federal government to reviewing and selecting from plans prepared by state library agencies. It presupposed that the government would accept such a passive role in dispensing its funds.

The immediate result of this proposal was failure to obtain direct federal aid to libraries; but at least one long-term goal was achieved: the establishment of a federal library agency. Since 1929, ALA conferences had been the scene of discussions centering around the need for such an agency. While many librarians objected to federal aid, there was almost no objection to the agency. Largely through the efforts of Forrest B. Spaulding, head librarian of the Des Moines (Iowa) Public Library, Congress rather reluctantly approved the bill creating the agency. The Commissioner of Education had included an item of $40,000 for the library agency in his 1936–37 budget request. He appeared before a House subcommittee in support of the item. However, in spite of favorable reaction in the subcommittee, the item was dropped by the director of the budget. Efforts by the subcommittee to restore the allocation were unsuccessful in the House, and so the campaign moved over to the Senate.

Acting as ALA's Washington representative, Spaulding almost single-handedly rescued the library agency from oblivion. He met with both senators and representatives repeatedly in order to secure a reconsideration of the agency item. He was eventually successful in his efforts. As passed by Congress, the budget provided for a first-year appropriation of $25,000. This was a reduction of 70 percent from the original request. Nevertheless, it was sufficient for the agency, renamed the Library Division, to begin serving libraries.[82]

RACIAL DISCRIMINATION

The selection of Richmond, Virginia, as the 1936 conference site posed a new problem for ALA: a state law, general at this time in the South, that forbade the mixing of white people with Negroes in meetings. The issue came to light in May, 1936, when Negro members of the association received a letter from the local arrangements committee in Richmond. The letter expressed the hope that large numbers of Negro librarians would attend, but with a knowledge of the conditions they could expect to find in the city. These conditions included the following: Negroes could use the same hotel entrances as white delegates, but they could not obtain rooms or meals at hotels the whites used; meetings held in conjunction with breakfasts, luncheons, or dinners would not be open to Negroes; seating for Negroes at meetings would at all times be reserved in the right-hand section.[83]

The angry response of librarians to these conditions was limited to a few letters to *Library Journal*. The *ALA Bulletin* took no note of the controversy until after the conference was over. The strongest criticism came from LeRoy Charles Merritt, a student at the University of Chicago, who demanded to know why there had been no advance explanation of the situation to the membership. Why had only Negro librarians received the letter, Merritt asked? He believed an apology was due the entire membership from the officers of the association. Merritt concluded,

> Let that explanation come forth in the contrite tone of an apology, and let it avoid the further error of seeking a justification of a situation that merits none.[84]

There were to be no apology and no explanation from the officers. The only periodical outside the profession to comment on the situation was the *New Republic*. An editorial published on May 20, just before the Richmond conference, said the meetings gave promise of being a "pleasant conference, except for those librarians who happen to be Negroes." The writer noted that the excuse for the discrimination was the laws of Virginia, over which ALA had no control. A question concluded the editorial: "Why should any civilized association, with Negro members, undertake to hold a convention in Virginia or any other state that makes such distinctions?" In spite of the law, five months later the traditionally conservative American Legion met in Virginia under different circumstances; the group found it possible to invite Negro members to eat in the same banquet room as the white members.[85]

At the Richmond conference action was taken to reduce the possibility of a repetition of this unfortunate discrimination. The executive board appointed a committee to formulate policy in this area. On December 28, 1936, the committee submitted three recommendations, which the council approved:

1. That ALA's freedom of action should not be affected by an insistence upon equal treatment of all members
2. That no section of the country should be eliminated from consideration for the annual conference because of anticipated racial discrimination

3. That in all rooms and halls under the control of the association for conference use, all members should be admitted in full equality.[86]

The executive board issued the following statement after the Richmond conference:

> The members of the board were unanimous in thinking that the association would protect its members against professional discrimination because of race or color, but that it was not the province of this organization to take up the question of general social or personal discrimination.[87]

As can readily be seen, these positions avoided the larger issue of racial discrimination in the South. They also avoided the responsibility of an association to seek for its members the elementary right of equal protection under the law. No concern was shown for what might happen elsewhere, and discrimination might well be experienced by members trying to obtain rooms and meals. Thus, while the reports indicated some progress towards a guarantee of equal treatment, much remained to be done. In the view of many members, this was by no means an adequate victory for civil rights in ALA.

The issue was allowed to remain somewhat dormant for almost four years. Then in 1940, a group of Southern librarians petitioned the council to reconsider the 1936 action, which had in practice eliminated Southern cities from consideration as conference sites, because it insisted on full equality in all rooms under the control of ALA.[88] President Ralph Munn appointed a committee of two to make a special study of the problem and report back to the council: Ernestine Rose of the New York Public Library and John Hall Jacobs of the New Orleans Public Library.[89] Later on, in a rather unusual move for a presiding officer, Munn appointed himself to also serve on the committee.

Even before the committee reported in May, 1940, many people indicated their unhappiness that ALA had even allowed the issue to be reconsidered. The discrimination seen at Richmond in 1936 was still fresh in the minds of some Northern librarians. Furthermore, this question was raised at a time when the anti-Semitic persecutions abroad were causing much protest in the United States. It seemed inappropriate that the association could possibly revert to what one librarian called the "older order of things."[90]

In all fairness to the Southern librarians who requested the reconsideration, it must be pointed out they were not asking the association to ignore the possibility of racial incidents. Instead, these members wanted the South to be given serious consideration in the selection of conference sites. They believed that ALA leaders had not previously pressed strenuously enough for equality of treatment. President Munn shared this opinion, as he stated to the council at the Cincinnati conference in 1940:

> From my own service on the executive board, I know that determined and forceful approaches have not been made; we have taken the word of local librarians, and hotel managers without pressing the issue.[91]

Southern areas were certainly not the only localities where Negro librarians would encounter segregation, of course. *ALA Bulletin,* in announcing plans for the Cincinnati conference, gave this advice:

> Colored delegates will find excellent accommodations at the Manse Hotel, 1004 Chapel Street, about four miles from headquarters and auditorium with several car lines passing close to both without transfers.[92]

Midwinter meetings held in Chicago presented the same situation. Neither the Palmer House nor the Drake Hotel, where the association often met, accepted Negroes on the same basis as Caucasians. Yet there was no public criticism of this discrimination. This left Southern librarians to wonder why the association allowed two standards to remain in effect.

The Special Committee on Racial Discrimination submitted its report to the council at the Cincinnati conference. It recommended no change from the 1936 policy statement. The report did suggest, however, that ALA make it known it desired to meet in all areas of the country. Then in considering any city, officials should exert every effort to obtain compliance with requirements. If any city found it impossible to guarantee compliance, the association should meet elsewhere. This report was accepted in its entirety by the council in May, 1940, thus presumably ending the problem.

While the association was confronting, and perhaps partially avoiding, the discrimination issue, it was also developing a code of ethics for librarians. For a long time, librarians had been discussing in committee and in conference the need for such a code, which would spell out a professional's responsibilities. An individual effort, C. K. Bolton's "The Librarian's Code of Ethics," began to appear in various public libraries about 1909 and, with a number of revisions, was later included in books and periodicals. There was some sentiment that Bolton's code should be adopted by ALA, but it was decided instead to develop a new set of professional standards. *The Annals of the American Academy of Political and Social Science* in May, 1922, carried an extensive code that served to further the discussion. A committee within the association was established to arrive at a consensus statement, which was presented to the council as a draft in

December, 1929. Another committee took up the work, and it was not until December, 1938, that the council finally approved the code. It was a statement of twenty-eight articles, covering the librarian's relations to the governing authority, the library's public, the library staff, the profession, and society in general. In general, it was a compilation of philosophical and practical concepts that librarians could easily accept without hesitation or argument.

SUMMARY

The dominating factors during this time were the depression and the nation's effort to recover from its ills. The economic conditions slowed down ALA activity through loss of members and the subsequent drop in income. Even the successful completion of the Endowment Fund failed to help the association significantly in its financial struggles. Fortunately, relief work of various types helped, in that fewer librarians were unemployed.

This segment of ALA's history was one of intense internal criticism. John Cotton Dana was the most vocal and successful of the critics, but he seemed to represent many members in his demands for changes. Dana's constant criticism led to the establishment of the Activities Committee, a group charged with the responsibility of reviewing the association's procedures and practices. The committee proved to be valuable in pointing out weaknesses, leading to eventual modifications.

One of the most difficult problems the committee had to deal with was library education. The Board of Education for Librarianship and the Association of American Library Schools found it difficult to work effectively with each other, and as a result the Activities Committee was forced to investigate. No permanent solution to the problem was formulated, but the open discussion seemed to help in the relationship. A great amount of criticism was also generated when ALA formed a Business Librarians Section. This move came after repeated warnings by SLA officers and even members of ALA that the new section was in direct competition with SLA, and therefore should be avoided. An open break between the two national organizations was averted only by the calming influence of SLA officers. Finally, for the first time in its history, the association faced the problem of racial discrimination. It had escaped the problem before only by refusing to admit that it existed. ALA's solution to the problem was only partial, since it did not really confront the basic issue of rights of members. But judged in the context of the times, it was perhaps a reasonable compromise that at least provided a means to help avoid future conflicts.

7

RECOVERY AND PREPARATION FOR WAR

*B*y 1937, unemployment among librarians had declined to about 600, compared with the 1,600 seeking positions in 1933.[1] Salaries also demonstrated a considerable improvement over the lowest period of the depression. Library budgets in many cities regained much of the ground lost during the previous eight years, but library service was still inadequate as judged by the suggested minimum standards. In 1937, the average per capita expenditure for library service in the United States was 40 cents, and a total of 45,000,000 people remained without any library service at all. Most of these people lived in rural areas, especially in the South. One-third of the counties in the country were without any public libraries.

In spite of these bleak figures, progress was being achieved. During 1937, four more states allocated funds for the development of libraries. County libraries increased in number and in size as a result of state aid and federal relief projects.[2] Through a combination of circumstances, the nation as a whole was moving along rapidly towards recovery. The year 1936 had been a "boom year," and the first three quarters of 1937 had shown similar characteristics. Immediately after Labor Day, however, there was a drastic setback in the business recovery. In place of the usual autumn upturn in business, there was a sharp decline; this reversal brought the economy almost down to the level of 1934. Fortunately, the recession was relatively short, and by mid-1938, business had resumed its upward surge. Libraries were not seriously affected by this recession because of its short duration.

135

PROPOSED CHANGES

Perhaps as a result of a lessening concern over economic conditions, librarians were becoming more concerned with the structure and activities of ALA. One librarian spoke of the period as the "Age of Reorganization," for the subject always seemed to be under discussion. In fact, between 1937 and 1940 the primary thrust of membership activity was towards a structural reorganization of the association. Meetings and periodical articles brought out the intense feeling that the association was not performing adequately. There were many questions over priorities, directions, and results of ALA efforts. What had been accomplished during its years of existence? To what extent had ALA been instrumental in the library progress achieved? Why didn't the leadership show more concern about the social issues facing Americans? Were librarians benefiting from the multiplicity of library organizations allowed and seemingly encouraged by the association? These and many other serious problems were enough to encourage speculation as to whether the organization would ever survive. In the event that it did, there were a great many suggestions for changes, some of which had been presented many times before. Discussion was principally concerned with the following major proposals:

1. A federation of library associations with one united organization, instead of separate national organizations. This federation would completely integrate local, state, regional, and national associations into the central organization.
2. A unified pyramidal organization with divisions representing public libraries, university libraries, special libraries, and school libraries. Divisions would also be formed to represent the various types of library work, such as acquisitions, cataloging, reference, and circulation. Regional organizations would be established for each section of the country.[3]
3. Classification of the membership according to level of education or position. Many members had long felt uncomfortable over the fact that anyone could join ALA simply by paying the dues. It seemed appropriate to them that there should be some minimum requirements for membership. At the very least, there might be several levels of membership based on education or experience.
4. The question of replacing the annual meetings with biennial meetings was raised again. This had been suggested many times during the history of the association. The idea never really gained extensive approval although it had obvious merits that deserved serious consideration.[4]

Of the proposals suggested, unification of library organizations seemed to be most evidently needed. The multitude of associations had been allowed to develop without any visible pattern or plan. Table 1 lists the national library organizations active at the time.

Table 1. National Library Associations

Name	Founded	Members	ALA Affiliation
National Association of State Librarians	1889	52	yes
Medical Library Association	1898	438	no
Bibliographical Society of America	1904	441	no
League of Library Commissions	1904	437	yes
American Library Institute	1905	100	no
American Association of Law Librarians	1906	345	yes
Special Libraries Association	1909	1,897	yes
Association of American Library Schools	1915	27	yes
American Merchant Marine Library Association	1921	1,362	no
Association of Research Libraries	1931	44	yes
Music Library Association	1931	85	no
Catholic Library Association	1932	463	no

SOURCE: *ALA Bulletin* 33:21 (Jan., 1939).

In addition, there was a multitude of local, state, regional, and interest-oriented organizations to which librarians belonged. Even in a profession of 40,000 people, such fragmentation appeared excessive. Yet it was exceedingly difficult to provide any coordination that would satisfy all the members of the various organizations. Furthermore, probably the greatest factor in the growth of the separate national organizations was dissatisfaction with ALA. If the association could have responded adequately to the specialized needs of all librarians, there would have been no reason for the existence of a number of the organizations. Now that they were established, however, it would be difficult to make changes. Librarians who had carefully nurtured the younger associations would be unlikely to agree to a complete consolidation within the oldest and largest organization—ALA. The proposal for federation was made as an alternative to consolidation. A federation could coordinate the activities of existing library associations and provide central leadership. At the same time, it would not require the dissolution of any group; this factor made federation much more attractive than consolidation. In spite of the advantages of having some overall leadership provided through federation, however, not enough support was generated even within ALA to make this proposal feasible.

In view of the protracted discussion during this period, it was only logical that the third Activities Committee would also focus its attention on the various plans to restructure the organization. The committee received its impetus from a memo that Milam sent to the executive board on April 30, 1937, suggesting the need for a new review of the association. The committee, under the direction of Charles H. Brown, reported two years later. It called for a more democratic government, specifically a council that would be "a 100 per cent elective body based on a recognition of specific interests and geographic distribution."[5] The council at that time consisted chiefly of ex-officio members. The committee called for major changes in the structure of ALA because "Its administration is not adapted to an association with 15,000 members. . . ."

The report carefully recognized the accomplishments of the secretary:

> It is questionable whether any other person in the profession would have accomplished as much for the national recognition of librarianship as a profession and could have built up so effective a headquarters staff as has the present secretary.[6]

The committee credited him with many of the accomplishments of the association since the war: an increase in memberships, an increase in revenues, and greater influence of the association. But while giving Milam major credit, it also charged him with two major failures, shared with the executive board. According to the committee, the two had failed to encourage the growth of groups representing special types of libraries, with the result that similar organizations had developed outside the association. Second, with the intention of developing an efficient organization, the secretary had "contributed to the building of a system of centralized control." This had led to a lack of democracy in the appointment of boards and committees. The result, as far as minority groups were concerned, amounted to a policy of taxation without representation.

While finding the organization less than perfect, the Activities Committee was also critical of the membership. Members' criticism of headquarters was often "faultfinding" and "heckling," rather than reflecting an honest effort to improve the organization. Younger members, especially, too often were asking the question What does the ALA do for me? The *Bulletin* alone was worth the three dollars they paid in membership fees, and most professional organizations charged more. A large share of the membership seemed ignorant of what the association had already done for them. As professionals, they should be more concerned with what they could contribute, the report stated.

The end result of studying and debating reorganization for three years was no change at all.

SELECTION OF LIBRARIAN OF CONGRESS, 1938–1939

At this time, ALA became involved in an unfortunate controversy regarding the national library and the selection of a new head of it. Since 1900, ALA has tried three times to intervene in the selection of the Librarian of Congress. In each case, the success or failure of the involvement has been measured against the success the association enjoyed in the selection of Herbert Putnam as librarian in 1899. Unfortunately, there is no evidence that the association has had any influence in the selection of the three librarians.

The first occasion for involvement in this century was the retirement of Herbert Putnam. As early as 1937, he had indicated a desire to retire after almost forty years as the Librarian of Congress. This was perhaps a tentative statement by Putnam, since no formal move was made until mid-1938. Apparently, there were two reasons for the delay in retirement plans: a desire by Putnam to select his own successor, and an inadequate pension plan.[7] Although the retirement had not been officially announced, association leaders knew it was inevitable and therefore began to make plans. They were anxious to duplicate the success the association had had with Putnam's appointment. The leaders immediately began the process of identifying possible candidates for the position when it became vacant. The first step was the appointment of a committee of five to represent the association.[8] Although no official decision was made, the committee seemed to agree informally that the two best-qualified candidates were Prof. Carleton B. Joeckel of the University of Chicago Graduate Library School and Carl H. Milam, ALA's executive secretary. Very shortly, the committee settled on Milam as its nominee.

The problems of the selection committee were compounded by two factors. First, Herbert Putnam had not yet announced his retirement, and did not seem to be in any hurry to do so. Second, President Franklin Roosevelt had indicated through his close adviser Harry Hopkins that the advice of professional associations in the matter of appointments would not be solicited. Through Hopkins it was also learned that the administration was annoyed with Putnam for his delay in retiring.[9] This problem was solved in June, 1938, when Roosevelt signed a bill allowing Putnam to retire at half salary. The librarian then announced his retirement as of August 1. The resignation gave the selection committee its opportunity to contact Roosevelt for the first time. In a telegram to the president, Harrison Craver stressed the importance of the position, suggested the necessary qualifications, and offered assistance in the selection of a new Librarian of Congress. The presidential office responded with a polite, perfunctory note of appreciation.

Putnam's resignation also allowed public discussion of a possible successor. John Vance, Library of Congress law librarian, announced his availability for the position. This caused friends of Carl Milam to urge the executive secretary to campaign openly. Milam refused to do this, although his friends were uninhibited in his behalf. He indicated that if the position were to come to him, it would have to be on his own terms: that he did not openly seek the job.[10]

However, some indirect steps were taken by both Milam and his friends. At Milam's suggestion, Harrison Craver wrote Frederick Delano, an uncle of the president. The letter offered to "suggest names if the President cares to have them suggested."[11] Delano did not respond to the letter. Milam next wrote to George Parker, editor-in-chief of the Scripps-Howard newspapers, regarding the urgency in filling the vacancy—apparently trying to encourage editorial support. The letter also discussed possible candidates. Of Vance he wrote,

> I do not know whether our committee would endorse him or not.
> I do know that it would put certain names ahead of his.

The only other name Milam mentioned in the letter was his own. He conceded that it had been mentioned, but said he did not know how seriously. He declared "I am in no sense a candidate."[12] Putnam did not help matters, since he did not offer public support to any candidate. Yet he seems to have privately supported Milam's secret candidacy, as indicated in the following letter from Craver to Milam:

> [Putnam] much prefers you to Vance. In fact, I think no other appointment would please him. . . . Even [William Warner] Bishop prefers you to Vance! Poor Bishop wants a scholar, which he says you are not, but is not able to suggest one.[13]

In December, 1938, and again in February, 1939, letters were sent to Roosevelt urging the appointment of Milam. In addition, the second letter included a comment designed to thwart the candidacy of Vance:

We have heard that a number of the present staff may be urged for consideration. Dr. Putnam has, however, frequently stated that there is *no* member of his staff whom he could confidently recommend as his successor, and we are sure that the selection of the man mentioned would be a disappointment to the profession.[14]

Members of the committee believed the failure of Roosevelt to name a a new librarian was due to his lack of interest in the position, but it appears that Roosevelt was having difficulty making up his mind. He admitted as much in a personal letter to Justice Felix Frankfurter, whom he had just appointed to the Supreme Court. The letter asked what Frankfurter thought of Archibald MacLeish. Frankfurter responded that he thought MacLeish would make an outstanding contribution. He predicted that MacLeish

> would bring to the Librarianship intellectual distinction, cultural recognition the world over, a persuasive personality and a delicacy of touch in dealing with others, and creative energy in making the Library of Congress the greatest center of the cultural resources of the nation. . . .[15]

On June 6, 1939, Roosevelt announced his selection of MacLeish. In his statement, Roosevelt said he had sought, and found in the poet, a "gentleman and a scholar." He was convinced the nomination would meet with the approval of the library world.

The reaction of the library world, however, was swift and negative. At Milam's request, the new ALA president, Milton Ferguson, sent telegrams to the directors of the largest libraries in the country urging them to protest the appointment.[16] The Senate Library Committee was a special target for the protest because it was charged with the responsibility of holding hearings on the appointment. Its members were deluged with letters and telegrams objecting to the nomination. Many senators responded that it was the president's prerogative to name whomever he wished. Therefore they felt it would be discourteous to oppose the nomination of MacLeish. The librarians continued in their efforts, however. Milton Ferguson, speaking as president of ALA, called a news conference to publicize the reactions of librarians. Ferguson said that he would no more think of the poet as the Librarian of Congress "than as the chief engineer of the Brooklyn Bridge."[17] In addition, when ALA held its annual conference in San Francisco, over fourteen hundred members signed an open letter to President Roosevelt. The letter stressed that no one questioned MacLeish's "ability and distinction as a man of letters," but "librarianship is not a literary pursuit." The letter concluded that it would be a calamity to have MacLeish approved as Librarian of Congress.[18]

The battle was lost, and most librarians realized it. Harrison Craver wrote to Milam:

> My sympathy for you is great. I know you would have filled the position capably, even brilliantly. We would have been proud of our representative. And aside from that, I wanted to see my friend get what he wanted.[19]

On June 29, 1939, the Senate confirmed the appointment. Two days later, ALA's newly elected president, Ralph Munn, wrote to congratulate MacLeish. He apologized that the association's battle had to take the form of a protest against MacLeish's nomination. He noted the sole basis was the poet's lack of training and experience.[20] MacLeish responded that he understood the reason for the protest, but he said, "I do regret the tactics adopted by certain representatives of the A.L.A."[21] Milam also sent his congratulations to the new librarian and included a denial that he had ever been a candidate for the position.[22] His denial was accurate only to the extent that his candidacy had never been made public.

There was very little publicity given to the activities of ALA in this struggle. The average member would not have known the extent to which the organization was involved, because only a small part of the story was told. After some public criticism was made over what one librarian called ALA's "holy war," the events that had taken place were briefly summarized in the *ALA Bulletin*.[23] Curiously, however, this summary made no mention of Milam's candidacy. There was no further discussion of the issue in the *ALA Bulletin,* and its editor refused to print a letter criticizing the association's leadership.[24]

Perhaps it was wise to cut off the discussion and to try to forget what had happened. Surely the campaign against MacLeish was a shrill, histrionic outburst that could only hurt a professional organization. In retrospect, it proved especially inappropriate in view of the outstanding reputation MacLeish gained during his short tenure as Librarian of Congress.[25] Furthermore, after an understandable period of coolness towards ALA, MacLeish became closer to ALA and Milam than Putnam had been during most of his later years.

CLOUDS OF WAR

As the war in Europe increased in intensity, it became clear that it would only be a matter of time before the United States also became completely involved in the conflict. Industry was gearing up for the expected demands

on its facilities. Production had already shifted in some respects from a con-
sumer orientation to a military orientation. Military conscription was
clearly in the near future, although in the summer of 1940 it had not yet
been passed by Congress. The executive board of the association urged all
types of libraries to help wherever possible with military training. To some
people, this seemed to be premature, but it was certainly in keeping with
the militaristic spirit that was engulfing the country.[26]

This spirit, and the steady drift towards war, alarmed a sizable minority
of Americans. The dissident faction was formally represented in the library
profession by a group called the Progressive Librarians Council. The council
aroused the ire of the executive board by sending a "peace telegram" to
Roosevelt during the 1940 conference. The message began with the following statement:

> Alarmed by the rapid drift of this country toward involvement in
> the European war, we librarians, assembled at the sixty-second
> annual conference of the American Library Association in Cincin-
> nati, May 26 to June 1, respectfully urge you to keep this country
> at peace.[27]

The board was angry over the possibility people might interpret this
statement as emanating from ALA, and it condemned the telegram as misleading. This in spite of the fact that the telegram had been signed "Progressive Librarians Council." The board then sent a telegram of its own to
President Roosevelt. It was a rather curious message, which said the Progressive Librarians Council represented the opinion of a very small group
and had no authority to speak for librarians on this or any other subject.
The telegram further stated that, if the members of ALA were polled on the
question, they would overwhelmingly reject the ideas reflected in the original
peace telegram.[28] This was a rather astonishing claim to make, since the
membership had never been polled on the subject and had never given
any collective indication of where it stood. The telegram was released for
publication by the White House, although no such treatment had been given
to the earlier telegram. Similarly, the text of the executive board's telegram
was reprinted in the *ALA Bulletin*. The text of the telegram from the Progressive Librarians Council was ignored.[29]

In a matter related to the "peace telegram," a minor controversy developed in the Junior Members Round Table between its officers and its membership. The round table, at its membership meeting during the Cincinnati
conference, endorsed the peace message to Roosevelt. This official action
was ordered deleted from the minutes of the meeting by the executive board
of the round table. The reason given was that the resolution "was out

of order inasmuch as it did not pertain to the affairs" of the round table. The chairman said the executive board was simply fulfilling its obligation to act when the entire group was not in session. Objecting members could raise the issue at the next meeting if they wished to pursue it. This was an arbitrary action on the part of the round table's leadership, and there seemed to be no adequate reason for it.[30]

INTELLECTUAL FREEDOM

The approaching war also increased fear over internal security. This fear was evidenced in the growing demands for strict control over the dissemination of propaganda and "subversive" publications. The question of whether or not libraries should restrict the use of this type of material was debated at the Cincinnati conference in 1940. Speaking for restriction was Gilbert Bettman, former attorney general of Ohio. The American people did not want their democracy undermined, according to Bettman, by the "purposely poisoned arrows" of totalitarian propaganda. Thus it was imperative for public libraries to restrict the circulation of propaganda. Taking the opposite view was Arthur Garfield Hays, counsel for the American Civil Liberties Union. Hays called restriction of any kind undemocratic and contrary to the American theory of government. He said our governmental system could not and should not be preserved by silencing the advocates of change.[31]

A special committee on censorship had previously been established because of the continuing pressure on libraries in regard to material thought to be subversive. This committee, composed of Sterling North, Alfred C. Nielsen, and Forrest Spaulding, reported at the Cincinnati conference. The report reminded the council it had adopted the Library Bill of Rights in 1939. If this document was to mean anything, then further action must be taken by the association to protect librarians. Any librarian or library board confronted by demands for censorship of materials should be strongly supported. The committee was careful to differentiate between censorship and book selection. The latter, it was felt, was a matter of strictly local concern.[32] As a first step, the committee recommended the appointment of a new Committee on Intellectual Freedom. This group would have the power to act for ALA in safeguarding the rights of library users. The council accepted the report and the Intellectual Freedom Committee was appointed in late 1940.[33]

At the time of its adoption, the Library Bill of Rights had been received with no objection. The Intellectual Freedom Committee was also accepted with no problem. The attitudes of some librarians, however, began to change as the two began to function. In 1944, pressure was exerted on the committee to strengthen the role of ALA in censorship disputes. The immediate cause of the pressure was the public outcry over John Carlson's *Under Cover,* an account of the author's ten years as a member of fascist organizations in the United States and abroad. The tremendous popularity of this book caused citizens in many areas to try to prevent public libraries from buying it. In addition, efforts were made to prevent its distribution within the armed forces. The result of this controversy was a recommendation from the committee to the ALA council to add the following sentence to the bill of rights:

> Further, books believed to be factually correct should not be banned or removed from the library simply because they are disapproved by some people.[34]

Although the proposal was approved by a majority of those council members who responded to the mail vote taken, the necessary two-thirds response was not achieved, and the proposal lost. However, the council later took another vote and the measure passed.[35] There were other books that often strained the relationship of the library with the community. For example, John Steinbeck's *Grapes of Wrath,* Lillian Smith's *Strange Fruit,* and Kathleen Winsor's *Forever Amber* evoked serious censorship problems.[36] The Intellectual Freedom Committee as a result became more active in gathering national data on book banning and began to compile reports on community incidents throughout the country. The basic problem, of course, remained unsettled. What was the recourse when the Library Bill of Rights was violated? What could be done to help the librarian under attack? The answer, unfortunately, was very little. The only force was moral force, and that could be effective only when librarians cooperated. The glare of publicity could be valuable in exposing attempts at suppression. This was the reason for the committee's search for evidence of censorship.

Yet it was abundantly clear that the profession was not united in its bill of rights. Letters to *ALA Bulletin, Library Journal,* and ALA headquarters indicated strong dissent over the trend literature was taking during this period. *Forever Amber,* with its preponderance of sex, provides an outstanding example. The book's popularity, and the problem of to buy or not to buy, was grist for many discussions, letters, and speeches. In a number of cases, it is difficult to discern the difference between censorship efforts by the public and book selection by the librarian. The result was often the same, and in many cases the reasoning seemed to be very similar.

While the association was willing to assert its concern over censorship attempts in libraries, it was unwilling to get involved with related censorship problems in radio. In 1938, radio station WTCN of Minneapolis created a storm of controversy when it began broadcasting Eugene O'Neill's *Beyond the Horizon*. When the Federal Communications Commission (FCC) took the role of censor, a protest resolution was introduced in a meeting of the executive board. The ensuing debate showed the majority of board members were unwilling to extend the principle of freedom of speech to radio. Ralph Munn stated:

> I don't think we ought to get mixed up in this radio business. It is one thing to have books which have too many "God damns" per square inch of printed matter on a library shelf, and it is another thing to have it coming into the home by radio.[37]

President Milton J. Ferguson countered that argument with the observation that "It is only a step from saying Eugene O'Neill's book may not be given over the radio to saying you can't put it in your library."[38] The board members, however, did not accept that prediction, and the motion to protest the FCC's action was defeated.

SUMMARY

The recovery from the depression marked this brief period of ALA history. Due to various factors, including the outbreak of war in Europe, the nation was again making significant economic progress. For the library profession, this was reflected in growing employment and increasing membership in the association. With librarians less concerned over the economic situation, there developed an alarming dissension within ALA. Serious questions were raised over how the association might become more responsive, more democratic, and more representative of the library profession. This led to a variety of proposals, all intended to accomplish these goals. Among the suggestions were federation, classification of membership, and biennial meetings. After protracted discussion, however, no action was taken on any of the suggestions.

The most difficult problem encountered by the profession during this era was intellectual freedom. At first the issue was almost academic, but in time it became a very practical problem faced by many librarians. In a number of ways, challenges were made to freedom of information and the library's right to supply the information unencumbered. The ALA made a significant response to these challenges with the Library Bill of Rights. There was no force to back up the statements, however. Only the glare of publicity would prevent individuals, organizations, or governments from abusing the right of free access to information.

8

WAR AND POSTWAR PLANNING

*T*he United States in 1941 was preparing for a war that most people knew was inevitable. Selective service had been established in 1940 to increase the size of the Army to 625,000 men. Although at this time the United States technically had no enemy, it was in a limbo between peace and war. Since September, 1939, the country had been in a state of limited national emergency. On May 27, 1941, the president changed the status to unlimited national emergency, which meant that, except for the absence of actual combat, the country was on a wartime basis.[1] With the attack on Pearl Harbor by the Japanese on December 7, 1941, the last vestige of peace was destroyed.

DEFENSE ACTIVITIES

As each step took the country closer to all-out mobilization, libraries and the American Library Association became more involved in national defense activities. In this development, librarians had three distinct advantages over the librarians engaged in similar work during World War I. The first was the steady reinforcing of the knowledge that the nation was going to become directly involved in the war. Even with all the warning signals prior to United States involvement in World War I, library involvement in the defense efforts came as a distinct shock. This war was different. While the attack on Pearl Harbor was indeed a terrible surprise, librarians had not waited until the actual moment of war to become involved. The involvement had been going on for some time and was steadily increasing.[2] The second advantage for librarians in 1941 was experience. They could draw on the previous work of others who had served in defense activities. The third advantage was the recognition by the War Department of the value of libraries and library service. It was not necessary to again demonstrate the worth of libraries to the military because this had been amply shown in the previous war.

Pointing up the value placed on libraries was the extensive program of library development, which was established and maintained by the War Department, not by ALA. In the army, libraries were organized at most of the camps and were under the supervision of the Morale Division. By March, 1941, there were already 75 camp libraries, each with a trained librarian, and this number was soon expanded to 125. Over $400,000 was allocated by the Morale Division for the purchase of books for these libraries.[3] The navy library organization was very similar to that of the 1920s. Libraries were operated in naval stations, hospitals, and vessels. Although there was room for improvement in the military library organization, it was far superior to the arrangement at the beginning of World War I.

Even though the War Department had taken over many of the library activities, there still remained much work for ALA to do. For example, its president, Charles H. Brown, noted that requests for ALA help and advice had increased sharply. He reported that during a trip to Washington, he had received such requests from officials of four federal departments and agencies.[4] Julia W. Merrill of the headquarters staff was loaned to the Office of Education to make a survey of library needs of defense areas and emergency needs of public libraries.

In cooperation with the American Red Cross and the United Service Organization (USO), ALA began planning a drive for books for servicemen. This became the National Defense Book Campaign, under the direction of Althea Warren of the Los Angeles Public Library.[5] It was estimated that between five and ten million books would be needed. This estimate took into account such needs as the day rooms for each company or battalion in the army camps; the 400 USO reading rooms for servicemen on leave; the needs of the Marine Corps; and the greatly enlarged capacity of the hospitals of the armed forces. Even before the actual campaign got underway, however, local library organizations throughout the country had begun their individual drives. Aware of the needs of the young men in the service, they worked hard to get books on the way. The Chicago Public Library collected 20,000 books for servicemen. In New Jersey, thousands of books were sent to camp libraries through the efforts of the New Jersey Library Commission.

On January 12, 1942, the national book drive began under the name

Victory Book Campaign. This, of course, reflected the change in national attitude after the attack on Pearl Harbor. With the slogan We Want Books, librarians began the massive effort to obtain ten million books for servicemen.[6] Libraries across the country acted as collecting centers, but the headquarters were in the Empire State Building in New York City. Althea Warren continued as director of the campaign until April 1, 1942, when she returned to the Los Angeles Public Library. John M. Connor of the Columbia University Medical Library was appointed to take her place.[7] The active publicity, resourceful leadership, and strenuous campaigning culminated in what President Roosevelt designated as Victory Book Day, April 17. At that point, the American people had contributed over nine million books. Later contributions brought the total to approximately twelve million. Of this total, about six million were considered useful enough to place in the various libraries. Most of the books received were fiction, as had been true of the book drives during World War I.[8]

Although librarians were in charge of the Victory Book Campaign, many other organizations assisted. The soliciting and packing of books was done largely by such organizations as the Girl Scouts, Boy Scouts, and Camp Fire Girls. Transportation of books was provided by such diverse groups as the American Trucking Association, bus companies, milk companies, the American Red Cross, and the American Women's Volunteer Services. Many authors contributed books, and also wrote newspaper columns and gave readings at meetings to encourage the giving of books. Thus it was a concerted national effort that enabled John Connor to call the campaign a success.

The following year, the decision was made to have another Victory Book Campaign, because of the demands of servicemen and the realization that the war would not soon be over. Connor again agreed to direct the efforts of librarians. Certain lessons learned in the 1942 drive were applied during this campaign. For example, the experience had taught the leaders that much of the reading material supplied from the nation's attics was simply unacceptable for servicemen. Thus Connor issued the following memorandum to librarians taking part in the drive:

> We ask that the book sorting be ruthless. Let's not have our men complain that "We're getting a lot of sentimental novels by early Victorian ladies."[9]

He then asked librarians to discard all books written for women and children; juvenile books (which had been received in large numbers) were also to be omitted. The public itself was more fully aware of the type of reading desired, because there had been much publicity concerning the reading needs of servicemen. As a result, fewer books were collected, but they were of higher quality than in previous drives. At the official close of the campaign, seven million books had been received; of this total, four and a half million were distributed to the service libraries.[10]

NATIONAL AND INTERNATIONAL ACTIVITIES

The association also administered funds provided by several foundations. The Carnegie Corporation had severely limited its gifts to ALA, but it still made small grants. Association president Charles Brown reported that, when he presented a tentative budget of almost $40,000 to the corporation, the immediate reaction was negative. Frederick Keppel, president of the corporation, said, "This is about double what we gave you last year." Brown explained the additional monies were to be used for defense activities. As usual, Keppel said that there was little chance of receiving favorable consideration for the full program.[11] However, the corporation did provide some special grants for new projects. Colleges for Negroes were given a total of $100,000 for the development of their libraries. At Atlanta University, a library school for Negroes was also established with the aid of a grant from Carnegie Corporation. Under the terms of a grant from the Rockefeller Foundation, the association continued to administer the Books for Europe program. Because of the war, books for research were purchased and stored in the United States. After hostilities were over, the books would be sent to the libraries in Europe to help rebuild their collections.[12]

In an effort to promote closer ties with Mexico, ALA in 1941 established a library in Mexico City. This was Biblioteca Benjamin Franklin, patterned after a typical American public library.[13] Its collection was made up largely of books, periodicals, and other publications from the United States. Its special emphasis was on services of international importance. The library was meant to act as an exchange center for research materials between Mexico and the United States. In addition, the library planned to offer classes and recordings to promote the learning of the English and Spanish languages. Funding for the project came from the Rockefeller Foundation, although the idea for the library apparently came from the United States Department of State.

The name of the library was chosen after considerable discussion between the State Department and ALA officials. One of the first suggestions from ALA was that it should be called the Dwight Morrow Library, but this was objected to by a State Department representative because it "smelled a bit of oil."[14] The library was finally named for Benjamin Franklin because he was known by the Mexican people not to have any political entanglements that would be offensive to the people of Latin America. In addition, he had been active in establishing libraries in America and had also urged the study of Spanish to further good relations with Latin America.[15] The library's first director was Harry M. Lydenberg, the retired director of the New York Public Library.

This project was part of a growing emphasis on the country's southern neighbors. Because there had been pro-German sentiment in Latin America during World War I, every possible step was taken to cement closer ties with the area during the Second World War. Thus in 1941 and 1942, United States foreign policy was heavily concerned with Latin America. Some of the other ALA activities showed this emphasis also. An experiment in the education of librarians was launched in 1942 when courses were given at the National Library of Colombia under the joint sponsorship of the Colombian Ministry of Education and ALA. Approximately one hundred librarians from Colombia and neighboring countries were enrolled. This project was funded by the Rockefeller Foundation, with some supplementary help from the United States Department of State.[16]

A Books for Latin America project was also inaugurated in 1942. It was basically similar to the older Books for Europe program, and its purpose was to supply books by United States authors to South American libraries. Minor projects were also sponsored by ALA in cooperation with other agencies; United States libraries were established in Montevideo and Managua, and librarians from Latin America were given fellowships to study in the United States. The need for more institutes on the history and government of Latin American countries was recognized. In this area an interdisciplinary approach in librarianship was suggested. It was hoped the increased scope would better prepare librarians for leadership roles in understanding international affairs.[17]

While these activities were demonstrating ALA's growing interest in the international scene, two other international projects suffered because of the war conditions. All United States citizens who were staffing the American Library in Paris were forced to evacuate the city in 1942 because of the German aggression. In spite of the difficulties, the library remained open.[18] The second project to suffer was the Books for Europe program. This had been funded by the Rockefeller Foundation and had resulted in the purchase of thousands of books for European libraries. War conditions made it exceedingly difficult to continue the work of the program, and it was therefore allowed to die when the funds were depleted in 1942.[19]

Despite these setbacks, ALA was engaged in a constantly expanding international program. In recognition of this fact, in 1942 the association finally changed its original charter in order to remain within its legal powers. The international activities already engaged in went beyond the powers of the charter, according to ALA attorneys, and therefore the words "throughout the world" were added to get away from any implied limitation to strictly national activities. At the same time, a limiting clause was included. It clearly restricted any further expansion to those activities approved by the executive board or the council.

COUNCIL OF NATIONAL LIBRARY ASSOCIATIONS

One potentially desirable outcome of the emergency situation was a move toward improved coordination within the library profession. From time to time, librarians had recognized the growing need to provide a more formalized system to encourage cooperation among the different national library associations. There was at this time a total of twenty-one national organizations, with an almost complete lack of cooperation among them. Most had a very loose affiliation with ALA, but this meant very little in terms of coordination. This problem had been discussed in the report of ALA's third Activities Committee, completed in 1939. According to the committee, ALA was to blame for the proliferation of organizations:

> The association has, unwittingly, acted in an autocratic and unprofessional manner toward group organization. The A.L.A. itself must be held primarily responsible for the formation of independent national library associations.[20]

The committee report recommended that ALA should clearly express its willingness to appoint members to joint committees with other national associations. In response to this suggestion, several joint committees were formed. In addition, an ALA committee on relations with other national associations was appointed. This was only a false step, however, since the committee took no action at all.

On June 19, 1941, the Special Libraries Association proposed that a council of library associations be established to bring the organizations closer together.[21] The immediate reaction of ALA officials was to wonder about the motives of SLA in suggesting the organization. On this point, Milton Lord tried to reassure members of the executive board:

> We don't suspect from what we can find that there was any ul-

terior purposes of any great consequences, but more than anything else perhaps a burning desire to move ahead quickly and to show what can be done in an emergency situation.[22]

A resolution was then passed favoring cooperation and "coordination of library activities on a national scale." It called for a committee of three to meet with officers of SLA to explore the "interesting" proposal of a coordinating council. Keyes Metcalf, a member of the newly appointed committee, commented that he considered the use of the word *interesting* sarcastic. President Charles Brown replied:

> Of course, in the strictest meaning of the word it is of interest. It is of great interest. But I am afraid of the interpretation that might be made. If it weren't funny, it would be the most interesting thing I have ever seen. It is almost entertaining. I think it is better to leave it out.

Two months later, on December 28, 1941, the executive board again discussed the SLA proposal. It was reported that SLA was interested in ways to form an organization that would not be dominated by ALA. Executive Secretary Milam stated that he suspected that

> there are some motives in the S.L.A. which are deeper than a desire to become equal to the A.L.A. and to have a part in some of the enterprises which will recognize that equalness. There may be, in the back of their mind, that there should be for librarians something corresponding to the American Council of Learned Societies. . . .[23]

President Brown expressed the opinion that ALA would have control in the new organization. He said, "It has enough allies in other associations, so that it has almost a determining voice."

A Joint Committee on Relationships between National Library Associations met with the presidents of fifteen of the associations. The committee then recommended that its own name be changed to the Council of National Library Associations. With Sidney R. Hill as chairman, the council became a reality and met formally with ALA at the latter's annual conference in Milwaukee in 1942.[24]

Unfortunately, hope for the council was unduly optimistic. Perhaps the organization's own goals were too broad and too ambitious: "to serve as a clearinghouse for information, a planning board, and a coordination board dealing with common problems."[25] *Library Journal* expressed the hope the time had arrived when there would no longer be "any room for [the] mutual misunderstanding and petty differences" that had plagued the profession for so long. This editorial suggested that the first priority of the new council should be to coordinate the war efforts of library organizations. Then, as its long-range goal, the council would be in a position to "raise the level of public recognition of the profession."[26] President Brown of ALA expressed the hope that the council would be able to weld together the diverse associations. But he felt that if it only served as an arena for discussion it would serve a very useful purpose.[27]

The council never really had an opportunity to try to achieve Brown's first idea, and it was only partially successful as an arena of discussion. The first signal of a problem came with a dispute over the inclusion of the word *coordination* in the council's statement of purpose. The word implied that the council would have an authority that some of the member associations did not wish to grant. The word was removed from the statement of purpose.[28] As a result of this dispute, the council became an agency for cooperation rather than coordination.

Two years later, when Milton Lord was president of the council, he reviewed its history for the newer members of the executive board:

> For those of you who may not be very familiar with the council, it came into being a few years ago. I should say, advisedly, perhaps as an activity on the part of some other associations that were desirous of sharing in the eminent position of the American Library Association in some of the things it does and perhaps also on the part of some associations, and I think frankly on the part of some individuals interested in obtaining a place in the sun for themselves and their associations.

Yet Lord now believed that the Council of National Library Associations had performed a useful function during its brief existence:

> One parting remark I might make about the council is that whereas it was conceived in a certain amount of distrust or envy of the A.L.A., there is also a perfectly natural desire to take part in a cooperative activity. Let us not forget that, despite the other aspect of it, I think that it has evolved so far . . . into an activity in which there is a disappearance . . . of antagonism toward the A.L.A.[29]

In retrospect, it is clear that ALA—and the council in particular—often were guilty of an uncharitable attitude toward the smaller national library organizations. This was brought out quite definitely in a statement by President Charles H. Brown during a 1942 executive board meeting:

> I am convinced that the A.L.A. itself needs a better understanding
> of its sister associations and members thereof. I believe some un-
> fortunate misunderstandings cannot be placed on any one group.
> I think the A.L.A. can only blame itself.[30]

The misunderstandings Brown was referring to are not difficult to identify,
since they have been referred to previously. The difficulty is in trying to
understand and rationalize the behavior of ALA in these relationships. For
the most part, the association's actions were unreasonable, unnecessary, and
indefensible.

A SHORTAGE OF LIBRARIANS

The oversupply of trained librarians that had reached alarming propor-
tions during the depression ceased to be a problem as the country made a
full economic recovery. Even before the outbreak of the war, library schools
reported 100 percent placement of their graduates. As a result, there was
no reserve of librarians to fill the unusual number of positions made available by the war. Hundreds of librarians left the profession to enter military
service or defense work, and others took jobs in government libraries or in
the newly established libraries of the army and navy. While this depletion
of the ranks was going on, a second factor was compounding the problem:
fewer people were entering the library schools. In 1942–43, there were only
1,200 students in the schools, compared with 1,800 in 1940–41.[31]

Not all of the decrease can be blamed on military and defense demands,
however. Perhaps an even more significant reason for the decline was the
low salary level for librarians. The Personnel Division of ALA reported in
October, 1943, that of the position requests received, over 95 percent paid
less than $2,000 a year. The majority of the openings paid less than $1,700,
and many were even under $1,500. These positions did not include any in
military or war industry libraries. The report pointed out that a high school
graduate without experience could command an annual salary of about
$2,000 doing stenographic work. To compound the problem, librarians in
public libraries were often very poorly paid even after years of experience.
Yet a young librarian recently out of library school could obtain a much
larger salary by entering a defense-connected library. As a result of this
situation, the division reported a tremendous turnover of personnel during
the previous year. Higher-paying positions were available elsewhere, and
librarians could not be expected to be so altruistic as to ignore the importance of compensation.[32]

Another problem that had been troubling the profession for many years was pointed out in 1942 by Charles C. Williamson, dean of the School for Library Service at Columbia University. In his annual report, he stressed the need for schools to reconsider the degree system.[33] The prevailing system of granting a second baccalaureate degree as the first professional degree in library schools had long been under attack. After waiting for ALA and the Association of American Library Schools to do something about the problem, several schools studied the feasibility of independent action. As Williamson noted, granting a master's degree for the first year of library school study was one alternative. A number of schools were considering this move, but only one accredited school was willing to adopt it at this time. Such a program was, in the view of many people, including Williamson, an undesirable lowering of the standards. The Board of Education for Librarianship was well aware of the problem and indeed had been studying it for a number of years. The board's annual report in 1943 indicated the committee concerned with the degree question had not been able to complete its study. The board said a decision would probably not be forthcoming until after the end of the war.[34]

WARTIME ACTIVITIES

Wartime restrictions on travel caused the cancellation of both the midwinter and the annual conference for 1943. The executive board of ALA proposed instead a series of institutes on methods of providing information about war and postwar problems. The board recognized that libraries and librarians could "make a substantial contribution to the enlightenment" of the people about vital issues. Librarians would encourage reading and thinking to help clarify questions while trying to avoid imposing conclusions of their own.[35]

The Carnegie Corporation provided the funding for the institutes. The first in the series was the National Institute on War and Post-War Planning. This was held in Chicago on January 30–31, 1943, and was meant to serve as a demonstration of what could be done in later institutes held at the regional level. Due to war restrictions on travel, attendance at this first meeting was restricted to about two hundred librarians. A number of discussion sessions were held to consider the major issues and practical problems and the role librarians should take. Speakers from other disciplines were invited to lead the discussions.[36]

No effort was made to have a single pattern for the regional meetings that followed the national institute. Many were one-day meetings, and the participants tended to be more concerned with practical applications than with general theoretical issues. In general, librarians reacted favorably to these meetings, for most realized the importance of becoming better informed about national issues. Of course, there were some dissenters. As Secretary Milam pointed out, these librarians wanted the association to "stick to our knitting" and to be more concerned with library methods.[37]

The membership was more concerned over the extent of the association's international activities. As Milam reported in his 1943 annual report, ALA had made an almost complete conversion to a wartime program. This change had not been accomplished without protest, since it seemed to some members to be at the expense of domestic library service. President Milton Ferguson was among those who questioned the acceptance of foundation funds to subsidize library service abroad when almost half the American people were without library service. He wondered if the foundations weren't assuming the leadership from the association and perhaps setting priorities. Milam answered that ALA had never "accepted money for a project which has caused us to do something which was contrary to our opinions."[38] Milam was apparently quite determined in this policy, judging from a dispute with a sponsoring foundation the following year. There was a disagreement with the Rockefeller Foundation over procedures in carrying through a project in South America. Milam wrote to the committee chairman involved:

> If the disagreement is sufficiently great, we might hand back the money rather than accept Foundation interpretation. . . . I feel very strongly that the A.L.A. should not be pushed into doing things which it does not believe in doing simply because the agency furnishing the money thinks they should be done.[39]

The wartime conversion Milam had written about included a great many international activities, funded by various foundations (largely Rockefeller) and the federal government, not from internal sources. President Althea Warren saw the association's activities as a starfish, attempting to reach out in five directions at the same time. These were (1) to build a relationship with our South American neighbors, (2) to help in rebuilding libraries in Europe by buying books for them, (3) to supply British troops stationed in North Africa with American publications, (4) to provide training programs for librarians so they would be ready to go into occupied countries at the close of the war, and (5) to continue the close cooperation with Mexico through the operation of the Biblioteca Benjamin Franklin.

Miss Warren admitted these new directions were being challenged by some members. They asked why the association should be so internationally concerned when so many of the inhabitants of the United States had no library service. In her beautiful presidential address called "Salute to the Dawn," Miss Warren described the problems in terms of the war atmosphere. There were "icebergs and submarines in ALA's organizational North Sea." However, reluctantly, the membership had to face its international responsibilities, just as the nation had already been forced to do. She believed there could be no turning away from the responsibility, for either the country or ALA.[40]

Although President Warren was eloquent in her address, describing the problems and trying to smooth over the discontent, she and other leaders were far from completely successful in this effort. For example, the executive board's decision to eliminate the annual conference was annoying, particularly to council members, who apparently were not consulted in the decision. One member, Ralph Shaw, was exceedingly disturbed over what he saw as the board's usurpation of "final authority" from the council—which, he said, made the council as efficient as a reichstag in a totalitarian state. In such a situation, according to Shaw, the "legislative body becomes mere window dressing."[41] President Warren discounted the attack, since she said she had come to "expect a chronic state of agitation from Mr. Shaw—I am resigned." She was concerned, however, with Shaw's attitude and motive regarding the executive secretary:

> . . . he is very definitely out with a curved knife on Mr. Milam's trail. I see no reason for Mr. Shaw to be belligerent if his purpose is as he states it: to have the council consulted frequently about A.L.A. policies.[42]

Whether or not Miss Warren was correct in her assessment of Shaw's motives, it is nevertheless true that Shaw played a major role in the early retirement of Milam, as described later on.

ALA's increased emphasis on international projects was further demonstrated in 1943 by the establishment of an International Relations Office in Washington to handle activities outside the United States. Its first director was Harry M. Lydenberg, formerly director of the New York Public Library and administrator of the Biblioteca Benjamin Franklin. Basic funding for this new project came from the Rockefeller Foundation; the grant of $25,000 covered the period from October 1, 1942, to December 31, 1944. Many of the activities carried out by this office were jointly sponsored by the State Department, the Coordinator of Inter-American Affairs, and ALA. Various philanthropic and educational foundations provided additional funding. For example, in 1943, the Rockefeller Foundation and the Canadian Library Council underwrote a three-year joint project to microfilm Canadian newspapers and other historical documents. The Rockefeller

Foundation also gave the association $3,800 to pay for the cataloging of the Jalisco State Library in Guadalajara, Mexico, and provided $70,000 for the purchase of scientific and scholarly periodicals to be distributed to European and Asian libraries after the war. The Julius Rosenwald Fund gave $800 for the publication of a reading list on racial problems in the United States. The Carnegie Corporation provided $5,000 for the purchase of scientific, technical, and reference books for Alaskan libraries.[43]

In the midst of the international efforts and the Victory Book Campaign, ALA was also planning postwar activities. The previously mentioned institutes that were held throughout the country in 1943 dealt largely with postwar issues—most of them international in nature but some domestic. The latter included changes in community living, financial issues, agricultural problems, juvenile delinquency, and race relations.[44]

ALA headquarters was also concerned with library development after the war. A study was undertaken to determine what library services would be needed to help ease the adjustment of demobilized servicemen and industrial workers to normal peacetime living.[45] Two librarians, Ralph Ulveling and Donald Coney, prepared a statement concerning the adjustment of librarians themselves to demobilization. This report discussed the problems likely to be faced by librarians when they returned from military service or government positions; the probable dislocation of those who had filled their places during the war; and the possible problems of library administrators who would face new conditions affecting salaries, hours, and recruitment.[46]

A new set of standards for the nation's public libraries also showed the association's forward-looking stance. Under the title *Post-War Standards for Public Libraries,* a new set of professional guides and measurements was set forth. The standards called for a greater role for libraries in the years ahead. A "positive program of leadership" needed to be assumed by the library:

> As a dynamic institution it offers to persons with certain intangible qualities opportunities for constructive service. The librarian should have a warmth of personality and should possess those qualities which mark him as a leader in the educational, cultural and civic life of the community.[47]

The future status of the profession would be determined by its success in maintaining and developing the services established under wartime conditions. Gains achieved because of the emergency should not be lost. It was clearly up to the librarians to see that the forward momentum of libraries be continued.

CONFERENCE IN PRINT, 1944

Again in 1944, wartime conditions prevented the association from holding its annual conference. Instead, papers and reports that would ordinarily have been delivered in person appeared in the *ALA Bulletin*. Retiring president Althea Warren, for example, reviewed the membership criticism in her address. In summary, the criticisms were as follows:

1. Publications, especially the periodicals, offered little to the membership. The *ALA Bulletin* had few articles valuable to small libraries and also lacked the "bookish" slant that would make it attractive to large libraries. The *ALA Handbook* was small additional reward for the dues paid in. Many members felt dues should also entitle a member to one of the divisional publications, such as *College and Research Libraries*.

2. The professional association did not seem to be sufficiently concerned with obtaining higher salaries and better working conditions for its members. More attention needed to be given to classification and pay plans. Trustees should be kept informed of rising salary schedules. Professional librarians could not be expected to continue to accept other compensations in lieu of higher salaries.

3. Members were concerned that the leadership seemed to be a gerontocracy. It seemed that presidents, especially, were chosen from "the elderly and pretentious." Other associations, such as the National Education Association, practiced a rotation scheme to prevent this from happening.

Miss Warren felt the blame for ALA's faults could not be placed entirely on the association's structure or its leadership. She was critical of the members as well. Of a total membership of over 15,000, fewer than 6,000 were active in committees or even divisional membership. Therefore, more than half of the membership received nothing because they gave nothing to ALA.[48]

Incoming president Carl Vitz also wrote of the need to change, to plan for the future, and to profit from past mistakes. To President Vitz, the need for organization in terms of larger service units was primary. Local jealousies had to be overcome. Only through expanded service areas, with the resulting larger financial bases, could the public be adequately served. Statewide and national planning was a necessity.

Vitz also called for a revision of library school curricula. In his view, library school training was too elementary and too general. Greater expertise in administration, subject areas, and public relations was necessary. Vitz thought there was an acute need for a two-year program in library schools: the first year to be devoted to a core program, and the second year allowing for specialization. Library educators were also criticized in this speech. Vitz said too many instructors were becoming strict academicians, too far removed from the actual library world. He suggested a program to put teachers back into library situations every few years. This would give them sound practical experience in addition to the theoretical background most of them already had.[49] This criticism was not new, of course, but it was perhaps the first time an ALA president had joined in the assault.

SELECTION OF THE LIBRARIAN OF CONGRESS, 1944

At about the same time, the problem of the selection of a Librarian of Congress was once again before the association. Through the news media, librarians learned of the resignation of Archibald MacLeish to become Assistant Secretary of State in charge of public and cultural relations. Memories of the controversy over MacLeish's appointment to the library, and the mistakes that had been made at that time, came back to librarians as rumors began to circulate. A report in the *Washington Star* on December 10, 1944, seemed to confirm the possibility of trouble once again. The newspaper announced that several nonlibrarians, including Carl Sandburg and playwright Robert E. Sherwood, were being considered for the vacancy.

In contrast to 1939, the role of ALA was subdued in spite of the apparent threat that another nonlibrarian would head the nation's most important library. An initial letter from ALA president Carl Vitz to President Roosevelt in January, 1945, offered assistance in selecting a new librarian. Roosevelt died on April 12, 1945, and Vitz then wrote to Harry Truman. The new president expressed a willingness to receive the advice of the association. Vitz then gathered the suggestions of various librarians by telephone and personal contact. On the basis of these recommendations, he decided that the following librarians should be considered for the vacant post: Keyes D. Metcalf, librarian of Harvard University; Ralph Ulveling, librarian of the Detroit Public Library; and Luther Evans, Chief Assistant Librarian and Acting Librarian of Congress. A personal conference between Vitz and Truman was arranged for May 7, 1945. The surrender of Germany on that date prevented the appointment from taking place, and Vitz made the suggestions in a letter dated May 8.[50]

On June 17, President Truman announced his selection of Evans as Librarian of Congress. The choice was a happy one for the profession, but there is no reason to assume that the recommendations of Vitz had any effect on the decision. The *Washington Star* had named Evans as a possible nominee in the article previously mentioned. Nevertheless, it was reassuring to the profession to know that the president would at least encourage advice from professional associations in the matter of appointments.[51]

It is interesting to note the role MacLeish played in the selection of his successor. He talked several times with Roosevelt about the choice and suggested at least two persons: Wilmarth S. Lewis and Julian Boyd. Both men were offered the position, probably before Carl Vitz offered the services of ALA in making the selection. Boyd, involved with the Thomas Jefferson papers, indicated that he could not abandon that responsibility. Roosevelt refused to accept that reason because, he said, the project could be transferred to the Library of Congress, and Boyd could spend "a few moments each day" supervising a staff. Boyd's reservations were dismissed

> with a wave of his arm, a genial smile, and the suggestion that I go home and seek the sensible advice of my wife.

In fact, Boyd had already made his decision. The only problem was:

> I simply did not have the courage to say no to a President I admired so much—at least not enough to say it to him in person. Hence it was not until the next day that I wrote and declined the offer.[52]

The death of Roosevelt prevented any further suggestions from MacLeish, and President Truman did not consult with the former Librarian of Congress. So MacLeish learned of the appointment of Luther Evans the same way most other people did—from the newspaper.[53]

EXPANSION OF FACILITIES

Even though ALA was not in very good financial condition, in 1945, it made an important purchase: it acquired the Cyrus McCormick mansion in Chicago to serve as the first headquarters owned by the association. The mansion was the central building of three residences on East Huron Street and was purchased for $175,000.[54] The building's thirty-five rooms offered much-needed space for expanding activities and increasing staff. Furthermore, the beauty and dignity of the old building seemed to be especially in keeping with the professional atmosphere of an association. At a more practical level, there was sufficient land in the purchase to allow for expansion if that should become necessary at some future date.[55]

Later in 1945, the association announced the establishment of a Washington office. It will be remembered that throughout most of the history of the association there had been some sentiment for relocating headquarters in Washington. The value of being close to the seat of an increasingly active federal government was readily apparent. Also, the earlier establishment of an International Relations Office had demonstrated the value of having a representative in Washington.

The new office, under the direction of Paul Howard, had three main functions:

1. To clarify the role of librarians in a federal research program that had recently been announced.[56] In the past, there had been various proposals for increased federal participation in research projects, with some evidence of official awareness of library needs. An important report of the Committee on Science and Public Welfare, U.S. Office of Scientific Research and Development, had increased this awareness. The report emphasized the importance of library and bibliographic services to research programs. It also suggested that an appropriate governmental agency should give consideration to problems of interlibrary cooperation, abstracting and translating services, and reference services. The report proposed the use of federal funds in solving these problems.[57]

2. To form a closer relationship with the Office of Education in particular, and library-related agencies in general. Officials of the association had often felt hampered in their contacts with government agency officials because of the geographic separation.[58]

3. Although many librarians felt an almost instinctive repugnance over the word *lobby* because of past experience, the Washington office was clearly meant to perform in this capacity. Following the lead of other organizations, ALA was going to strengthen its influence by establishing an office close to Congress.[59]

To support its Washington office, the association embarked on a new campaign for money. It began a drive called Library Development Fund, which was planned to extend over a five-year period. Both the fund and the Washington office were started at the suggestion of Althea Warren.[60] During a council meeting in October, 1944, Miss Warren spoke of the many benefits that would be derived from having a full-time representative in Washington to promote library interests. She concluded her remarks by moving that such an office be established and that a campaign be held to raise money for it. One year later, the office had been established and the campaign for funds completed. Secretary Carl Milam reported that $87,645 had been collected; the original goal had been $105,000. It was believed that in spite of the near success of the fund drive, continuing it for four years as planned would not significantly increase the amount. Even though the goal was not met, the amount collected was remarkable in view of the wartime conditions.

SUMMARY

World War II dominated this period of ALA history. The war prevented the holding of conferences, and so in 1944 there was a "conference in print"—the publication of papers that would ordinarily have been given in person. The war also resulted in two major book campaigns and in drives for funds to support library defense work. During this time, the association increased its activities in international relations. Many interesting projects, such as the Biblioteca Benjamin Franklin and the Books for Latin America program, were administered by ALA.

Two domestic problems also confronted the association. Instead of the unemployment problem of the previous period, there was a serious shortage of librarians. There were two main reasons for this: inadequate salaries in domestic libraries and the demands of military and defense operations. The second problem facing ALA and the profession was the lack of coordination of effort. This had been evident for some time. A Council of National Library Associations was formed to overcome this problem. However, opposition developed, and the powers of the new council were severely limited.

In 1945, the association finally obtained its own headquarters building. After almost seventy years of making use of free or rented quarters, ALA purchased the McCormick mansion and adjacent property in Chicago. Although the buildings purchased were old, the property was valuable. Thus it appeared that, in terms of an investment, the organization had made a wise move.

9

POSTWAR PROGRESS AND
REORGANIZATION

*T*he cessation of hostilities in Europe and then in Asia meant a sudden change in priorities for librarians. Readjustment to a peacetime world became a matter of prime importance to the profession, as it was to the rest of the country. The abrupt release of millions of people from military and defense activities meant a massive displacement of civilian personnel, which had to be softened as much as possible. Advanced education was one of the methods used, and it proved to have an immense appeal. One of the major factors was the Servicemen's Readjustment Act of 1944, better known as the "G.I. Bill of Rights." Even preliminary estimates indicated that two million young people in the service might take advantage of the educational provisions of the law.

The impact of demobilization was felt immediately by the library schools. For the first time since 1940, there was an increase in enrollment. The 32 accredited schools showed a total of 1,032 students in the fall of 1945.[1] Most library schools indicated a willingness to be flexible in their requirements for the returning veterans. Among the adaptations were refresher courses, admission of students at irregular times, and the granting of college credit for experience and education obtained in the armed forces. Such concessions were common among institutions of higher learning after the war.[2]

THE PROBLEMS OF CHANGE

While the old problems continued and new projects proliferated, a serious question faced ALA and its membership. What direction should the organization take in the postwar world? The question was often posed and often debated. A similar problem had faced the organization after World War I, and insufficient planning then had helped lead to the embarrassing debacle of the Enlarged Program. The leaders of the association were anxious that the same kind of mistakes should not be made again. There were many demands on the resources of the association, and there would be new ones to be faced in the future. Part of the problem was the fact that programs had been allowed to proliferate without adequate planning and control. Some projects had been undertaken largely because funding was available through a foundation or from the federal government. The funding rarely compensated the association completely for its time and effort. Thus additional burdens were placed on the main financial structure of the association, which was based on the dues paid by members. This also meant less money would be available for worthwhile projects proposed by the membership.

Dissension was the ultimate result of this situation. There was serious question as to whether all the activities were truly legitimate for a voluntary professional association. Were not some actually the function of society in general, working through governmental agencies? There was already evidence of duplication of effort by ALA and the government. For example, there was a public library specialist on the headquarters staff and a similar specialist in the Library Services Division of the United States Office of Education. There was like duplication of personnel in service to schools and to children. A logical extension of this situation would be to provide specialists in college work, library extension, and young adult work in both ALA and the Office of Education. One function of a national library association should certainly be to ascertain what services are needed and then to decide which agencies should provide them. Some services can best be provided by governmental units, and some services can be provided most effectively by a professional association. The association needed to define more specifically its own role in the profession and in society.[3]

This lack of overall direction led to an impasse in several areas within ALA in 1945 and 1946. The most serious problem was with the Association of College and Research Libraries (ACRL). This was not a new problem area. ACRL's predecessor, the College and Reference Section, had often accused ALA of neglecting scholarly and bibliographic work. In 1930, dissatisfaction was so strong that there was considerable pressure to withdraw from ALA. The first Activities Committee, established to review the work of ALA, found there was justification for the unhappiness. It recommended greater activity in scholarly fields as a partial solution to the problem.[4] Eight years later, the third Activities Committee also criticized ALA for its treatment of the divisions, especially ACRL. The committee's report stated that divisions were not encouraged to develop any strength. Instead,

ALA had taken responsibility and authority from the divisions. To improve the situation, the third Activities Committee suggested that divisions

> establish a more permanent form of government, receive as income a share of the dues of the association, participate through elected representatives in its policy-making program, and direct within their own fields.[5]

The particular responsibility of ACRL, as defined in its constitution, was to direct a program of activities that would advance the standards of library service in college, university, research, and reference libraries. This program was to be designed to promote the continued professional growth of librarians practicing in those fields. To carry out its program, ACRL in 1945 had an income of $1,753. This was in spite of the fact that it had a total membership of 223 who had paid in $7,000 to ALA for dues. As ACRL president Blanche McCrum declared, this was a "starvation" program in which all areas suffered. There were other serious problems preventing efficient service, but the financial arrangements were undoubtedly the major stumbling block.

The members of ACRL believed that it was time for a change. Expressions of sympathy and understanding, so frequently given in the past by ALA, would no longer be acceptable to the division. President McCrum assured the ALA members there was no desire "to climb on the fallen bodies of its sister divisions." But she made it clear that ACRL had reached the moment of decision regarding its status as a division of ALA.[6] Now it was necessary for the parent organization to make the modifications necessary to preserve the relationship between the two groups.

The situation was also bluntly stated by a member of the executive board, Ralph Ellsworth of Iowa State University. In a letter to Milam on January 10, 1946, he accused the "public library crowd" of "ruling the roost" in the association. He said he did not blame the situation on Milam's "personal attitudes, inclinations, or idiosyncracies," nor was he accusing Milam of "personal perfidy." But, Ellsworth wrote, there had been too much mixing up of academic and public library activities for the good of either group. And the academic librarians were not getting their fair share of the dues paid into ALA. As for the rumors about secession,

> I think it would be a serious mistake if A.C.R.L. were to secede from A.L.A., at least on any permanent basis. But I do think the present situation is intolerable and that changes . . . are in order.

He closed with the assurance that he was an easy person to work with, but he warned that "I am not easily talked out of things."[7]

The immediate result of the increasing hostility between the two groups was the appointment of a Committee on the Relations of the ACRL to the ALA. The committee made its report at the 1946 ALA conference in Buffalo, and seldom in the history of the association had a committee report caused as much controversy. The chief response to the report was the accusation that ACRL was trying to split ALA by its demands. However, the committee had voted at its first meeting that ACRL should remain within the association if reasonable changes could be made. The committee was unanimous in its belief that the autonomy promised in the constitution and bylaws of ALA must be delivered to the divisions. If autonomy were not forthcoming in the foreseeable future, then separation from ALA would probably be necessary.[8] In the hope that changes could be effected, the committee made the following recommendations for the improvement of relations between the two organizations:

1. ACRL headquarters should be at a college or university near Chicago, rather than at ALA headquarters. This was an unusual recommendation, but it was perhaps logical. As the committee pointed out, institutions of learning were often willing to provide space, staff, and other services either free or at a reduced rate to such organizations because of the prestige involved. This had been the case with *College and Research Libraries,* the ACRL periodical. Its editorial work was done at Columbia University, and at less expense than would have been the case at ALA headquarters. ACRL was presently paying for its share of the overhead at ALA headquarters, including salaries of administrative officers, clerks, and other ALA employees.

2. ACRL should collect its own dues from its members and turn over a proportionate amount to ALA. The fact that ACRL received in 1946 only one-fifth of its dues was particularly galling to the division. If this proposal were adopted, the opposite situation would exist. As opponents pointed out, ALA would be forced to go "hat in hand" to ACRL for money. That would be a demeaning position for a national organization, but it was exactly the position in which ALA had put its divisions.

3. Control over the use of endowment funds should be more democratic. These funds were largely from the Carnegie Corporation, but some of the money had been obtained from memberships as a part of the endowment program. In the past, some of the funds had supported activities concerning college and reference librarians. However, ACRL claimed it had not been represented on the gov-

erning board of the endowment fund, or even consulted regarding the distribution of funds. Decisions affecting large groups of members should be made by those affected, rather than in the paternalistic fashion employed in the past.

4. The committee suggested that ALA respond to its recommendations by the end of the year. If a reorganization along these general principles was not being carried out by that time, the committee promised to proceed as "rapidly as possible with proposals for the organization of a separate association."[9] This was widely interpreted within ALA as an ultimatum to act or face the consequences. However, in view of the long delays encountered in the past in getting a response from ALA, the statement seems to be reasonable. An example of a previous delay was in the request for a college library specialist. In 1932, the ALA council approved the request of the College Library Advisory Board for the position. Fourteen years later, it was noted, the position had still not been funded.

Fortunately, the ALA council and the executive board on June 17, 1946, acceded to most of the demands of ACRL. The council agreed to give encouragement and assistance to all divisions wishing to increase their autonomy within their own fields of interest. It was agreed that the proportion of dues going to the divisions would be reconsidered. An executive secretary for ACRL was approved, pending the availability of funds. Perhaps the most significant statement was the following:

> The executive board believes that the idea of the ALA as a federation of autonomous organizations is worthy of exploration by all library organizations in the United States and Canada.[10]

The only recommendation of ACRL that was not covered in the council's response concerned the location of the division's headquarters. In general, the response seemed to be calm and accommodating. This was underlined by Carl Milam's statement to the council regarding ACRL's complaints:

> . . . I am sure you recognize that they stem from a genuine dissatisfaction with our present machinery and represent an earnest desire to make the association and all its parts more effective instruments for the advancement of libraries and librarianship.[11]

Over a period of several years, significant changes were made in the relationship between the association and its divisions. One important result of the new attitude was the appointment of an executive secretary for each of the divisions. Another was the more equitable allocation of funds from the dues collected, which took longer to achieve. During the 1952 midwinter conference, the executive board agreed to an experimental arrangement for one year. This was a division of monies from dues on a "60–40" basis. Under this system, ALA would receive 40 percent of the dues income, and each division would get 60 percent of the money paid in by its members. Devised in 1950, this plan was first applied to ACRL on a provisional basis in 1951.[12] For most of the divisions, the plan meant a sharp increase in their budget.

The third response of ALA to its divisions was an attempt at decentralization. This was apparent in the placing of more responsibility with the divisions. The appointment of divisional executive secretaries made the decentralization even more important. It was obvious that a clear demarcation between their responsibilities and those of the ALA executive secretary was necessary if chaos was to be avoided. An initial step in this direction was the series of meetings that the executive board held with divisional officers in 1952.[13] During these meetings, it was possible for misunderstandings to be cleared up and for problems to be discussed openly.

These responses, of course, did not satisfy all the critics. ALA had seemed to act in part to stem the growing demand for a form of federation: greater freedom for the divisions was a more desirable alternative to ALA leadership than federation. However, the association did seem to be evolving towards a more democratic organization. This was pointed out by Robert B. Downs, president in 1952, in his inaugural address:

> Through democratic processes of change over the years, the association has continued to be fully responsive to the evolving needs of the profession. . . . At the same time, a high degree of autonomy has been achieved, to prevent the activities of any group from being unduly hampered or restricted by an all-powerful headquarters organization.[14]

Surely some people would have found reason to dispute Downs's view of headquarters in relation to the divisions. Few people, however, would disagree with the observation that ALA was trying to become a more democratic organization.

A SHORTAGE OF LIBRARIANS

One of the most serious problems facing the profession in 1947 was the acute shortage of librarians. In part, this shortage was a result of the war.

The wartime economy had forced salaries upward in almost all fields. But librarians had not benefited enough from the general increases awarded. Most libraries, in fact, lost ground in the race with rising costs. The natural result of restricted budgets was a level of compensation not competitive with other professions. A survey by the ALA Board of Personnel Administration revealed that hundreds of professional librarians had still not reached the recommended minimum salary of $2,100. Positions in libraries paying poor salaries often went without any applicants, since even inexperienced librarians had a number of jobs to consider.[15]

The 1947 report of the Placement Office of ALA gives an indication of the situation. There were 2,232 requests to fill positions, compared with 1,653 positions listed during the previous year. For those positions, there were only 401 librarians registered, and most of them already had positions. Enrollment in the library schools was up significantly over 1946, but the increase was not enough to meet the demand. It had been estimated in 1944 that 18,000 additional librarians would be required to meet the demand until 1951. Later, ALA changed the estimate to an additional 64,160 librarians needed between 1947 and 1960. The shortage in 1947 alone was believed to be in excess of 4,900 librarians.[16]

The response of the Board of Education for Librarianship and the library schools was directed to two areas. The first was increased recruiting of young people into the profession. This activity was hampered by the lack of special funding for the project, and was therefore basically intended to instill in professional librarians a sense of personal responsibility for recruiting. While promoting increased enrollments, library educators apparently rejected the idea of additional schools for training librarians. The board of education warned against taking precipitate action in meeting the shortage of librarians, and this included the establishment of new agencies for their preparation.[17] At this point, however, the accredited library schools estimated that they could add only 700 students to the 1,800 enrolled in 1947. Obviously, if the projected shortage figures were correct, the schools would continue to be inadequate in erasing the deficit.

The second area of activity was in proposals for undergraduate work in library science. This, too, seemed to be included in what the board of education termed "precipitate action," for the response was less than enthusiastic. There were a number of advantages to be gained by introducing some library science courses at the undergraduate level. Among these were (1) to provide a basic education in the field, on which a graduate program could justifiably be built; (2) to serve as a device for recruiting young people in college who might not otherwise be aware of the existence of the profession; (3) to provide the necessary preparation for positions that do not really require five years of college work. There were problems, of course, related to such a departure from the established type of program. For the library schools, it would mean having to determine whether to accept students with such a baccalaureate degree. The schools that did accept the degree would have to revise the curriculum in order to provide a more advanced form of instruction.[18] Libraries would have to change their classification of employees to accommodate persons with the new undergraduate degree.

The Board of Education for Librarianship suggested in a policy statement that it hoped there would be a great deal of thinking on the matter "and some experimentation."[19] This statement would seem to suggest that experimentation was not really advocated. However, in 1947 the board of education did approve one program that was a radical departure from the established pattern. That year, the College of Librarianship of the University of Denver began to offer a group of undergraduate courses for seniors, who would receive a regular baccalaureate degree. The fifth-year program would include graduate courses in both library science and in subject areas. This program would lead to a master's degree in library science. The experience gained by the University of Denver in this experiment would be of value to other library schools considering a revision of their curriculum.[20]

As the experimentation continued, however, the Board of Education for Librarianship realized that a serious problem was developing. During 1948 and early 1949, the board gave its approval to innovative programs in a few library schools on an experimental basis. This did not constitute accreditation, however. Even though experimentation was desirable and was to be encouraged, the board was not yet ready to evaluate completely the new programs, since the standards for accreditation then in effect were clearly inadequate. Furthermore, the board, at its meetings on June 6–8, 1949, decided that provisional approval of any more new programs would be unwise. It advised library schools to postpone the establishment of the new programs until minimum requirements could be established. This moratorium would be of indefinite length because funds had not yet been obtained for a preliminary study.

As might be expected, the moratorium was not universally well received. Schools that had already submitted new programs to the board were in some respects in a favorable position. Although accreditation was not given, at least there was an "approval" to go ahead with the programs. Schools that had not formally submitted a program were somewhat less fortunate. The board promised only to review and comment on their proposals. Furthermore, the statement of the board had the effect of discouraging further experimentation.

In one of the most scathing editorials ever printed in *Library Journal*, this decision was called "pontifical" and "officious." The control of the board of education over library education was called "strangulatory," amounting to a closed shop. The editorial commented that differences between library schools should be encouraged; there was danger in requiring that the programs of Illinois, Columbia, and Berkeley "be like peas in a pod." In a final slap at the board of education, the editorial suggested that the day for setting standards was over. Standards were needed in the early days of library education, but they had outlived their usefulness.[21]

Jerrold Orne, director of libraries of Washington University, criticized the board for its neglect of the so-called unrecognized library schools: schools that offered extensive undergraduate work in library science. The absence of the "stamp of the union," as he put it, did not accurately reflect what these programs were accomplishing. Yet both the schools and their students suffered because of the stand taken by the board of education, according to Orne.[22]

The moratorium on accrediting graduate programs continued far longer than was originally believed necessary. Board of education members had thought the revision of the standards would take a relatively short time, but delays in funding and disagreement on guidelines became major problems. Because it was thought that suspension of accreditation would not last long, the thirty-six schools then accredited were allowed to keep their status while the new standards were devised.

Working with the Association of American Library Schools and the Library Education Division of ALA, the Board of Education for Librarianship produced the new accreditation standards in 1951, and the council accepted them in July of that year.[23] However, the National Commission on Accrediting then placed a moratorium on all accrediting programs for 1951–52.[24] The purpose of the moratorium was to give that agency opportunity to make a survey of all accrediting organizations. At the same time, the commission suggested that specialized accrediting agencies work with the regional accrediting associations to develop institution-wide accreditation. This suggestion provoked a great amount of criticism from many quarters. The result was a revised statement that recognized that not all of the regional associations were ready to assume the responsibility for overall accreditation of institutions.[25] The Board of Education for Librarianship agreed to work experimentally with the regional associations to develop the concept of institution-wide accreditation. In the meantime, the board was to establish, maintain, and apply its own standards. With this compromise effected, the board of education resumed accrediting schools, using the standards adopted in 1951.

A second part of the new accrediting procedures was to establish revised standards for undergraduate library science programs. These programs had long been a problem for the profession. In 1934 the Board of Education for Librarianship had presented to the council its "Minimum Requirements for Teacher-Librarian Training Agencies," and at that time, Keyes Metcalf, chairman of the board of education, said,

> The board is a bit embarrassed in seeming in this way to approve of any standards below those of the regular schools, but it realizes that we must face the situation.[26]

As Metcalf pointed out, 30 library schools then offered a one-year graduate program in library science. But 150 schools offered library science courses at the undergraduate level. ALA could not continue to ignore the undergraduate programs or refuse to set standards for them, according to Metcalf.

The difficulty remained in 1952, so it was still necessary to set guidelines for the institutions involved. In February, 1952, the board of education presented its new standards to the American Association of Colleges for Teacher Education. That organization began to apply them experimentally in 1952–53. These standards, however, were to be used simply as guidelines in the overall evaluation process. The board of education decided not to assume responsibility for accrediting the undergraduate programs.

PLANNING FOR THE FUTURE

During 1947, ALA completed one study and began another that were both important milestones in library planning. These studies helped to answer the frequent criticism that national library planning was almost nonexistent. Several years' work had gone into the formulation of the National Plan for Public Library Service, which was released and adopted at the 1947 conference of ALA. This plan was primarily the result of the efforts of the Postwar Planning Committee, whose chairman was Carleton B. Joeckel. The plan was the most visionary and most ambitious blueprint for action that the association had ever produced. Its basic premise was that all Americans should receive library service, and that existent library arrangements were inadequate to provide that service.

Under the provisions of the plan, the 7,500 public library agencies in existence in 1947 would be supplemented by 1,200 large unit libraries. The latter would have "second-line" reference centers that would provide assistance when needed. Each state would have an effective state library agency. At the top of this pyramid would be a national bibliographic and library center, the Library of Congress. An essential feature of this pyramid would be its interlocking federated system.

The program would not be inexpensive, as it called for a per capita expenditure of $1.50 for minimum service and $3.00 for superior service. No unit would receive less than $37,500 annually. The annual cost for services would be $200,000,000; the cost for new and enlarged buildings would be $500,000,000; the cost of stocking new and substandard libraries would reach $175,000,000. The plan also called for new and improved types of service, more extensive use of audiovisual materials, and improved library methods.[27] This was indeed revolutionary, and perhaps too visionary a proposal for the time. Funding was not available, and the American people had not come to view adequate library service as a necessity rather than a luxury. As Carl Milam so succinctly put it in his annual report, the association with its national plan was "all dressed up and no place to go."[28]

The second study was the Public Library Inquiry, which was first proposed in 1946 and got under way in April, 1947. This two-year study was to investigate how well the existing public libraries were servicing American communities. It was also to help decide whether public libraries should be the future custodians of films, television, and noncommercial radio. Although proposed by ALA, the inquiry was to be the responsibility of the Social Science Research Council. The intent in delegating the work was to ensure a study on broad social terms rather than in narrow professional terms. The Carnegie Corporation underwrote the inquiry with a grant of $175,000.

Robert D. Leigh, former president of Bennington College, was appointed to conduct the inquiry. In addition to his background in education, Leigh had experience in analyzing major American institutions. He had completed studies of mass communications, secondary education, and higher education in New York. A special committee of the Social Science Research Council was chosen to supervise the study. Its members were Ralph A. Beals, director of the New York Public Library; J. Frederic Dewhurst, economist of the Twentieth Century Fund; Donald Marquis, psychologist from the University of Michigan; Mary U. Rothrock, ALA president; Richard H. Shyrock, professor of American history at the University of Pennsylvania and acting director of the American Council of Learned Societies; Malcolm M. Willey, vice-president of the University of Minnesota; and Leigh as chairman.

The committee decided to cover the following aspects of the library as an institution:

1. The evolution, functions, and objectives of the public library
2. The internal operations and management of libraries, including personnel, costs, processes, and controls
3. Governmental and other overhead controls and services relating to the library

4. Present services to, and relationships of the library with, the community

5. Relation to the library function of new technical and commercial developments in the field of communication.[29]

To implement the study, the research team selected forty-nine representative American communities ranging from metropolitan cities to rural towns. In each of the communities selected, the character of the library facilities and their relation to the needs of the population were to be studied. In addition, a series of research projects covered such topics as foreign and international library development, the state of civic enlightenment, and the effects of communication.[30] In all, it promised to be an extremely comprehensive survey of the effectiveness of the traditional public library in the United States.

FINANCIAL AND ORGANIZATIONAL MATTERS

Warnings over the financial crisis facing ALA had become an almost annual event in the postwar period. Secretary Milam had alluded to this problem in 1947 when he said that the association was all "dressed up" as far as planning was concerned, but unable to carry out many of the plans because of the bleak financial picture. As 1948 ALA president Paul Rice pointed out, inflation was the primary cause of the trouble. To perform the same services as in 1940, the association needed approximately 60 percent more income. More services were being attempted, and the income had not kept pace with the expenditures.[31]

Several steps were taken early in 1948 to reduce the amount of deficit spending. In January, the *ALA Bulletin* carried advertising for the first time in its forty-two year history. In a further economy move, the *Handbook* was removed from the *ALA Bulletin* and published as a separate work. At midyear, the Placement Service at headquarters was suspended. This service had been expensive because it had attempted to be selective. It had required professional staff to match employers with prospective employees, and at a time of acute shortage of librarians, this selectivity was probably not an essential feature of a placement service.[32] As a substitute for this program, a new plan was put into effect in September, 1948. This was a short-lived experiment known as the ALA Employment Register; it failed because librarians felt it was a poor substitute for a placement service.[33]

Negotiations also began for the sale of part of the property acquired in 1945. At first, only the property on the east side of the headquarters building was involved, but later, the property on the other side was included also. The Community Development Trust purchased the first piece of property for $125,000; the property west of headquarters was sold to the Catholic Diocese of Chicago for $100,000. This reduced ALA's net investment in the property to about.$65,000.[34] The transactions returned some of the original purchase price to the endowment fund, a move that increased the income of the association.

The final major reaction to the financial situation was the consolidation of the two Washington offices. This move was made necessary by the depletion of the special funds that had financed the separate offices.[35] The 1948 grant from the Rockefeller Foundation to the International Relations Office had been designated as a terminal grant. The funds for the National Relations Office, provided by the Library Development Fund, would be exhausted by mid-1949. The consolidation of the two offices was seen as a temporary move necessitated by the economic conditions.

Unfortunately, as the executive secretary said in his 1948 annual report, ALA's financial problems were not solved by all these economies. It was clear that means of support beyond the regular budget would be required if all the association's activities were to be continued.

It was with this background that the fourth Activities Committee presented its report, a document that was to have a major effect on the organization and leadership of the association. The committee began its work following a directive by the executive board on December 27, 1945, to take the responsibility of

> considering relations of the ALA in general to regional, state, and local chapters . . . and consideration and evaluation of ALA Headquarters activities. . . .[36]

It soon became clear that, under the chairmanship of Ralph Shaw, the committee would indict the basic structure of ALA and the leadership of Carl H. Milam. The financial arrangements at headquarters came under close scrutiny which resulted in heavy criticism. The committee recommended that some of the activities connected with membership be decentralized, so that expenses could be reduced considerably. According to the committee, the accounting system used showed that the publishing activities of the association were a drain on its resources. If a more accurate system were used, and publishing were considered a separate entity like a university press, an entirely different picture would emerge. Likewise, the system of reporting treasury balances at the end of the fiscal year was questionable and certainly presented the financial status of special projects inaccurately.

Headquarters, in particular, came in for heavy criticism. The report implied that the staff was too large and the building too expensive to be justified. Only 10 percent of staff time was devoted to professional work, with the remainder concerned with clerical jobs such as record keeping. By decentralizing some of the activities, and reducing the "housekeeping elements which cause the present high overhead costs," the headquarters staff could be reduced to under forty, and therefore the expensive headquarters building would not be necessary.[37] The committee pointed out that, unless the association was really interested in reducing overhead expenses, which amounted to 40 percent of the operating budget, there wasn't any point in reorganization.

The present organization was that of "a highly centralized state," with some external resemblance to a confederation. However, even that characterization was probably inaccurate, in the view of the committee, because there was no provision for joint action on the part of the members. The organizational structure included no real means for membership involvement on a day-to-day basis. Indeed, total control was centered in the council, at least theoretically. In practice, it was the executive board, the executive secretary, "and to a lesser extent," the headquarters bureaucracy that ran the affairs of the association. Since the executive board had to depend to a large extent on the advice of its secretary, the result was a "highly centralized operation with a minimum of membership participation."[38] The committee called for decentralization based on region, type of library, and function. The result would be a federation of library groups, with carefully delineated areas of interests and responsibilities.

Milam could not be blamed for the structure of the association provided in the constitution, but it was clear that he was the target of much of the criticism. The policies and practices he had developed during his long tenure as executive secretary were difficult, if not impossible, to separate from policies established by either the board or the council. The two were almost completely interwoven, in the view of many people, and to criticize one was to criticize the other. The fourth Activities Committee report was meant to be a criticism of long-established policies of the executive secretary, and it was regarded as such by Milam.

THE END OF THE MILAM ERA

The council met on January 29, 1948, and endorsed much of what the report advocated: that responsibility and authority be decentralized, that the dues structure be kept as simple as possible, that the work of the council and the executive board be integrated more closely, and that the association's activities be carried out primarily by voluntary effort.[39] On February 1, Milam informed the executive board that he was considering leaving ALA to take a new position.[40] His method of informing the membership of his decision to resign was characteristic. In what was merely a postscript to his monthly newsletter in the *Bulletin,* he indicated that he had accepted the position of director of the United Nations Libraries. It was a surprise to some members, because he was to retire from ALA in 1950.

For Milam, the new position presented a challenge to try his hand at one last position "before turning myself out to pasture," as he put it.[41] For the association, the loss was indeed serious. Milam had been the secretary for twenty-eight years. To many people, Carl Milam and ALA were almost synonymous. In a sense, the two had matured together. Milam was fresh from work in the Library War Service at the end of World War I when he was appointed to the ALA position. As *Library Journal* pointed out, seldom if ever had a job fit more exactly the measurements of a man.[42] The position changed immensely as the organization developed, and Milam responded to meet the new challenges. Under his leadership the membership increased from 4,400 to 15,000. Income grew from $32,000 to almost $1,000,000. A permanent endowment fund of $2,000,000 was secured, and the association had its own building.[43]

The intangible benefits under Milam were even more important to the association and to the profession. It was largely through his efforts that ALA took on its international emphasis. His defense work during World War I had undoubtedly helped him see the need to broaden the work of ALA at the international level. The missionary role that had so characterized the activities of the association during its early days was applied to library-poor countries. At home, Milam was active in strengthening the role of the federal government in library activities.[44] There were many other contributions that could as well, at least in part, be ascribed to Milam.[45]

As Milam's successor, the executive board on April 21, 1948, chose John MacKenzie Cory. At that time, Cory was associate librarian at the University of California, Berkeley. He was a graduate of the School of Librarianship at the University of California and had also attended the Graduate Library School of the University of Chicago. In addition to holding numerous government positions during the war, he had been the director of libraries at the University of Alabama. Although he could not have been considered one of the most active leaders in ALA at the time of his appointment, Cory had been on a number of boards and committees of the association.[46]. Since he was not available to take office until September 1, 1948, Harold F.

Brigham became the interim executive secretary. Brigham was at that time the treasurer of ALA.

Less than a year after Carl Milam left his office, the association found itself in an embarrassing and awkward position regarding the former secretary. The difficulty began with a well-intentioned effort to honor Milam by nominating him for the office of vice-president (president-elect). For a number of years, it had been the custom for the nominating committee to list only one nominee for each office. This practice had led to criticism, but nominating committees reported that prominent librarians refused to compete with one another for ALA offices. To be nominated by the committee was of course tantamount to election, since nominations were seldom made by the other methods possible. Although not a democratic procedure, as it resulted in no choice at all, the practice was clearly constitutional. Thus, the 1948–49 nominating committee followed precedent in naming one person for each office, including Milam for the vice-presidency.[47]

As usual, the nominating committee presented its report to the council at the midwinter meeting. A great deal of discussion followed the report, centering on the desirability of having two nominations for the vice-presidency. President E. W. McDiarmid called for a voice vote on the motion to adopt the committee's report. He then ruled that the motion had carried. A storm of protest broke out in the audience of 1,400, forcing a show of hands. The second vote showed that the motion had lost by a vote of 47 to 15. The president then ruled that the constitution did not require acceptance of a nominating committee's report. After two days of stormy meetings, and with an atmosphere reminiscent of a political convention, this decision of the president was allowed to stand. It was unpopular, but correct according to the constitution. A sizable proportion of the membership present at the midwinter meeting showed its unwillingness to let the nominating question remain settled in this manner. At the last session of the meeting, the executive secretary announced that the name of Clarence R. Graham had been placed in nomination for the vice-presidency by petition, an alternative method allowed under the constitution.[48] Other nominees selected by the nominating committee remained unchallenged by the membership.

The situation was embarrassing to Milam as well as to the association. For several reasons, he had originally declined when the nominating committee had asked him to run for the office. He would be retired from the library at the United Nations by the time he assumed the presidency of ALA. Therefore, he would have no secretarial assistance available during his term, usually a necessary requisite of the office because of the limited budget. Officers of the association assured him that this would not be a serious problem. Milam was also concerned over the possible embarrassment to the new executive secretary in working with his predecessor. This, too, was checked out by the committee and refuted. When protests began during the midwinter meeting over his nomination, Milam again attempted to have his name removed. Friends and officers prevailed on him not to do so.

The opposition to Milam's nomination was based on a number of factors. First was the general feeling that, despite executive secretary Cory's denials, having Milam as president would put Cory in an unpleasant situation. Milam as executive secretary had been a strong and dominating leader. The natural tendency might be to have power and influence gravitate towards him once again as president.[49] The second reason put forth for the opposition was in connection with the proposed reorganization of ALA. The fourth Activities Committee had suggested certain basic changes in the organization's structure. To some members, it seemed incongruous that Milam would be taking office just when the reorganization might be taking place. The sum of this argument was that Milam was considered too closely connected with the "old" ALA.[50]

The third reason perhaps had little to do with Milam himself. There seemed to be a deep resentment and frustration over the fact that the membership actually had very little control over the operation of the organization. Lack of opposition in the election of officers was, to many people, simply a glaring example of the lack of democracy in ALA.[51] The nomination process was of course established by the constitution, which had been approved by the membership. Younger members were not mollified by that fact. Basic changes were desired by the group in order to end leadership by a few older people. Finally, opposition to Milam's nomination was engendered by personal antagonism towards the former secretary. Although he was highly respected and generally liked during his twenty-eight years in office, it was only natural that there should have been some conflicts and unhappiness.[52] Many people undoubtedly felt that he had been at the helm long enough, and that other people should be given the opportunity to provide leadership. The mixture of these factors was enough to ensure Milam's defeat. He received only 3,104 votes out of the 8,335 ballots cast.[53]

INTERNATIONAL ACTIVITY

When the end of World War II came, the immediate response was to emphasize the domestic situation. However, ALA's international role was not neglected. In some respects, there was an enlargement of these activities. The work in Latin America previously described, was continued. In addition, grants from the Rockefeller Foundation subsidized the following projects: a study of the National Library of Brazil; work on the Mexican Union Catalog; attendance of Latin Americans at American library schools; and fellowships enabling Latin American librarians and archivists to visit important libraries in this country.[54] Grants from the United States Department of State enabled ALA to administer American libraries in Nicaragua and Uruguay. In June, 1945, an American Book Center was organized with the cooperation of other national library associations. Its purpose was to coordinate efforts at restocking the libraries in war areas of the allied nations. Its major project was to be a book drive to obtain 1,000,000 volumes.[55] A Books for China program, similar to earlier ones for Europe and South America, was also started in 1945. This program was funded for two years with a grant of $100,000 from the State Department.[56]

There followed a period of relative inactivity when the international program of ALA became almost negligible. The Rockefeller Foundation grant in 1948 was a terminal grant, which meant there was very little money for other than domestic work. In 1950, emphasis on international relations increased again. The start of the Korean conflict in June, 1950, probably contributed to the change. While the association did not become involved in defense activities as it had in the past, the war called to mind the need for greater international awareness once again.

ALA and its member associations administered a number of small projects. The old Books for Europe program had grown into the United States Book Exchange, which coordinated efforts to supply foreign libraries with materials no longer needed by American libraries. The association was one of the sponsors of the exchange, with funding coming from the Rockefeller Foundation.[57] The association directly administered a Rockefeller grant for the International Youth Library in Munich, Germany.[58] It also administered a Department of State grant for a foreign translation program.

The biggest project at this time was the opening of a Japanese library school. Plans for the school had been under way since May, 1950. A preliminary survey had been done by Robert Downs of the University of Illinois Library School. Final arrangements reflected most of his suggestions, and the school opened in 1951. Robert L. Gitler, director of the School of Librarianship at the University of Washington, was appointed the first head of the school. Although the Department of the Army financed the project, ALA was given full responsibility for its administration. This included the establishment of academic policies, admission standards, and the selection of the faculty. After fifteen months, the school was supposed to become the responsibility of a Japanese university.[59]

Similar in nature was a grant in 1955 for the establishment of the University of Ankara Library School.[60] With funds from the Ford Foundation and the cooperation of the University of Ankara, the program got under way on March 1, 1955. Robert Downs served as the first director. After seven months, control of the school was turned over to the cooperating university, as had been planned.

In 1956 ALA received a three-year grant from the Rockefeller Foundation for the establishment of a new International Relations Office.[61] Although it had the same name as the previous office, its function was much narrower. The new office was concerned primarily with library education in foreign countries, including archival work, documentation, "and other activities usually associated with the work of libraries and information centers."[62] The director of the office was to investigate library development and library education throughout the world. On the basis of this work, he was to assist in the development of proposals for foundations, government agencies, and foreign groups. The establishment of library schools in foreign countries would, of course, be a continuing concern for the association and this new office.

In spite of the creation of this new agency, the old International Relations Committee continued to exist. The committee, along with other groups within ALA, was responsible for such programs as the exchange of librarians between the United States and other countries. In some areas, the line of authority was not clear. The problem was in the stated purpose of the new International Relations Office. While it seemed to be completely concerned with library education, the inclusion of "other activities usually associated with the work of libraries" in its purpose made its sphere of activity quite large. The lack of coordination made for confusion and duplication of effort.

OTHER FOUNDATION ACTIVITY

In 1955 ALA received a major grant from the Fund for Adult Education for a project to determine the role of the library in the community. The project, headed by Ruth Warncke, was intended to broaden and develop previously funded activities. It had three major aspects: a partial continuation of the American Heritage project, first announced at the seventy-fifth anniversary conference of ALA; the training of consultants for adult education; and the development of adult education programs in four states, to be chosen as pilot projects.[63]

Undoubtedly the most significant foundation project to begin during this time was the Council on Library Resources. Made possible through a grant of $5,000,000 from the Ford Foundation, the council was established on

September 19, 1956. Its president, Verner W. Clapp, was formerly the Chief Assistant Librarian of Congress and had been associated with that institution for thirty-three years.[64] The new council was to act as an initiator of new ideas and as coordinator of developments. Grants-in-aid to individuals and to institutions would support efforts to identify obstacles to efficient library service and to find new ways of overcoming the impediments.[65] The council was to be especially concerned with new procedures and applications of technological developments in libraries. It was an imaginative venture that was to have significance for libraries in the future. As for its director, David Clift wrote,

> In Verner Clapp, the council has an executive officer whose fertile and imaginative mind and great energy will accomplish all that the venture promises—and more; to him, librarians in every field of endeavor will be eager to give the help and counsel that he may need and desire and the cooperation that he has himself always so freely given.[66]

Although the association's relationship with foundations in the administration of grants was usually satisfactory, such projects added little besides prestige and staff to the association. Most projects were self-sustaining, but they did not help to reduce the financial strain on the association.

A CHALLENGE TO INTELLECTUAL FREEDOM

The anti-intellectual activity of the prewar period was more than matched by the censorship activities during the postwar years. Fear of communism, increased by the cold war that developed between the United States and Russia, at times almost reached hysteria. It was, as one author called it, the period of "The Great Fear":

> Between 1949 and 1954 the nation was gripped by a pervasive fear that Communism was about to subvert the Republic. Any program or any idea traceable to Communist ideology became suspect; mere accusation of having been a Communist was sometimes enough to condemn a man to loss of job or friends. A veritable witch hunt of suspected traitors and disloyal citizens was carried out by government and by private groups.[67]

Censorship activities against libraries seemed to be on the increase everywhere in the country. At its conference in Atlantic City, New Jersey, ALA responded with two measures designed to strengthen the role of librarians in guarding intellectual freedom. The first was a revision of the Library Bill of Rights by the Intellectual Freedom Committee. The result was a stronger and more explicit statement of rights and responsibilities than the original. Book selection, according to the new statement, should not be done on the basis of the race or nationality or the political or religious views of the author. The earlier statement had said that these factors should not influence the selection process. The new policy also stated that censorship attempts by individuals or groups must be challenged by librarians as part of their responsibility to provide free access to information. The new statement, also named the Library Bill of Rights, was adopted by the ALA council on June 18, 1948.[68]

On the same day, the council approved another statement in the area of intellectual freedom. David K. Berninghausen, chairman of the Intellectual Freedom Committee, presented a resolution protesting loyalty investigations in libraries. Although it was adopted, this resolution did not receive the support that the Library Bill of Rights had.[69] The loyalty investigations were a postwar development that had grown out of the fear of communism and communist-affiliated organizations. Many Americans could not understand why any noncommunist would object to the investigations. As the resolution pointed out, it was only on the surface that the investigations were harmless and innocent; underneath was a serious violation of intellectual freedom. The basic premise of the investigations was the desire to require an acceptable conformity in the thinking of public employees. In a strongly worded statement, ALA condemned the use of such loyalty investigations. The action did not reveal the division over the question within the council. Some of the members were not opposed to loyalty investigations per se, but only to "improperly framed" orders that obviously violated individual freedom.[70]

The problem of loyalty investigations and loyalty oaths surfaced again and again, for it was too complex a matter to be solved by a resolution. Furthermore, some librarians began to question the wisdom of the resolution. The "unqualified condemnation of the use of loyalty investigations," as the resolution stated, was too strong for some people. The following year, the council substituted the word "abuse" for "use," in what was interpreted as a clarification of the wording. The point was made that loyalty oaths had been used in the past and would be used in the future; so it would be foolish for ALA to take an intransigent stand against their use.[71] Another member expressed the view that, in its original stand, ALA was placing itself alongside other subversive organizations.[72] Although there were members of the association who believed otherwise, they were apparently in the minority at this time, since the council action was allowed to stand.

A *Library Journal* editorial stated it was still unconvinced that loyalty oaths were necessary or desirable in a democracy. The only exception would be where there was a clear and present danger, a qualification that was not apparent at the time. The editorial pointed out that loyalty checks were concerned not only with acts, but also with private opinions. If a person's views were not orthodox, then he would lose his job and perhaps any chance for future employment. The whole concept was contrary to American ideals, in the view of the editors.[73]

As long as the problem remained a theoretical one, librarians could still believe that the *abuse* of loyalty oaths represented their only real danger. However, when individuals began to lose jobs over refusal to sign an oath, the danger became more apparent. The first ALA member to lose her position over the loyalty oath issue was Elizabeth Haas of the Enoch Pratt Free Library in Baltimore. Miss Haas had become a Quaker after serving in World War II as a member of the Women's Air Corp. Her refusal to sign the oath in March, 1950, was based on both religious and political grounds. She said that the oath itself contained nothing that she could not affirm without any reservation. But the law on which it was based, Miss Haas stated, was "a positive evil and a denial of principles."[74] It was the dismissal of this kind of employee that pointed out the potential tragedy of the loyalty oaths.

Another case demonstrated to librarians the stake they had in the issue. The first loyalty oath case to reach the United States Supreme Court involved a Los Angeles librarian. Julia Steiner, an employee of the Los Angeles County Library, had been asked to reveal whether she had ever been a member of, or a supporter of, any of the 144 organizations that the California Un-American Activities Committee had characterized as "subversive." Miss Steiner refused to answer and appealed through the lower courts to the United States Supreme Court. That court dismissed the case on the grounds that the lower courts had failed to establish that Miss Steiner actually faced dismissal if she did not sign the oath.[75]

The two court cases revealed to many people the true danger of the loyalty oaths. Oaths were not necessarily effective in fighting subversive activity, since dishonest people might not be intimidated by them. But they had the undesirable effect of causing the dismissal of loyal, strong-principled employees such as these two women, who refused to believe that a democracy needed to resort to such tactics.

In retrospect, it would seem to this author that ALA retreated when the word *abuse* was substituted for *use* in its resolution against loyalty oaths. The first resolution was a strong, unequivocal stand. When altered, the resolution became weak or even meaningless, since the substituted word *abuse* could be defined as suited the individual. It is true that the resolution was only a paper statement, and included no enforcement machinery. However, a strongly worded statement might have helped to marshal public sentiment against loyalty oaths and to provide moral support for the librarians who were faced with losing their jobs because of strong principles.

The need for a new resolution on loyalty oaths was clear. The ambiguity of the amended statement had placed ALA in the embarrassing position of criticizing something it could not define. Return to the original, strongly worded resolution condemning the *use* of loyalty oaths was probably not possible. Berninghausen, as chairman of the ALA Intellectual Freedom Committee, was the most effective leader in attempting to clarify the association's position. He said it was naïve to believe loyalty could be ensured by an investigation, or a threat of investigation, into one's personal opinions. Unorthodox opinions must be allowed, however objectionable they might seem to others. He continued:

> In a democratic society the only true loyalty which can be considered desirable is that which is a result of unrestricted individual choice. Firm faith in the democratic way of life and freedom of inquiry cannot result from any sort of coercion.[76]

In response to the work of this committee and of various individuals within the association, the council in 1950 approved a stronger statement on loyalty oaths. It condemned programs that investigated a librarian's personal background, unless his actions warranted such inquiry. It also condemned programs that allowed dismissal of employees without a fair hearing in which all of the evidence was presented. The new statement approved the "affirmation of allegiance to our government."[77] As can be seen, this resolution was a compromise. It satisfied the need for a new statement, and it was stronger than the previous stand of the association. But it was certainly less than what Berninghausen and others had recommended. The resolution was explicit regarding what were considered abuses of loyalty oaths. At the same time, the resolution did not condemn loyalty oaths per se. In view of the political climate, however, it was perhaps the best that was possible to achieve at this time.

In 1951, another aspect of intellectual freedom came under attack. For some time, librarians had been reporting attempts by various organizations to force library staffs to label materials. Many of the organizations were patriotic groups, such as the Sons of the American Revolution. The labels were meant to alert the patron of the library to the "type" of material being read. For example, labels were to be applied to publications advocating communism or issued by a Communist agency. The Sons of the American

Revolution further suggested that such materials should not be readily available to library patrons. Such activities were not, of course, limited to patriotic organizations, as religious organizations had also exerted pressure to prevent access in libraries to material they found objectionable.

The Intellectual Freedom Committee was contacted in April, 1951, by a pressure group in New Jersey. The organization asked the committee to adopt its plan of labeling communistic or subversive materials.[78] The result of this attempt was a strong statement by the committee condemning the labeling of library materials, adopted unanimously by the ALA council on July 13, 1951. The statement reaffirmed the association's belief in democracy but condemned any attempt "at closing any paths to knowledge." It called labeling a tool of the censor and a violation of the Library Bill of Rights. This was a forthright statement that would allow no interpretation by librarians or other individuals.[79]

Early in 1953, it became apparent that the principle of freedom of information was being severely tested in some United States libraries located in foreign cities. The problem came to light as a result of a commencement address by President Dwight D. Eisenhower. Speaking extemporaneously, the President urged Dartmouth College graduates not to join in with the bookburners. This seemed to be a reference to communist-hunters like Senator Joseph McCarthy, who had been putting pressure on the State Department to remove books by communist authors from department libraries.[80]

On June 16, the day following the President's address, Secretary of State John Foster Dulles revealed that United States Information Service libraries had already destroyed eleven books, but refused to give details.[81] In the days that followed, the Eisenhower administration's confusion on this subject became very apparent. The President added to the problem by stating that he did favor the destruction of books advocating the overthrow of the United States government, if those books were in government libraries overseas. At the same time, he angrily denied that his original remarks had been aimed at Senator McCarthy. McCarthy also said he had not been the target of Eisenhower's address: "He couldn't very well have been referring to me. I have burned no books."[82] It developed, however, that the action of the State Department libraries had closely paralleled criticism from the Senate Investigations Subcommittee, chaired by Senator McCarthy. Under pressure from McCarthy, the State Department had issued a number of directives to its overseas libraries. A March 17 directive ordered the removal of all periodicals containing material detrimental to the United States. A directive of May 13 listed sixteen authors whose books were to be removed from information center libraries. No reason was given for the removal. All the authors listed, however, had appeared before McCarthy's subcommittee and had refused to state whether or not they were communists. A survey of government libraries by the *New York Times* indicated that the purge extended far beyond books by the authors cited in the May 13 directive. Approximately two hundred titles by forty authors were involved, although not in all libraries. There seemed to be no real pattern followed by the Information Service libraries in the removal of the books.[83]

Alarmed by this attack on the freedom of information, Robert Downs, president of ALA, on June 15, 1953, wrote to Eisenhower to express his concern. Although lacking in specifics, Eisenhower's answer was reassuring:

> We know that freedom cannot be served by the devices of the tyrant. As it is an ancient truth that freedom cannot be legislated into existence, so it is no less obvious that freedom cannot be censored into existence. And any who act as if freedom's defenses are to be found in suppression and suspicion and fear confess a doctrine that is alien to America.[84]

When Eisenhower's letter was read at the membership session of the 1953 conference in Los Angeles, there was prolonged applause. Downs continued the counterattack in his message to the council when he decried the

> current wave of anti-intellectualism, manifesting itself in attacks on books, on free speech, freedom of inquiry, freedom to teach, and all those rights which we have long held to be guaranteed. . . . A virulent disease, presently diagnosed as "McCarthyism" but antedating the distinguished Senator for whom it is named by centuries, is infecting nearly every segment of our government structure, from national down to local levels.[85]

On June 25, 1953, in response to this situation, ALA adopted a strong statement condemning the interference in American libraries in other countries. It expressed dismay at the "fearful" response of the State Department to criticism. The libraries could be useful only if their users could be reassured they contained the truth. The statement agreed that books considered to be harmful to the United States did not belong in the Information Service libraries, but book selection should not be based on an arbitrary and offensive scheme of security clearance. The Overseas Library Statement concluded,

> The American overseas libraries do not belong to a Congressional Committee or to the State Department. They belong to the whole American people, who are entitled to have them express their finest ideals of responsible freedom.[86]

A further step was taken in conjunction with the American Book Publisher's Council. Meeting early in May, 1953, the two groups adopted the Freedom to Read Statement, an eloquent attack on censorship and the attempts at suppression of reading materials. The statement pointed out that the freedom to read was essential in any democracy, yet citizens were constantly being threatened with censorship from both the public and the private sector. It recognized the widespread fear of communism:

> Such pressure toward conformity is perhaps natural to a time of uneasy change and pervading fear. Especially when so many of our apprehensions are directed against an ideology, the expression of a dissident idea becomes a thing feared in itself, and we tend to move against it as against a hostile deed, with suppression.[87]

Publishers were called on to continue to make available a wide diversity of books; librarians had a similar obligation to the public. Obscenity laws should be enforced, but efforts to impose personal standards and tastes must be resisted.

> ... no group has the right to take the law into its own hands, and to impose its own concept of politics or morality upon other members of a democratic society. Freedom is no freedom if it is accorded only to the accepted and the inoffensive.[88]

This statement was also adopted by ALA on June 25, 1953.[89] The following year, Emerson Greenaway called the Freedom to Read Statement "one of the documents of the century" as he described its importance to librarians.[90] Perhaps that is too strong an accolade, but nevertheless the association had taken an important and courageous step in defense of this liberty during a period when such affirmations were not always popular.

In 1956 an incident occurred that concerned ALA's relationship with the Fund for the Republic. The fund had been established with a $15,000,000 grant from the Ford Foundation, and some of its activities had generated a certain amount of controversy. It had been called a "vicious communist propaganda machine" by Senator Joseph McCarthy, because the fund had subsidized bibliographic work in the area of communist influence.[91]

In December, 1954, the fund had given the ALA Committee on Intellectual Freedom $6,000 to be used principally to support the publication of the committee's *Newsletter.* In September and October, 1955, the *Newsletter* was attacked in the Hearst newspapers. An article written by E. F. Tompkins, columnist for the Hearst syndicate, described the *Newsletter* as a miscellany of leftist items, rather than a librarian's professional information sheet.[92] The incident that followed was reminiscent of a Don Quixote tilting at windmills. Apparently taking its cue from the Hearst papers, the American Legion *News* of Punxsutawney, Pennsylvania, took up the attack and expanded on it. In the December, 1955, issue, the *News* referred to the American Library Association as "leftist," "red front," and a "Communist organization." The local library was attacked for its adoption of the Library Bill of Rights and for stocking books the legion post considered to be subversive. A telegram was sent to the United States Attorney General to inquire whether his office had ever cited ALA as subversive.[93] The answer, of course, was negative.

Naturally the problem, in spite of its ludicrous aspect, raised the question of the propriety of any continued relationship between ALA and the Fund for the Republic. This was answered effectively in the following letter from David Clift:

> I believe that these attacks are unavoidable at this particular time in our history and that they are lacking in substance. It is probably true that the Fund for the Republic has been inept on occasion, but I am convinced that this is no reflection on its principles and objectives.
>
> I feel strongly that the American Library Association has no reason to avoid association with the Fund.[94]

Although the criticism of the fund continued in the press and in Congress, this did not have an adverse effect on its relationship with ALA.

APPOINTMENT OF CLIFT

The announcement of the resignation of John Cory as executive secretary of ALA was the surprise of the midwinter conference in 1951. His tenure of three years had been a period of financial difficulty, self-study, and internal dissension for the association. Undoubtedly it had been a frustrating experience, since there was so much that needed to be done and so little to do with in terms of financial backing. In announcing his resignation, Cory spoke of the need for the association to change its personnel more often than in the past. The executive secretary had great power and heavy responsibilities. It was therefore best for the association and for the individual that one person should not hold the office too long. Cory believed that there was a large reservoir of qualified librarians who could capably fill positions in the headquarters staff without becoming career officers. By his resignation, Cory was putting into practice his own philosophy.[95]

Evidently the executive board was convinced of the logic of Cory's philosophy. At the same midwinter conference, the board voted to limit the length of time professional staff members were to remain employed at headquarters. Regular staff were to be kept on only as long as their services were essential. Staff at the executive level should be employed for no more than five years, subject to extension. This was a radical departure from established policy and was naturally extremely unpopular with the headquarters staff. Although the execution of this policy would lead to excessive turnover of the professional staff, its basic premise was logical. New personnel would bring in new ideas. There would be a closer connection with the profession. Time alone would tell whether the theory worked in practice.[96]

The selection of Cory's successor took several months of searching and discussion. The executive board met in special session in May, 1951, to make its decision. The unanimous choice was David H. Clift, the associate librarian of Yale University. Clift was a graduate of the Columbia University School of Library Service. His first professional position was with the New York Public Library, where he remained for six years. In 1937 he became assistant to the director of libraries at Columbia University. Following service with the army during World War II, Clift went to Germany for the Library of Congress. The work of this special mission was to seek out books in enemy countries for the use of American research libraries. Upon his return to this country, he was appointed Yale University's associate librarian.[97]

The appointment of Clift coincided with the association's seventy-fifth anniversary. The total membership stood at 20,202. It was estimated that there were over 50,000 librarians in the United States, so the organization still did not represent the majority of librarians. Yet the growth rate had been quite phenomenal. Membership had tripled in the twenty-five years since the celebration of the fiftieth anniversary.[98] Although the conference in Chicago attracted only 3,800 librarians instead of the expected 6,000, it was a successful and happy celebration. The theme chosen for the occasion was "The Heritage of the United States in Times of Crisis." Probably the most exciting moment of the conference was the announcement that the Ford Foundation had given the association $150,000 to assist public libraries in promoting discussions of the American heritage. In view of the topic of the conference, the announcement came at an especially appropriate time.[99]

FEDERAL AID

A ten-year struggle for the enactment of federal aid to libraries reached its successful conclusion in 1956 with the enactment of the Library Services

Act. Every year since 1947, a bill of this nature had been introduced in Congress and supported in hearings by ALA. President Dwight Eisenhower, on signing the bill into law, said:

> The Library Services Bill, which I have today signed into law, represents an effort to stimulate the States and local communities to increase library service available to rural Americans. It shows promise of leading to a significant enrichment of the lives of millions of Americans, which, I am confident, will be continued by the States when this limited Federal program comes to an end.[100]

This act authorized federal appropriations of $7,000,000 annually for five years to extend library service for rural areas. A basic annual appropriation of $40,000 was allotted to each state, in addition to an amount based on the proportion of rural population of the state. Each state was to match the federal funds on the basis of its per capita income. No state, however, was to fall below 34 percent or exceed 67 percent of the federal appropriation. When Congress passed the appropriation bill funding the Library Services Act, librarians were disappointed to learn that only $2,-050,000 had been allowed. In effect, the decreased appropriation meant states would receive only the basic $40,000 during the first year. Congressional leaders commented that any future increase would depend entirely on what the states did with the initial funds granted them.[101] The burden was thus placed on the states, although in actual fact very little could be done at the state level with such limited funding.

In spite of the setback in financing the new program, the enactment of the library services legislation was a major victory for the library profession. Despite its limited resources, it did set a precedent for federal participation and the matching of state funds for library programs. Future programs would benefit from the pioneering effort. In attempting to give credit to those who achieved this goal, it must be remembered that many people were involved in the ten-year effort to secure federal aid. Paul Howard, as director of the Washington office in 1948, had been instrumental in introducing the legislation. At that time, the Senate passed the bill, but the House of Representatives did not take any action on it. Julia Bennett, head of the Washington office in 1956, devoted a great deal of time and effort to securing the votes necessary to ensure victory. Perhaps the greatest accolade belongs to Senator Lister Hill of Alabama. He sponsored every library services bill during the ten-year effort. In recognition of his efforts, the executive board awarded an honorary membership in ALA to Senator Hill in 1956.[102]

SELECTION OF THE LIBRARIAN OF CONGRESS, 1953

While ALA was achieving one victory at the federal level, it was only partially successful in the continuing battle to gain a voice in the selection of the Librarian of Congress. The tenure of Luther Evans at the library was short, and he combined that work with an increasing amount of effort devoted to the United Nations Educational, Social, and Cultural Organization (UNESCO). Many members of Congress were very critical of Evans for the time spent away from the library. A report of the Senate Committee on Rules and Administration, published after Evans's resignation, commented,

> It would appear that the last two Librarians of Congress [MacLeish and Evans] were not wholly fitted by background for the post, and in addition were engaged in activities apart from their duties.[103]

In March, 1952, in appearing before the same committee, Evans's assistant, Verner W. Clapp, had seemed to agree with Congress that the librarian should decide between UNESCO and the Library of Congress. He said, in response to criticism of Evans, that "UNESCO badly needs the wisdom of a man like Dr. Evans."[104]

In 1953 Evans resigned to become director general of UNESCO, and ALA reacted almost immediately. President Robert B. Downs appointed a special committee to offer its services in selecting a new librarian. The committee met at the Los Angeles conference of ALA in 1953. It then wrote to President Eisenhower requesting an appointment with him in order to present the essential qualifications for the position. Charles F. Willis, Jr., special assistant at the White House, acknowledged the letter and asked that the committee meet with him. On July 15 the committee went to the White House, where they presented a statement of qualifications and a list of six well-qualified librarians to be considered for the position. Senators and representatives on the Joint Committee on the Library were also contacted at this time. One week later, members of the committee were contacted by telephone regarding two men who were being considered for the position. Committee members rejected both names as being unsuited for the librarianship.[105]

This incident, combined with rumors that nonlibrarians were being considered for the position, forced the committee to take additional action. On January 4, 1954, several of the committee members met with representatives of the National Research Council, the National Academy of Sciences, the American Council on Education, the Social Science Research Council, and the American Council of Learned Societies. After reviewing ALA's statement of personal qualifications needed, this group drafted its own statement, enlarging and reinforcing the original one. More names were added to the list of librarians qualified for the vacancy. Both the enlarged statement and the original names were then presented to Sherman Adams, assistant to the President, on January 4, 1954. In accordance with the wishes of the White House, the names suggested were not made public.[106] There the matter seemed to rest for an uncomfortable length of time. It was rumored, and printed in the *New York Times,* that Verner Clapp had been ALA's first choice. If that were the case, politics soon changed the situation:

> Some political maneuvering has developed in connection with the post, although the learned societies would like to keep it above politics. In this maneuvering, Mr. Clapp has been elbowed aside, although apparently not eliminated from consideration.[107]

It was also indicated in the *New York Times,* but not confirmed by the administration, that a Republican was desired for the position. Finally, on April 22, President Eisenhower named L. Quincy Mumford, librarian of the Cleveland Public Library, as the new Librarian of Congress. The nomination was confirmed by the Senate on July 29, 1954. Mumford's nomination was unique in that he had already been chosen as the president-elect of ALA. Thus he had the honor of assuming the two highest offices in the profession at approximately the same time.

PLANS FOR THE FUTURE

Planning for the future seemed to be the emphasis of a number of officers and members during the 1950s. Three plans will be discussed here—those concerning the headquarters library, the relocation of headquarters, and a management survey preliminary to a complete reorganization of ALA itself.

Ironically, the library had long been a neglected feature of headquarters. It was inadequate, poorly housed, and had lacked proper administration during most of its history. A statement submitted to the executive board in September, 1955, commented:

> . . . in order to give adequate service of any kind, the Library should be well organized and well cataloged. Such is not the case in the Headquarters Library.

The historical archives of the association, stored in the headquarters building, received similar criticism:

The archives of ALA are also in a deplorable condition. The American Library Association has a rich history, but it will not have any way of locating the material if something is not done soon about its archival collection, much of which is at present rotting away from dust, dirt, and heat in the basement storage room in which it is housed mostly in cartons.[108]

Unfortunately, a number of annual reports would have to repeat the criticism before adequate provisions for the library and archives would be made.

The second example of future planning concerned the headquarters building and the possibility of relocating the association in another city. Within ten years of the purchase of the old McCormick mansion, officials had become well aware that the building was costly and inefficient. During the fall meeting of the executive board in 1955, the members noted the deteriorating conditions and the need for extensive repairs. This caused the board to appoint a committee to look into the whole matter of location of headquarters. The committee report was submitted to the executive board at the 1955 midwinter conference. The report indicated that the association should move to Washington, for the following reasons:

1. The move would eliminate the need to maintain a second office close to Congress.
2. Washington was more convenient to nonlibrary associations, institutions, and other agencies with which the ALA maintained relations.
3. Washington was more convenient to a majority of the membership.

In making its recommendation, the subcommittee admitted that

no ground swell of membership opinion has yet supported this suggestion to move to Washington, yet the opinion of a few informed members had persistently supported it.[109]

By a majority vote, the executive board accepted the report and directed that it be placed on the council agenda for the 1957 annual conference. On June 24 in Kansas City, the executive board presented the following recommendation to the council:

That the executive board be authorized to negotiate the sale of the present property and their rental, purchase, or construction of other quarters with a view towards moving on or before January 1, 1959.

That the new quarters be located in downtown or near-downtown Washington, provided a suitable arrangement can be made at reasonable cost. If it cannot, that a new Chicago site be sought.[110]

After considerable debate, the council approved both of the resolutions, which ordinarily would have been the final decision. However, acting in accordance with the provisions of the constitution, a group of members filed a petition to set aside the action of the council on the second resolution. The constitution provided for a mail ballot by the membership in such cases. The response to the question was an overwhelming rejection of the move to Washington.[111] Thus the membership in effect approved the acquisition of a new headquarters building by 1959 and at the same time, made it clear that ALA should remain in Chicago.

The third project in planning had actually been started in 1954. During the annual conference of that year, held in Minneapolis, the membership had approved the employment of a firm to conduct a management survey of the organization. It was hoped that the result of this survey would be a more efficient, productive, and capable ALA. On October 26, 1954, the firm of Cresap, McCormick, and Paget began work on the survey, which included the following aspects:

1. A study of ALA organization structure to determine the effectiveness of the relationships within the structure;
2. A review of personnel administrative practices;
3. A survey of the financial structure and practices of the association;
4. An examination of the membership policies and their effectiveness;
5. A review of central services performed at the headquarters.[112]

In order to obtain a comprehensive view of the organization, a number of methods were used. Interviews were held with a large number of individuals connected with the association: the headquarters staff, almost all executive board members, officers and directors of the divisions, board and committee chairmen, and a cross section of the membership. Minutes of the council, the executive board, and the division boards of directors for the previous five years were read. Reports of the executive secretary to the council and the executive board were reviewed. A questionnaire was sent to the leaders of regional and state library associations. The firm also reviewed the publications of the association and its divisions.

The final report of the management firm was released to the membership at the annual conference in July, 1955. It summarized the strengths and the weaknesses of the association better than had ever been done before. The report spoke of a "measure of success" first of all. These achievements were: improvement of techniques in cataloging and classification; special services for children, adult education, publishing, activities in international education; raising standards for professional education; and other activities that contributed to the advancement of the profession. The association had cast itself in the role of spokesman for the modern library movement and, to a great extent, had been successful in this role.

There were also weaknesses and a "degree of failure," according to the management firm. ALA had not developed as the single organization representing all phases of librarianship. Because it failed to pursue the special needs of some librarians, other associations developed. Some, such as the Special Libraries Association, developed outside ALA, while others, like the Association of College and Research Libraries, developed within the framework of ALA. The management firm found that, as groups within the association had developed, the possibility of secession had brought changes in order to meet the needs of these groups. Some of the changes created serious problems for the parent organization. The basic problem, the study revealed, was the lack of a "sound, progressive, and consistent management policy."

The following specific weaknesses and needs were pointed out in the final report:

1. The council and executive board were involved in too much detail to function effectively.
2. There was insufficient integration of the activities of ALA and its chapters.
3. There was lack of coordination of the functions of the executive board and the divisional secretaries, which handicapped all concerned.
4. The executive secretary lacked the authority and resources to effect overall action and coordination.
5. Reorganization was needed to eliminate overlapping boards and committees.
6. There should be a clear distinction between the divisions as to their proper functions.
7. The divisions should be delegated the responsibility to act for ALA "on matters solely within the limits of their distinct fields of jurisdiction."
8. The existing organizational structure was too complicated, and the delegation of responsibility was too inadequately provided for.

The report concluded with a number of recommendations to remove the weaknesses noted in the organizational structure. These recommendations were based on the assumption that the divisions would be willing to relinquish some of their autonomy in the common interest of the association. The management firm pointed out that its plan would make it possible to delegate more responsibility to the divisions than they then had, notwithstanding the loss of some autonomy. The major recommendations were as follows:

1. The council should be renamed the General Assembly and should function as the governing body of ALA.
2. The executive board should be renamed the Executive Committee of the General Assembly and should act as the central working body of the association.
3. Consideration should be given to fixing a five-year term for the executive secretary, with provision for reappointment if desired and appropriate.
4. The dues system should be based on the ability to pay and on the benefits received.
5. Divisional income should be allotted partly on the basis of membership and partly on the basis of need.
6. Every division needed an executive secretary, although sharing such an officer might be necessary for the very small divisions.
7. Subgroups should be organized by type of library and by interest as well as by geographic area and state.
8. Publishing should be centralized under a Board on Publications. However, publishing falling into the jurisdiction of a particular agency should be the responsibility of that agency.

In spite of the many weaknesses noted, the management report was generally optimistic over the future. The challenges of the growing population in the country would mean an ever increasing role for libraries and librarians. They would be called on to provide services that had never been provided before. The report concluded.

> Thus, the American Library Association appears to be on the threshold of a great opportunity. This opportunity can be met successfully only if there is an elimination of divisive tendencies, a de-emphasis of parochial points of view, and a strengthening of the association's unified capacity to fulfill its broad mission.[113]

An enthusiastic council unanimously accepted this report on July 6, 1955. It approved a plan of implementation that would call for a major reorganization if finally accepted. This plan called for extensive study of the recommendations before final action could be taken by the association. After a number of preliminary steps, a Special Committee on Reorganization was appointed to work on the restructuring of the organization as suggested by the management report. Although there were many facets to this work, the guiding principles were as follows: (1) a closer relationship between the organization and its twenty thousand members, accompanied by greater membership participation; (2) decentralization of responsibility and authority; (3) strengthening of the council as the governing body of the organization; and (4) allowance for more planning, control, and flexibility in managing the financial resources of the organization.

While the constitution had not yet been completely revised, and some of the problems of reorganization had not been worked out, the major aspects had been completed by the end of 1957. Therefore, it is possible to examine the reorganized association at that point to see how effective the work had been.

The attempt at providing a climate for closer contacts between headquarters and the membership was achieved through the decentralization of responsibility. This meant a general restructuring of the divisional framework. The Special Committee on Reorganization subdivided divisions into type-of-library groups and type-of-activity groups. In doing so, the committee said it recognized that ALA "is by nature a two-dimensional pattern of overlapping interests." Librarians were usually interested in types of libraries as institutions and in types of library work as professional activities. However, for the purposes of clarifying the organizational structure, it was necessary to delineate between the two in order to avoid duplication.

Type-of-library divisions were "focused upon planning in and evaluation of the whole library as an institution and upon the synthesis" of functions as they relate to the services of the library. The type-of-library divisions were the American Association of School Librarians, the Association of College and Research Libraries, the Public Library Division, the Association of Hospital and Institution Libraries, and the State Library Agencies Division.

Type-of-activity divisions were to be concerned with the study and development of such functions as reference, children's work, and administration. The following divisions made up this second group: the Adult Services Division, the Children's Library Association, the Library Administration Division, the Library Education Division, the Reference Services Division, and the Resources and Technical Services Division. The committee originally suggested the merger of the Library Education Division and the Library Administration Division, but this suggestion was withdrawn when the two divisions involved showed a lack of interest.[114]

The management survey had been quite firm in its recommendations for divisional realignment:

> It is recommended (1) that a division . . . encompass a field of interest clearly distinct from that of any other division, (2) that the area of responsibility of each division be clearly defined, and (3) that the governing body of each division be delegated authority to act for the ALA as a whole on matters related exclusively to the field of interest of the division.[115]

The firm had warned the association that this was the most important part of the reorganization, and that the conditions it was designed to correct had caused many problems. Under the old organizational structure, the fields of interest and activity of the divisions were not clearly enough defined, and therefore it had been impossible to delegate responsibility to divisions. The number of divisions in the new structure totaled twelve, whereas the old organization had had seven. If divisional areas of interest and responsibility were not carefully defined, the problems would be even larger than before the reorganization. There was some evidence that serious overlapping did exist in the new framework. For example, reference was included in both the Reference Services Division and the Association of College and Research Libraries; children's work was included in both the Children's Library Association and the Public Libraries Division.[116] These and other problems would have to be worked out in order to avoid the recurrence of the problems of the old organization.

In the previous structure, there had been some question as to whether the council or the executive board was the ultimate authority. The council seemed to be, since it was the policy-making and legislative body of the association. However, since it met infrequently and had its powers restricted severely by the constitution, there was a serious question as to its authority. The restructuring endeavored to change this by clearly designating the council as the policy-making body of the association. Further, the executive board was to have its origin in the council. The council was to elect board members from the council membership, so it was clear that the executive board was to act *for* the council. Council representation was made more democratic under the new structure, and the election process was also simplified. Some council members represented geographical areas, some represented divisions, and some were elected at large. Unfortunately, the council was still too large to act efficiently and speedily.

The next major change brought about by the reorganization was in the evaluation of the financial needs of the association. There had been two outstanding characteristics of the financial arrangements under the old organizational structure. First, there was no adequate, knowledgeable review of the relative need of funds by various groups within the organization.

Budgets were often developed out of politics, relative strengths, and the amount of complaining done. Second, although the divisions had developed a sense of autonomy, this did not really extend to their finances. The bylaws of the association explicitly denied the divisions the authority to incur expenses on behalf of ALA. Furthermore, until the development of the formula basis of budgeting funds to divisions, they were without adequate funding. Both characteristics of the old system were changed in the reorganization.

Budget preparation became the responsibility of the Program Evaluation and Budget Committee (PEBCO). Through this committee, ALA obtained the reviewing agency so greatly needed but lacking under the old organization. The committee had the authority to judge the relative merits of proposed programs. Its membership reflected the new status of the divisions. Of the fifteen members, twelve were past officers of the divisions. The other three were the ALA treasurer, immediate past-president, and president-elect.[117]

Second, the divisions gained a measure of financial autonomy. Since they could now act for the association, they could incur expenses on behalf of ALA. This authority, of course, was only within the division's sphere of responsibility. Although limited, the new responsibility and authority were particularly important from the divisional point of view. The lack of autonomy had been a matter of great concern in the past, especially for the more powerful divisions, such as ACRL.

The results of the reorganization were such that, at least on the surface, it could be considered a success. Decentralization had been promoted by the reorganization, although not to the extent wished by some members. In the process of decentralizing authority, the divisions had been expanded and strengthened. At the same time, the council was also strengthened. Its position of authority in the general areas of librarianship, was confirmed as second only to that of the membership itself. The selection of its members was made somewhat more democratic and somewhat less complicated. To promote financial planning, the reorganization had provided for a logical, systematic, and careful review of the overall spending of the association. At the same time, it had allowed for greater flexibility in the funding of new programs.

Problems and weaknesses in the reorganization, however, had already made themselves evident by the end of 1957. A careful delineation of areas of responsibility for divisions, sections, and committees had not been provided for adequately in the new structure. Perhaps it was not possible to delineate spheres so concisely that problems could be avoided. A second problem related to constitutional change. The association was, in 1957, still working under an outmoded and inadequate constitution. The third problem concerned the democratization of the organization and the closer involvement of the membership. Although this was one of the major reasons for the reorganization, it was not one of the notable successes. The only significant changes were in the composition of the council and the delegation of authority to the divisions. For the individual member, there was little direct change. He was no closer to the organization than before, and no more involved in its direction. Provision for this involvement could have been made with the chapters at the local, state, and regional levels. However, the reorganization did not place enough emphasis on them to make extensive use of their features.[118]

SUMMARY

During this period, ALA was preoccupied with internal problems that needed to be confronted before any real progress could be made with external issues. The largest and most difficult problem was concerned with the overall direction of ALA. Where should it go in the postwar world? Although much time was spent in the consideration of this issue, it was not completely resolved. Certainly no comprehensive statement of objectives or directions came out of the discussions. The most immediate problem facing ALA was that of its relations with the divisions, specifically ACRL. Some concessions were made in meeting the demands of ACRL, but at the close of the period, it was not certain that the problems had actually been resolved. The reorganization had been in partial response to these issues, yet after the expenditure of time and money, ALA could not be sure that the new structure could handle the problems any better than the old framework.

This postwar era saw a great amount of ALA activity financed by foundations. With the help of these philanthropic organizations, ALA administered library schools, libraries, and other projects in foreign countries. On the domestic scene, the two major undertakings were the studies on adult education and the establishment of the Council on Library Resources. Although not directly connected with ALA, the council was to play an important part in research and development in library science. A major victory was achieved by the association in the passage of the Library Services Act. This ended a ten-year struggle to achieve federal aid to support library services. The act established a much-needed precedent that would be useful in the future.

10

RESPONSE TO A CHANGING WORLD

*T*he testing of the reorganization began almost immediately. In line with ALA's long tradition of establishing a structure and then almost immediately having second thoughts about it, several problems soon began to develop. The major area of conflict seemed to be centered in the divisions and the responsibilities given to them. As had often been the case in the past, ACRL was among the first of the divisions to raise questions and wonder "about the workability of the new ALA."[1] As was true for a number of other divisions, the basic problem was in the fields of responsibility of ACRL. Only a very strict interpretation of the assignments received by the seven divisions and the five associations could avoid problems of duplication, competition, and perhaps even outright conflict.

Another area of potential trouble was the provision added to give more autonomy to the divisions. According to the bylaws,

> A division shall have the authority to act for the ALA as a whole on any matters determined by council to be the responsibility of the division.

An early sign of potential trouble occurred at the council meeting of January 31, 1957, when the Committee on Organization submitted a report clarifying the divisional fields of responsibility. President Ralph Shaw ruled the motion to accept the report out of order because it was "in clear contravention of provisions in the Constitution and By-laws."[2] The council upheld the ruling in a narrow vote, and Shaw added:

204

Honestly, I don't like this a bit better than you do. I am sorry, but I think there are matters of high principle involved here. I think we voted things into the constitution, and that we have to . . . decide whether we are going to stick with them or not.

A special committee was appointed to rewrite the divisional responsibilities, and it submitted its recommendations at a council meeting on March 4, 1957. The report also dealt in part with Shaw's refusal at midwinter to accept the report of the Committee on Organization. The special committee called the ruling "within the limits of permissable parliamentary practice. . . ," but went on to at least mildly censure Shaw for his decision:

We believe the interests of the association would have been better served had he found a way to accept the report as progress in the direction of reorganization. This leads us to observe that . . . President Shaw exceeded the bounds of authority and propriety as presiding officer, particularly in his use of statements which were clearly argumentative rather than expository.[3]

At the same meeting, executive secretary David Clift also contributed to the wrist slapping, although, characteristically, in a much milder tone. He pointed out that when "responsible arms" of the association devote time and effort to carrying out requests of the council, the interests of the association would be better served by placing the resulting reports before the council. He noted that, in the "present tentative state of the council and board," many reports ordered by the council could be technically barred from discussion. Clift concluded that any further public comment on the incident would accomplish nothing.

Although that ended the discussion of whether or not to receive the report, the basic issue of the autonomy of the divisions remained unclarified. It was certain that the granting of authority "to act for the ALA as a whole" did not agree completely with the constitutional mandate that the ALA was to be "the governing body of the association" and was to "determine all policies of the association." A collision course on this issue seemed to be inevitable, especially in view of the issues that had often in the past separated ALA and its divisions. As a result, at the 1958 San Francisco conference the Committee on Constitution and By-laws, proposed the following amendment limiting the divisions' authority to act for the association:

. . . except that the council shall have the right to review such actions. Adoption of policies and standards by a division in the name of the association shall be reported to the council prior to their promulgation. The divisions shall have the privilege of asking the council to consider and adopt such policies as would, in the division's opinion, be strengthened by such adoption.[4]

The committee asked how a division could have authority to act for the ALA if the council was, in fact, the policy-making body of the association. The council, according to the committee, should be the only group with power to commit the association in matters of policy.

When the proposal was presented to the council at the 1959 Washington conference, the amendment was adopted by the decisive vote of 86 to 43. However, four days later the membership overthrew the council decision. Leading the successful fight was the immediate past-president, Lucile M. Morsch, who reminded the membership that the council had unanimously approved in 1955 what it had just rejected. She also charged that the amendment would "negate much of the basic reorganization" of ALA by taking authority away from the divisions and from the membership.[5] After additional work by the Committee on Organizations, the matter was settled by a compromise statement that ensured the delegation of authority to the divisions "within assigned fields of responsibility and in accord with general council policy."[6]

A NEW BUILDING

While the association continued to suffer through the pains of the reorganization, it was also feeling the physical inadequacies of its headquarters building described earlier. For some time, there had been preliminary planning for a move, resulting in the appointment of a Headquarters Location Committee. A subcommittee of that committee recommended on January 31, 1957, that the present headquarters be sold and the association move to Washington. Its report was accepted by the executive board, which then voted 6 to 4 to place the question on the council's agenda at the annual meeting that year at Kansas City. At the same time, the board decided not to reveal the close vote in the report to be given in the *ALA Bulletin*.[7] Following the defeat of this proposal by the membership, the committee again took up the major task of finding a new home for the association. In 1958 at San Francisco, the committee presented its report, with the result that the executive board shifted its emphasis from planning for a rented building to buying or building offices. Again the committee, under the leadership of Gertrude E. Gscheidle, went back to work on presenting alternate plans of construction and financing. Several months later, as a result of the committee's work, the council settled on what was termed "Plan B"—to build on the present site while occupying all or part of the old building. Financing plans remained to be resolved by the committee.[8] Possibly to allay suspicions that the leadership was going to persist in moving out of Chicago, the Headquarters Location Committee became the Headquarters Building Committee, under the same leadership.

It soon became apparent that there would be no painless way of obtaining the large amount of money needed for the new building. The building committee, after being refused by the Carnegie and Kellogg foundations, concluded it was "highly unlikely" that any foundation would contribute a substantial portion of the needed funds.[9] For a short time, however, it appeared as if the association had indeed found a wealthy benefactor. Just before the close of the 1959 conference in Washington, David Clift received a call from a Marion Argyll representing a group that planned to build a twelve-story "national association" building in Washington. She said that all the necessary funds and land needed were assured already, but the group wanted one of the national associations to actually have legal ownership of the building. In a letter to officers of the association on July 10, 1959, the executive director[10] wrote:

> This is either an amazing philanthropic offer—or it is a promoter's hope to secure certain advantages of a financial and tax nature through the use of a tax exempt organization such as the ALA. My view, after considerable pondering of the matter, inclines me to the latter viewpoint.[11]

Clift cautioned that the news must be kept in strictest confidence or any fund-raising attempts for the association's own building might be seriously jeopardized by rumors. A letter of clarification from Mrs. Argyll's group soon made it clear that Clift's suspicions were correct. ALA would be expected to sign a mortgage for $3,410,000, would have to pay "land" rent of $40,000 a year during construction, and would be responsible for the real estate taxes of $5,600 a year. The matter was dropped, and the association's leadership went back to more realistic planning. The endowment fund would supply the major part of the needed financing, approximately $900,000 (later increased to $1,150,000), and it was hoped that a fund-raising campaign would bring in the remaining amount.[12] With that decision made, planning began in earnest on ALA's new building.

Through the combination of endowment funds and contributions, the association's first headquarters building slowly became a reality. The address remained the same, 50 East Huron Street, since the new building was constructed around the old. In December, 1961, one wing was completed, enabling the entire staff to move and the old mansion to be demolished.

Dedication of the finished building took place during the 1963 conference in Chicago. It was a proud occasion for the association: its first new home after eighty-seven years in makeshift quarters.

Built in the shape of an L, the structure had five stories in addition to a basement. Its outer facade was largely glass, bringing to the rooms an airy, bright appearance. The one exception was the executive director's office, the only one without any windows. The *Bulletin* commented that "the general impression made by the interior design and furnishing is one of dignity, good taste, and elegance without ostentation." In addition to the executive director's office, the first floor housed a fairly spacious lobby, the board room, and other offices. The Publishing Department occupied the entire second floor and, in addition, used much of the basement for storage. On the third floor were the division executive offices, public relations, and the offices of the *Bulletin*. The final two floors contained the offices of various projects and the library. It was a practical building without pretentions. "Nothing in the building is designed to make an impression by its richness or monumentality."[13] Most of all, it was large enough—a valuable consideration to the staff after years of working in cramped spaces without any privacy.

SUPPORT FOR PROGRAMS AND LIBRARIES

While the building situation was finally being resolved, ALA scored other notable successes in financial and legislative matters. The first was the announcement from the Council on Library Resources that ALA had been given $136,395 to finance the first two years of a Library Technology Project. The project was designed to provide librarians with accurate information about machines, equipment, and systems, and to guide inventors in developing new techniques and devices. Working with such agencies as the National Bureau of Standards, LTP would set standards of quality and performance, determine specifications, and disseminate information through a publication that would be a source of income.[14] It was an ambitious program for an area of the profession that sorely needed research and results.

The second success was in the area of federal aid. The passage of the National Defense Education Act (NDEA) of 1958 was a major victory for libraries, secured in part by the lobbying of the association. Although the act itself did not mention the words *library* or *library book*, it became an important asset in its generous support of the purchase of printed materials in science, mathematics, and modern foreign languages. Millions of dollars were poured into education programs at all levels, and through the various state programs initiated, a large amount was devoted to the purchase of library materials. The Russian launch of Sputnik, the first successful earth satellite, is often given credit for the impetus behind NDEA, but the lobbying of ALA's Washington office and the individual efforts of hundreds of librarians helped to direct some of the act's focus to libraries.[15] Earlier, at the San Francisco conference, librarians had also received the good news that the Library Services Act had been continued for another year, with an appropriation of $6,000,000. This, too, was a major victory in the fight to gain more solid and continuing support for the nation's libraries.[16]

There followed a veritable flood of federal programs that helped libraries and librarianship, although in a number of cases the benefits were incidental to the main thrust of the legislation. NDEA itself was amended a number of times, so that its original emphasis was enlarged to include more assistance to higher education. Next came the Depository Library Act of 1962, expanding the number of libraries eligible to receive government documents as part of the depository system. This act also established a regional library program for depository libraries and specifically included non–Government Printing Office publications in the distribution arrangement. In 1963 the Academic Facilities Act established an important precedent in providing for matching funds for the construction of library buildings. A unique feature of this legislation was the provision for grants to both publicly and privately supported institutions.

The Great Society of President Lyndon Johnson included a number of acts important to libraries. The year 1965 alone included the Medical Library Assistance and Hospital Construction Act, the Higher Education Act, and the Elementary and Secondary Education Act. Both HEA and ESEA included large amounts of money for the purchase of library materials. HEA was particularly important because of its assistance in library education (both fellowships and support of research) and for its provision that the Library of Congress would establish an international program of acquisitions and cataloging for research libraries.[17]

Under President Richard Nixon, the costs of the Vietnam War and the tremendous financial burden of the Great Society programs led to a slackening of federal support to libraries. The decrease was also due to the philosophy of the Nixon administration, which saw libraries as the responsibility of state and local governments. As one official noted:

Libraries simply are not a national government responsibility. . . . This program is a good case of a federal program that should be turned back to the states and localities.[18]

It was only through the resistance of Congress, urged on by the Washington office of ALA, that appropriations continued in support of acts previously passed.

While the Nixon administration was withdrawing financial support from libraries, it also took a significant step in the recognition of the importance of libraries. This was the creation of the National Commission on Libraries and Information Science, a bill signed into law by Nixon on July 20, 1970. This commission grew out of discussions in 1962 between the Kennedy administration and members of the Library of Congress. When a follow-up meeting was scheduled at the White House on January 22, 1963, David Clift represented ALA in suggesting the need for and the possible shape of such a commission.[19] As approved by Nixon, the new organization was to have fifteen members, including the Librarian of Congress as an ex officio member. It is still too early to evaluate the work of the commission, but it is likely to have a major impact on the profession. As Edmon Low has written,

> The creation of this commission with its distinguished membership brings a national recognition of libraries never before achieved and acclaims them as a major national concern.[20]

THE VOICE OF ALA

During much of its history, the association had never defined the role to be played by its official publication, the *ALA Bulletin*. How far, for example, could the magazine go in voicing or reporting criticism of its parent? This problem became more than academic in 1960, when the *Bulletin* accepted an article critical of library standards for junior colleges. ACRL, which had promulgated the standards, opposed the publication of the article on the ground that it would tend to weaken support for the standards. However, the editor of the *Bulletin* decided to go ahead with the article, and, despite strong pressure, Clift supported him:

> So long as Samray Smith is Editor of the *Bulletin,* it is, in my judgment, his decision to make—and I will stand back of him.[21]

Clift pointed out the two opposing views concerning the *Bulletin:* (1) that it would be unwise for ALA to put in its official journal anything that might damage the association's official position; (2) that the *Bulletin* should always be open to "critical, thoughtful, contributory articles" on the programs and actions of the association. It was clear where Clift stood on the matter, and on August 19 he requested Smith to go ahead as planned. But Clift also saw the problem as a natural and undesirable outcome of the constitutional provision giving divisions authority to speak for ALA. If the ACRL standards had been reviewed by the council, according to Clift, "we would have had a better set of standards."[22] And, by implication, no critical article by an author who refused to soften his criticism.

PROGRESS ON HUMAN RIGHTS

The beginning of the new decade also saw the first official reaction to the changes that were taking place in white-black relationships in both the South and the North. Progress in the country had been slow since the 1954 U.S. Supreme Court decision that separate educational facilities were inherently unequal and unconstitutional. Change was speeded up when "sit-ins" began to be organized in various buildings (including libraries) in segregated communities. As a later report commented,

> When, in 1960, ALA searched its statements for an adequate representation of its stand on discrimination in access to library service, it found none.[23]

That is not to say, however, that the association had totally ignored the rights of minorities. But its concern had been almost completely directed towards the rights of members at ALA conferences. Both the bill of rights and the code of ethics had ignored the issue of equal treatment. It may be conjectured that the "separate but equal" doctrine in effect in the country from 1896 to 1954 had legalized segregation and had also made it a matter of local determination—therefore outside the scope of ALA policies. In addition, as the report referred to above stated,

> ALA seems to have cherished the expectation that the situation, as regards library service to Negroes, was improving and would automatically correct itself.

Therefore, when it was suggested that sooner or later the association would be asked to comment on integration efforts in libraries, the first response of the executive board was a rather defensive reply that its position was already clearly stated in the Library Bill of Rights and in the non-discriminatory policy governing its meetings. Further than that, the board said,

> It was recognized that the association, while striving for service, cannot, nor does it attempt to, intrude on local jurisdiction.[24]

But it was clear that this response was inadequate for many people within the association. Furthermore, the sudden publicity on segregation and the many attempts to maintain it helped to solidify opinion in favor of equal rights, and the association was moved toward a policy statement even if that was outside strictly library matters. News articles in the *Newsletter on Intellectual Freedom, Library Journal,* and *ALA Bulletin* on the problems of desegregating libraries attracted attention. Suddenly the "vertical plan" for fighting integration (removing chairs and prohibiting the reading of books in the library), which was practiced in the Danville (Virginia) Public Library and elsewhere, focused national attention on library service. It was clearly no longer possible to totally ignore the situation and to hope that segregation would magically disappear.

A Special Committee on Civil Rights (also referred to as the Committee on Civil Liberties) was appointed by President Benjamin E. Powell on May 17, 1960, to

> . . . examine the existing statements of ALA and either recom-
> mend operating upon these, or prepare some alternative statement
> that the association could support in the area of civil liber-
> ties. . . .[25]

That committee, with a great deal of trepidation, presented its report at the 1961 midwinter meeting, commenting that in the tension of the times, the adoption of any civil rights statement would seem offensive to some and overdue to others.[26] Nevertheless, the committee forcefully stated that, whatever the risks, the association must add to the Library Bill of Rights a new paragraph that would be a simple and unambiguous statement of basic principle. The amendment proposed by the committee was as follows:

> The rights of an individual to the use of a library should not be
> denied or abridged because of his race, religion, national origins,
> or political views.[27]

The council immediately accepted the statement with very little debate and only one negative vote.

This relatively simple step, long overdue that it was, raised the question of further involvement or direct intervention by the association. It is clear that many members viewed the addition to the Library Bill of Rights as only the beginning of what should be extensive involvement in civil liberties.[28] Yet such action was strongly opposed by a very vocal segment of the association, including the *ALA Bulletin*. As its editor pointed out, there was a certain amount of satisfaction to be gained from the belief that ALA could use its power and influence to do all the things that its members might want to do. But, said the *Bulletin,* there were many things the association was not designed to do "and by its present nature and structure cannot do." The Special Committee on Civil Rights, the editorial continued, was operating within the sphere of the Intellectual Freedom Committee, and so perhaps the special committee should now defer to the work of the older group. Completing its lashing out, the *Bulletin* criticized the council's charge to the Intellectual Freedom Committee to recommend such steps as might be necessary to safeguard the rights of library users:

> This statement is misleading unless interpreted strictly within the framework of the ALA Charter and Constitution. As a membership organization with no regulatory powers, the association has expressed its stand on freedom of access to libraries. It can make its influence felt in many ways, but it has no authority to act in individual situations to safeguard the rights of library users.[29]

The editor was not alone in seeing the need to limit direct intervention by the association, as can be seen in the disagreement between the editors of *Library Journal* and the *Wilson Library Bulletin.*[30] Although there was basic agreement in the two editorial positions, the main difference was in *Library Journal*'s more activist attitude. The *Journal* thought it necessary for ALA to intervene in lawsuits precipitated by segregation struggles. Intervention was opposed by the *Bulletin,* which saw potential harm and ill will created by a northern-based professional association overtly interfering in a local situation. It was a controversy that would be resurrected many times during the next decade.

KENNEDY AND THE LIBRARIAN OF CONGRESS

The ALA leaders at the 1961 midwinter meeting were also concerned with what appeared to them to be political meddling at the Library of Congress. A report in the *Washington Star* on Jaunary 1, 1961, indicated that the incoming Kennedy administration was "shopping around" for a replacement for L. Quincy Mumford as Librarian of Congress. According to the column written by Mary McGrory, the "culture-conscious New Frontier" wanted a "great humanist in the Archibald MacLeish tradition." Although some librarians may have already been aware of Kennedy's plan, it was the article that galvanized the association into action. Germaine Krettek, director of the Washington office, sent a copy of the column to David Clift. On January 4, the executive board sent the following identical telegrams to Kennedy and to his advisor, R. Sargent Shriver:

The executive board of the American Library Association has noted story in Washington, D.C. Star, January 1st, suggesting new appointment of Librarian of Congress might be made. We hope strongly that no such change is contemplated and that the practice of the last one hundred years under which the Librarian of Congress has remained in office through succeeding administrations will be maintained.[31]

One week later, Shriver responded with a brief note that promised "to take your comments into consideration."[32] It was the only communication from the Kennedy camp, and the only acknowledgment, however faint, that a change was indeed being considered. Although some of the library leaders thought it might have been just a "trial balloon" to test public reaction, the threat seemed real enough to schedule a session of the executive board with Mumford on January 31. A committee was appointed by President Frances Lander Spain in February to consult with Kennedy or his advisors should the opportunity present itself. The opportunity never developed, and the committee never met. A month later, Clift learned in a rather offhand way that the removal of Mumford was no longer under consideration.[33] The problem was over, and in retrospect it seems likely that the quick response of the ALA leadership nipped the move early enough to be effective.[34]

The association's support for Mumford was strong and sincere, but there was considerable unhappiness with him as head of the library. The McGrory column had noted this, saying that the "library-like silence" of ALA in suggesting possible nominees to Kennedy resulted from its philosophy regarding the position and not necessarily from its approval of Mumford. This situation resulted from a general reluctance of the library, under his direction, to become committed to national service instead of remaining simply the service library of Congress. In addition, as David Clift noted in reviewing the situation, "There was a cautiousness and slowness (even for a government agency) about his administration which caused much unhappiness among librarians."[35] Clift thought the Kennedy incident and the "Bryant Report"[36] the following year had the positive effect of encouraging change at the Library of Congress.

LIBRARY 21

On the brighter side, ALA's participation in Seattle's world's fair enabled librarians and the public to glimpse one concept of what the library of the future would be. Library 21, as it was called, was intended to dramatize the importance of making fuller use of recorded knowledge and of providing an efficient organization of information considered essential to business, industry, and government. Although there were a number of specialized areas in the exhibit, the most popular and newsworthy display was the automated library service center, sponsored by Remington Rand. Its computer, UNIVAC, was programmed to show potential uses for libraries, such as providing personalized bibliographies and answering ready-reference types of questions. Library 21 was a very successful exhibit, and its $2,000,000 cost (subsidized by grants from the Council on Library Resources, the U.S. Office of Education, and business and industrial firms) seemed well worth the investment, at least for the companies involved.[37] Although interesting and eye catching, like an expensive toy it promised more than it delivered. In what was billed as a "marriage between the computer and the humanities," the thoughts of 74 different authors on 6 subjects were fed into the computer. At the request of a visitor to the exhibit, the computer memory was searched and the information was printed out automatically. The result, one reporter commented, was a "bloated and ill-printed Bartlett's *Quotations.*"[38]

FOUNDATION SUPPORT

Much more significant to librarians and library service was the announcement of a grant of $1,130,000 to ALA from the Knapp Foundation late in 1962. This was for a project developed and to be carried out by the American Association of School Librarians (AASL) to demonstrate the value of school library services to the program of a school. During the five-year program demonstration, school libraries would be established and improved to show how the national standards for school libraries could be used to improve a school's educational program. The pilot programs would be established in schools selected to represent different geographical areas. An important part of the project would be a national program of information services that would ensure widespread dissemination of the findings of the project.[39] The Knapp School Libraries project became one of the most important special projects ever engaged in by the association. It directed national attention to libraries, focused new emphasis on school library standards, and established model programs that were undoubtedly imitated throughout the country.

Ironically, at almost the same time that the association was working out the final details of the Knapp project, another agency of the association was questioning the proliferation of special projects so willingly undertaken by ALA during recent years. In a report submitted to the executive board on

November 9, 1962, the Headquarters Building Committee strongly suggested that the organization begin to consider much more carefully the assumption of library-related projects for other organizations. The committee asked:

> *Are special projects the blessing or bane of ALA? . . .* it is time that we looked gift horses carefully in the mouth. . . . The committee does not recommend getting out of the project business. *It does most urgently recommend that we only pursue those projects of such unique value and overwhelming appeal that they are irresistible.*

Although the committee was not particularly successful in convincing the executive board or council of the urgency of its recommendations, its report represented some careful thinking on the subject. Furthermore, it was echoing warnings given by others much earlier, who believed that special projects often actually drained ALA's resources in spite of the fact that funding was provided by outside sources. Projects also had a habit of steering the activities of the association rather than being completely under the organization's control. Undoubtedly the special projects, on the whole, had been beneficial to librarians and others in many parts of the world; the Headquarters Building Committee was simply warning that careful judgment had to be exercised even in accepting gifts. The implication was that perhaps ALA had been too willing in the past to accept gifts without a careful consideration of all of the ramifications.

CIVIL RIGHTS ISSUES

The civil rights issue, after being somewhat dormant for a year, came to the surface once again at the 1962 midwinter meeting. The chairman of the Intellectual Freedom Committee, Archie McNeal, had surveyed the various state chapters and determined that there were three with no Negro members. In passing this report on to council, the executive board indicated that, while the chapters were meeting ALA requirements for chapter status, it was "clear that some of the chapters involved are not providing all their members with the fundamental rights of membership. . . ." The causes of the problem, according to the committee,

> are to be found in state laws and local ordinances which prevent fully intergrated chapter meetings and a consequent lack of facilities for integrated meetings.[40]

McNeal's committee recommended that the following actions be taken by the association:

1. That ALA determine precisely which chapters were meeting the minimum requirements for chapter status
2. That the executive director be empowered to request board action against any member discriminating against its users
3. That after "due deliberation and hearing," any institutional membership could be declared void by the board because of discrimination
4. That any institution applying for membership be required to sign a statement of assurance that no discrimination was practiced against users on the basis of race, religion, or personal belief.[41]

In passing along the statement to the council, the board warned against drastic action requiring chapters to ensure equal rights to all members, because such action would "surely force the withdrawal or expulsion of some chapters." As the board pointed out, the chapters were operating under state laws and therefore had no real control over the situation. Concerning the second part of the statement from the Intellectual Freedom Committee, the board said its enactment would "cause a regrettable and . . . an unwilling loss in ALA membership and support." Among the librarians who criticized the board statement was Lawrence Clark Powell, who call it "monstrously cynical" and warned that its endorsement would be an admission of "moral bankruptcy." Acceptance, he said, would lead to its wide use and might even help to prolong segregation. He urged the association to stand strongly on its principles and to take a position of leadership.[42]

Opposition to Powell and the action he was urging came from those who could not accept this involvement by the association in social responsibilities. Jerome Cushman reminded the council that ALA's prime responsibility was librarianship, not social change. He pointed out that Powell's position, if adopted, would

> place the association squarely upon the philosophy it holds, [but] such a position would neither change the situation it might seek to combat nor provide a unified leadership in the advancement of library service in the few areas that would be affected; it would perhaps bring about a southern library association and cause American librarianship to lessen its impact through the forces of disunity and fragmentation.[43]

Following protracted and often heated debate, the statement was sent back to the executive board for further work, with instructions to submit a report at the Miami Beach conference in 1962.

The result of what seemed to some people to be endless debate and quibbling was a very unequivocal declaration adopted by the association at Miami Beach. It was called the Statement on Individual Members, Chapter Status, and Institutional Membership, and it indicated quite clearly that membership in the association, including that of the chapters, must be open to everyone regardless of race, religion, or personal belief. Chapters were to examine their charters in terms of specific rights of members (which were stated) and to certify that they were meeting them. If chapters needed additional time to ensure compliance, they would be given a maximum of three years; chapters unwilling or unable to satisfy the requirements would be asked to withdraw from the association.[44] The statement was less forceful and less demanding for institutional members. Libraries that were already members were urged not to discriminate among their users, and if they did discriminate, they were urged to stop doing so "as speedily as possible." Libraries applying for membership in the future were to be informed of ALA's attitude regarding public access, and that in accepting membership they were

> also accepting the responsibility for working toward free and ready access to libraries by all persons regardless of race, religion, or personal belief.

No enforcement procedures were established for institutional members who could not or would not accept the statement. This was emphasized two months later, when the public library of Albany, Georgia, refused to allow Negroes into the building. Two members of ALA sent a telegram to President James Bryan requesting that "appropriate action" be taken against the library. Bryan responded,

> It has not been the policy of the American Library association up to this time to take action on individual instances or circumstances of this nature.[45]

Thus it would appear that the segment of the statement regarding libraries and their relations to patrons had a very serious weakness. It was a paper policy that sounded good, but it was entirely lacking in specifics about enforcement.

However, several major results did stem from the adoption of the Miami Beach statement. First came the withdrawal of four chapters that could not or would not meet the requirements outlined in the statement. The secession was led by the Louisiana Library Association, which wrote,

We feel that we could not honorably ask for a three year extension because to do so implies that we would take steps to meet the requirements for membership, and this we are unable to do.[46]

Louisiana was joined by the state associations of Georgia, Alabama, and Mississippi in leaving ALA. This, in turn, led to a demand at the 1964 St. Louis conference that ALA officers not be allowed to attend functions of chapters that were segregated. It was introduced by Elonnie J. Josey, who had not been allowed to attend a Georgia Library Association meeting at which an ALA staff member had been the principal speaker. After long and heated debate, combined with several attempts to delay action, the membership voted that all officers and staff of the association should refrain from attending in official capacity the meetings of any state associations unable to meet the requirements of chapter status in ALA.[47]

The complaint by Josey, and the response of the membership, seemed especially appropriate during a week when President Lyndon Johnson had signed the Civil Rights Act. Further, a week after the membership vote, the White House announced a similar policy: "the administration would not expect Government officials to speak before segregated audiences."[48] For the association it was a major step: action matching words, policy with an intent so clear that there could be no doubt as to the goals of the membership. Eric Moon, as editor of *Library Journal,* commented:

> ALA has necessarily, like society and government, had to grope somewhat toward the point where its actions are as consistent as its intentions. But it has probably never taken a firmer stride toward authoritative definition and implementation of its words than it took in St. Louis. We have come a long way from our tentative murmurings in this area only a few years ago.[49]

In spite of the rather definitive statement and apparent intent, the executive board the following month decided to define "officers" as any person elected to an office at any level within the association. Immediately after publication of the new guidelines, so many protests were received that the board decided it might have erred in its interpretation. It sought help from its legal counsel, and was told that only the officers named in article VIII of the constitution could be called ALA officers. With that sage advice, the executive board drafted a new interpretation of "officers" (limited to the five constitutionally named officers) and sent it on to council for adoption.[50]

For good measure, the executive board also investigated the possibilities of the council reversing an action of the membership. The results were not encouraging. The Constitution and Bylaws Committee, in its report, reminded the council that, although it was the "governing body" of the association and its decisions were binding on the association, the constitution specifically gave membership the right to set aside any council action. The constitution did not authorize the council to reverse an action of membership. "Under existing circumstances," said the committee, "it does not seem advisable for council to attempt to reverse this or any other actions of the membership."[51] The board also asked ALA's legal counsel for advice, and the response was also in the negative. Basically, the legal firm suggested that it would be best for all concerned if council would remove any question about the propriety of the membership resolution; this could best be done by viewing that action as a "consensus of the membership" and translating it into a policy resolution.[52]

In spite of all the advice, when council met at midwinter, 1965, it was presented with a motion to accept the executive board definition of "officer." While this did not rescind the membership resolution, as some charged, it certainly narrowed and restricted it. It raised the very constitutional question that both the legal counsel and the Committee on Constitution and Bylaws sought to avoid. When the motion was introduced, the parliamentarian advised that it was out of order because it was unconstitutional. President Edwin Castagna overruled her, saying that the constitutionality of the interpretation was precisely the question that council wished to consider. The uproar that followed ended with a whimper when suddenly the motion was adopted without opposition. Laughter filled the room at the sudden and inexplicable change. As President Castagna noted, "There are some very surprising things that happen at ALA meetings—but this beats them all."[53]

Many people did not view the council action as a laughing matter. They saw, instead, the clear intent of the membership being ignored by the council—without any clear legal right to do so. It was, as Eric Moon said, "a gray day for democracy.[54] The action also raised further questions in the minds of members about the role membership played in the governance of the association. If membership decisions, hitherto thought by many to be binding on the council, could so easily be reversed or ignored by the 150-member council, then the potential for future problems seemed to be extensive. Fortunately, however, the immediate problem that created the constitutional crisis (relations with former chapters) was solved by the imminent return of the state chapters that could satisfy membership requirements.

One other major event could be traced back to the Miami Beach Statement on Individual Members, Chapter Status, and Institutional Membership. This was the impetus the statement gave to a study of access to libraries. The access study apparently had its official start in 1960 following a proposal by Archie McNeal, then president of the Library Administration

Division (LAD) and chairman of the Intellectual Freedom Committee. Preliminary planning and discussion led to the development of a more definite proposal to be undertaken by LAD. By the conclusion of the 1962 Miami Beach conference, the association had approved the study and was actively looking for funds.[55] Once those were obtained, it chose (after several individuals and firms refused) the International Research Association of New York to begin work on January 1, 1963.

When completed that year, the *Access to Public Libraries* report provoked as much controversy as any other report in the association's history. It identified two types of discrimination found in the libraries. *Direct discrimination* referred to the complete exclusion of members of one racial group from use of a library's resources. *Indirect discrimination* referred to inequitable location of library branches and unfair distribution of resources to these branches in terms of quantity and quality, giving one group less access to library resources than another. Among the principal findings were the following:

1. Direct discrimination was limited to the sixteen states classified as constituting the South, but indirect discrimination was found throughout the country.
2. Library segregation in the South was far more prevalent in rural areas and smaller towns than in the more densely populated cities and towns.
3. Discrimination against nonwhites in location and resources of branch libraries was found to be a serious problem in Birmingham, Washington, D.C., and Detroit.[56]

Discussion centered on what the study called indirect segregation—found in northern city branch libraries. Each of the cities criticized in the study responded with a barrage of facts, opinions, and countercharges. The methodology and validity of the study were questioned. The report itself was rumored to be in danger of being shelved or appearing in expurgated form.[57] These rumors proved to be unfounded, or at least incorrect, for the study appeared in print in August. However, as controversy increased and criticism mounted, LAD was called on by the executive board at its November, 1963, meeting to issue a report that was to consider all aspects of the problems raised by the study and to make recommendations. The result was an eight-page report, "Review and Evaluation of Access to Public Libraries," which the council ordered attached to all copies of the original access study.[58] The review included background on the development of the study and a number of conclusions: (1) the scope of the survey was too broad to be successfully supported by the funding available; (2) the section on access to libraries (which dealt basically with segregation in the South) was done in depth and provided useful information; (3) the section on resources of branch libraries (which basically criticized access in northern libraries) was too shallow, the methodology was in question, and the conclusions should be rejected. The report also called for additional studies on library service to the underprivileged, all aspects of branch library service, and patterns of discrimination in the employment and promotion of minority groups.

President Frederick Wagman included a letter in the copy sent to each library referred to in the access report. He said, in part,

> it gives me profound satisfaction to call your attention to page 7 of this report which questions the methodology applied to this section, takes issue with the incompleteness of the measurements employed to determine adequacy of library service, . . . voices strong disagreement with this section and rejects its conclusions.[59]

Did this letter, along with the LAD report appended to the access study, constitute labeling? LeRoy Merritt thought so, and so did Robert Vosper; both reminded the council that librarians were usually resentful when special interest groups asked for statements to be inserted in publications with which they disagreed.[60] Did it matter when ALA labeled one of its own reports? Perhaps not; at least the council did not regard it as a matter of principle and hurriedly passed over the disquieting idea.

The access study itself, when viewed in retrospect and with some additional hindsight, has fared better than the ideas of its detractors. Several years after its stormy acceptance, another committee was working on freedom of access to libraries, and it viewed the 1963 study "as a better and sounder document than it seemed initially when criticism . . . obfuscated its very real worth."[61] David Clift, in a 1973 interview, saw some valid criticism: reliance on secondary sources and not enough field work. But he believed it to be "basically factual." In a difficult area, it had produced statistics and conclusions that librarians have since used extensively. As for its critics, Clift commented:

> It shocked the hell out of some Northern cities, who thought that geography had placed them above the report. The outcry was primarily from those whose toes were stepped on.[62]

The access study, then, could be criticized on a number of counts, but it was largely valid. Like the *Public Library Inquiry*, the access study was a response to the changing world in which librarians found themselves—a world changing socially and politically, but perhaps not intellectually. The social order was on the brink of disorders that were to change forever the world they lived in. The access study was a response, however inadequate, to those changes, and its findings were to cause emotional reactions for many years.

ALA'S RESPONSE TO CHANGE

Much of what the association did and talked about in the remaining years of the Clift tenure can be considered part of this response to change. It was a period of disorder, disruption, riot, and dissension. Major cities saw huge sections burned and gutted as riots jumped from one urban ghetto to another. Yet it was also a time of great wealth and great aspiration: the Great Society of President Lyndon Johnson. It helped lead to an overly optimistic National Inventory of Library Needs, which was to be the faulty basis for future library and library-education planning. As the Vietnam conflict continued to consume a larger share of the nation's wealth, budgets began to contract and employment opportunities began to disappear. Within a few short years, the rosy picture of the Great Society had disappeared, to be replaced by one of rather grim reality.

Discrimination in the nation's libraries continued to be a major issue within the association. The Detroit conference in 1966 set the pace with timely coverage of poverty and economic opportunity, library service to the disadvantaged, and a discussion once again of institutional membership. The council had placed one item on the membership agenda: Shall library institutional membership in ALA be open only to libraries that are integrated? The response of the membership meeting was to adopt by unanimous vote a recommendation to council that the constitution be amended to eliminate libraries that discriminated on the basis of race, religion or personal belief.[63] In spite of the backing given to that recommendation by the executive board, the council at the 1966 midwinter meeting voted it down.[64]

The decision stemmed in large measure from a strong reluctance to make the resolution (aimed at segregation, which was already illegal) a part of the constitution. It seems apparent that the majority of the council were in sympathy with the spirit of the amendment and were opposed only to the machinery provided.

The council was immediately challenged in that direction by a resolution by Verner Clapp calling for a review of action taken by the association since it had expressed its determination in 1964 to use "every means at its disposal" to promote freedom of access to libraries for all people.[65] A committee was appointed in April, 1966, for this purpose and it reported in July at Detroit.

> ALA has, through the progressive attitudes of its members influ-
> ential in their communities, done much to promote full library
> service . . . it has helped bring about Federal legislation which is
> the greatest force and lever in eliminating direct discrimination.[66]

As for the question of what ALA had done officially to promote freedom
of access, the committee was very blunt: "The answer is, inescapably,
'Nothing'." A second access report was called for to provide in-depth information not then readily available. This report, written under the leadership of Keith Doms, left the association with a number of recommendations
dealing with services to the disadvantaged. But its significance lay, not so
much in its conclusions and recommendations, which were neither new nor
startling, but in its overall tone. It was almost unique among ALA reports
up to this time in its acknowledgement of the crisis in American society and
the need for libraries to respond to the situation. The authors had investigated the situation carefully and had arrived at the decision that there had
to be a major commitment on the part of ALA.

> We unequivocally suggest that the development and improve-
> ment of library services to the culturally disadvantaged and under-
> privileged be viewed as a major goal of the American Library As-
> sociation as long as may be necessary.[67]

That report was given before the council at the 1968 conference, and it was
symbolic of a change that was beginning to become more evident within the
association.

The unrest, the outspoken dissent, and the violence that had characterized American society during much of the 1960s finally touched ALA at
the 1968 conference in Kansas City. As *Library Journal* noted, Kansas
City might seem an unlikely place for a revolution to begin, but the changes
that began in that city can hardly be called less than revolutionary in an
organization long known for its complacency.[68] As with the latest access
report, the tone and the spirit of the conference were perhaps more important
than what was said and done. It was in the membership meeting, of course,
that the forces for change were the most noticeable and the most insistent.
A number of major issues were raised there, but the most important was
the request for the establishment of a Round Table on the Social Responsibilities of Libraries. The spokesman for the requesting group, Kenneth
Duchac, spoke of the crises of the year: the assassination of two national
leaders; a divisive war in Asia that already had taken over 25,000 American
lives; looting and burning of inner cities, which might eventually turn into
a "black and white civil war"; and hostilities of students and faculties at

institutions of higher learning. He called for the creation of the round table
to

> provide an outlet for expression of libraries' and librarians' con-
> cerns on these issues—race, violence, war and peace, inequality of
> justice and opportunity—creating a Round Table on the Social
> Responsibilities of Libraries, . . ."[69]

Duchac asked for and received membership support to bypass the Committee on Organization (charged with the responsibility of studying requests for new organizations), with the expectation that the council would
then approve the establishment of the round table. However, the chairman
of COO led the fight against the request, branding it a brazen power play
and warning that to give in would be to open the door to other pressure
groups. He was supported by the chairman of the Intellectual Freedom
Committee, who criticized the procedure and said the urgency was "spuri-
ous."[70] The council, as a result, turned down the request for immediate establishment and instead asked COO to consider the problem and act expeditiously. One may question whether the approval came expeditiously, as
the new group (SSRT) officially began in January, 1970; however, it was
allowed to meet earlier, to organize and to hold programs.

While the pressure for change from without at Kansas City was perhaps to be expected, there was also an unexpected attack from within the
power structure of the organization. Ralph Blasingame took the opportunity
of his retirement as treasurer to deliver as scathing an attack on ALA as
there had ever been; not even John Cotton Dana, in hurling his recurring
diatribes against the ALA bureaucracy, did so with as much bluntness,
acidity, and brutality. Blasingame charged that:

1. The ALA is an old organization—its policies and practices are con-
   trolled by old people.
2. The ALA is a bureaucracy in itself, dominated by members of other
   bureaucracies. Thus, ALA can consider all issues and place prece-
   dence on none. We are marvelously able to ignore the climate of
   membership opinion, to alter policies without seeming to, and to
   locate the treasured younger people who are prone to early sociali-
   zation.
3. The ALA has virtually no ability to plan its future in any respect.
4. ALA is out of control, with insufficient information about its own
   activities so that intelligent decisions could be made.

Blasingame had a few suggestions for change, which were almost as painful:

1. Younger people should be involved to a much greater extent at all levels of the organization.
2. There should be a return to the policy of putting a ten-year limit on the tenure of certain staff officers. This should include the executive director and his principal assistants.
3. There should be a reorganization of council and committee structure. Members should be limited in the number of offices occupied at one time.
4. There was a need for a new method of operation of the central offices of the association.[71]

Had the new spirit of the membership also found its way into the council, considered by many members to be the last bastion of conservatism in the organization? It was a short-lived dream, based more on hope than on realism. If the council was capable of ignoring the cries of social protest, it was also capable of ignoring a cannon fired in its midst. There was no discussion of the report.

The Committee on Organization did however, make one recommendation, suggested also by Blasingame, regarding committee appointments. It said no member "shall accept nominations or appointments which could result in simultaneous service in any two or more of several categories."[72] The council accepted this recommendation as a matter of policy. Although seemingly of small importance, the practice of giving several appointments to the same person had been particularly bothersome to some, for it was one sign of concentration of power and influence among relatively few people. For example, in 1968, 52 people had 5 committee assignments; 27 people had 6 assignments; 1 person served on 12 committees. Under the new policy, this centralization was diminished somewhat, but it was still a problem. In 1971, 46 people had 5 committee assignments; 24 people had 6 assignments; 1 person served on 13 committees.[73] In spite of the well-known reluctance of many people to serve on committees, it was difficult to believe that the distribution could not have been better.

The "revolution" that had started at Kansas City took on an increased intensity at the resort of Atlantic City in 1969. The movement began early, in Washington, where 100 young librarians took part in the "Congress for Change," and in New York, where "Librarians for 321.8" and "Libraries to the People" were organized. These groups became rallying points for those who wanted to change ALA and felt that their time had come. The changes they called for ranged from rather simple changes in procedures (such as asking candidates for council to prepare a statement of views) to taking an activist role in intellectual freedom, library education, and recruitment.[74]

The leadership of the activists included Bill DeJohn, John Black, and Patricia Schuman, but these were just a few of the articulate dissidents demanding change. Although these people were often referred to as "young activists," most of them were probably at least thirty, and many were veterans within the association. The threat of a disruption of the conference by radicals had been rumored for some time, with the result that security was far more stringent than it had ever been before. Meetings were monitored by guards, and badges were required for admittance. However, it was also obvious that the ALA leadership was doing everything possible to reduce tensions by allowing even nonmembers to speak at meetings and by avoiding unnecessary confrontations where possible. One area where conflict was avoided was a controversial measure giving membership only ninety days in which to override a council decision. Although scheduled for a membership vote, it was first postponed and then forgotten about. [75]

As for results, the conference was a mixture of victories, defeats, and delays for the activists. Some successes were achieved in the membership meetings, which approved Gordon McShean's move to strengthen the role played by the Intellectual Freedom Office and began a fund for legal defense. Resolutions were passed opposing the Vietnam War, favoring a revitalized effort to recruit people from minority groups, and urging a study of library education.

One response of the conference was the suggestion by incoming president William Dix that a new committee be appointed to examine the objectives and program of ALA and to give its findings at the 1970 conference. It was promptly dubbed the "Dix Mix" because its membership of twelve was to be selected from six nominated by SRRT, six by the president, and six by the Junior Members Round Table (JMRT). Although some members, particularly the activists, thought the move to be another delaying tactic, it seemed to be a sincere effort to prove that ALA, underneath all its bureaucratic layers, could really be responsive to its members.[76] An attempt by A. P. Marshall to turn the "Dix Mix" into a full-fledged Activities Committee was unsuccessful.[77] A proposal to strengthen the association's intellectual freedom efforts, although not as tough as McShean had suggested, was accepted by the council. The plan provided for written complaints to the Intellectual Freedom Committee, with appropriate action to be decided upon by IFC. With executive board approval, actions could include publicizing of information on the case; aid in locating jobs for those dismissed; suspension of a member for violation; and publicity listing those individuals or institutions in violation of the Library Bill of Rights.

A number of times during the conference, and many times thereafter, the specter of the loss of tax-exempt status haunted the association (or at least some of its members). The fear apparently had a basis in fact, but some members thought it was raised as a scare technique to discourage ALA journeys into social protest. At this point, it was clear that the requirements of tax-exempt status, the cost of losing it, and precisely how that might happen were all rather unclear to the members, and possibly to the leadership. Ervin Gaines tried to get the council to explore this problem through the "Dix Mix" committee and to have ALA express its willingness to give up its tax-exempt status if need be in order to pursue its goals uninhibited. He declared that

> I, for one, am unwilling to have the Internal Revenue Service influence decisions which the organization needs to make. Let's not be cowed into inaction by a coupon-clipping mentality.[78]

However, his motion was lost on the grounds that it needed more study and that ALA's basic philosophy was at stake. McShean's original proposal embodying a defense fund was also lost through a motion to refer it back to the Intellectual Freedom Committee.

On the surface, then, it would appear that the gains made by the various groups demanding changes were slight indeed, as viewed by the vocal part of the membership. The council's propensity to reject, refer, postpone, or table new ideas was in startling contrast to the mood of the membership. Ervin Gaines perhaps best summed up the reaction of many members when he said:

> I share many of the sentiments expressed in a variety of ways this week about the slow response of ALA to the actual crisis that surrounds us. There's without a doubt a cautious attitude that pervades some of the council and committees of this association that tends to inhibit and frustrate much-needed action. Sometimes I think we would love to live dangerously without unbuckling our safety belts.[79]

The winds of change, however, were too strong to resist for long. And it was from the groundwork provided at Kansas City and Atlantic City that many of the changes, when they did become reality, could be traced. The young insurgents, and many who were not so young, worked under various names: Librarians for 321.8, the National Call for Library Reform, the Congress for Change, the National Freedom Fund for Librarians, and the various groupings within the Social Responsibilities Round Table of ALA. From within the association itself came a move to reduce conflict and tensions: the "Dix Mix," under its new name of Activities Committee on New Directions for ALA (ACONDA), began to study the priorities of the organization.

ACONDA, under the leadership of Frederick Wagman, began its work in September, 1969. Other committee members were George Alfred, Arthur Curley, Keith Doms, William Hinchliff, David Kaser, John Lorenz, Edmon Low, Albert P. Marshall, Glenn Miller, Shirley Olofson, J. Maurice Travillian, and Katherine Laich. The first step taken by the group was to decide the major broad areas of current priorities, as follows:

1. The social responsibilities of the association, including its commitment to the fundamental values of society
2. Manpower, including specifically recruitment of minorities and the improvement of library education
3. Intellectual freedom, including the need to provide support for members under attack
4. Greater democratization of the association by involving more members in activities and decision-making and by demonstrating greater responsiveness to concerns of membership
5. Increased effectiveness in support of progressive legislation
6. Better planning and research, along with more thorough refinement of projects in which outside support should be requested.[80]

With the possible exception of the priorities relating to progressive legislation and research, these were all, of course, based on the demands of the activists. Thus the association's leadership was showing its responsiveness but clearly indicating at the same time that it intended to follow the usual channels in making any changes. It remained to be seen whether ACONDA was a "ploy" or "sop," as some of the dissatisfied members saw it, or whether ALA was really serious in its attempt to become more relevant, responsive, and democratic. The makeup of ACONDA, with its members largely nominated by JMRT and SRRT, should have been considerable reassurance to the activist members.

ACONDA made what was supposed to be its final report to the council on July 3, 1970. Katherine Laich had replaced Wagman as its chairperson, and it remained for her to present the conclusions to the association. Among the ACONDA recommendations were the following:

1. ALA should continue to be an organization of librarians and libraries, with the "overarching objective" being to improve library service and librarianship.
2. An office for Social Responsibility (changed by council to Office for Library Service to the Disadvantaged and Unserved) should be established.
3. The Intellectual Freedom Office should be expanded.
4. ALA should establish a policy with just procedures whereby any

member who violates the Library Bill of Rights may be suspended from the association.

5. The budget of the Washington office should be increased.
6. ALA should elect all council members at large, eliminate past-presidents from automatic membership on the council, and fix the number of voting members of council at ninety-six.
7. Each candidate for council should prepare a statement of concerns to be included on the ballot.
8. The divisional structure of ALA should be realigned to provide three types of library divisions and four types of activity divisions.
9. The association should be restructured. Several alternatives, including a federation and a functional organizational structure, were suggested.[81]

Council approved the first three recommendations; it sent several items back to ACONDA, and it established a special ad hoc committee of the council (ANACONDA) to work with ACONDA in a further study of the recommendations.[82] Action on the complete ACONDA report was promised by the Dallas meeting in 1971.

When ACONDA reported again at midwinter, 1971, in Los Angeles, it reiterated its strong feeling that ALA needed restructuring. In its research into membership and ALA staff opinion, a major point had emerged: "ALA's job is not getting done as well as it should." ACONDA was blunt in its criticism:

> Proliferation of units and subunits has resulted in overlapping interests, duplication of effort, increasingly complex administrative procedures, and a continuing increase of cost for headquarters and operation. . . . Protocol and red tape created by the sprawling structure strangle the association's output, making it necessary to spend a disproportionate amount of time coping with organization problems at the expense of productive work.[83]

The makeup of the council was also criticized by the report, which pointed out the following major flaws: (1) The council was too large and unwieldly to act as fast as the membership desired; (2) the group's composition violated the basic democratic principle of "one man, one vote." ACONDA recommended that the size of council be reduced to one hundred and that its members be elected on a district basis. That change would, of course, result in the removal of past-presidents as automatic members of council—a recommendation that seemed to have widespread approval within the membership.

ANACONDA's role was to study those parts of the ACONDA report not acted upon or discussed at the 1970 Detroit conference. Its first observation was that everyone had expected too much from a part-time membership committee such as ACONDA; what was needed in order to provide a complete review of ALA, and to suggest alternatives, was a thorough study by management experts. However, ANACONDA did review the ACONDA recommendations and came up with rather similar suggestions: the establishment of an Office of Library Manpower; increased support of the Washington office; and the democratization and reorganization of the association. But in addition to chapter representation, ANACONDA wanted council to include various categories of nonvoting members: presidents of chapters, divisions, and affiliates of ALA, and chairmen of ALA committees.[84]

The successes of ACONDA and ANACONDA were not conspicuous, however sincere and hardworking these committees were. In retrospect, the accomplishments seem very short-lived in relation to the problems they were meant to deal with. Offices concerned with the disadvantaged and with research were established, but funding for these and other priorities pinpointed by ACONDA proved to be difficult to obtain and sustain. The important principle of "one man, one vote" for council representation was not quite attained, but there was progress in the democratic direction. Furthermore, the council's reduction in size improved its ability to respond faster, and the removal of past-presidents gave it a more representative tone. But these were rather minor changes in view of the demands, the promises, and the amount of time devoted to ACONDA and ANACONDA.

INTELLECTUAL FREEDOM

Although organization and reorganization had been of major concern during this period, there had also been continuing interest in intellectual freedom and a strengthening of ALA's role in fighting for individual freedom. This was emphasized in its 1967 Goals for Action, a statement of major goals and priorities. Regarding intellectual freedom, it called for

> continued efforts to secure and retain the commitment of all concerned with libraries to the Library Bill of Rights and the Freedom to Read statement and to inform all people of the positions enunciated in these documents.[85]

In the same statement of goals, there was also an implementing statement:

> Support for state and federal library legislation until every individual has equal access to good library service.

The statement would appear to suggest that the road to freedom of access lay only through legislation, which would be supported by the association.

The Library Bill of Rights was at this time under revision. Work began in 1965 when a question was raised about a phrase in paragraph two of the statement: "of sound factual authority." This seemed to open the door to library collections becoming deliberately or accidentally biased through the exclusion of unpopular or unconventional points of view. At least one example of this came to the attention of the Intellectual Freedom Committee, and the potential for further trouble in this area was readily recognized.[86] A subcommittee, under the direction of Martha Boaz, worked on the 1948 document; the offending statement was removed, and other parts were updated. The result was a shorter document, with the "rhetorical flourishes" of the older statement removed, but nevertheless unequivocal in its defense of the doctrine of free access to all.[87] It was approved by the council at San Francisco in 1967.

While the council was approving a new statement on intellectual freedom, members were listening to and applauding a speaker who seemed to be the very antithesis of what ALA stood for. And librarians picketed and protested the speech of another speaker, former ambassador to South Vietnam Maxwell D. Taylor—an action that seemed to indicate that they weren't truly committed to intellectual freedom. The first speaker was Maxwell Rafferty, California's superintendent of public instruction. Rafferty criticized the California Library Association's statement that "there is no evidence that anybody committed a crime as a result of having read a book," saying it was the "most asinine, irresponsible statement that I've ever heard."[88]

> Every law enforcement officer in the land knows the high probability of finding whole stacks of pornographic books among the personal effects of minors picked up for sex crimes, and the grislier the crime the higher the probability.

As for censorship, the speaker said that librarians practiced it every day. "Oh, we may call it 'screening' or . . . some such fiddle-faddle, but it's censorship nevertheless." Hurting probably as much as his words was the standing ovation given Rafferty by his audience, the American Library Trustee Association.

Taylor was well received by his audience, in spite of threats of boycott, walkouts, and disturbances. The walkouts and disturbances did not materialize, but boycotting librarians turned their backs and their conference badges on the meeting in protest of his selection as a speaker without inviting a speaker representing the antiwar point of view. Like Rafferty, Taylor received a standing ovation at the conclusion of his speech. These receptions were good indications of the diversity and complexity of ALA as an organization.

Two other events at the San Francisco conference helped to shape future ALA action in areas of intellectual freedom. Daniel Gore, formerly of McMurry College, told of his skirmish with censors in Abilene, Texas. Pressures were brought to bear over a publication considered obscene by some members of the community, and when the college administration gave in to the pressure, Gore resigned. Among his suggestions for ALA action in such future cases were (1) to establish a clearinghouse to receive information on censorship attempts in order to ascertain the extent of the problem; (2) to establish some form of sanction to be placed on institutions that permit censorship.[89]

Gore's suggestions were taken up immediately by the Intellectual Freedom Committee. Its chairman, Ervin Gaines, called the council's attention to the distance between promise and performance of ALA:

> We have urged our members to be brave and we have given them words as weapons because we believe in words. But words are often insufficient when a librarian faces the implacable hostility of an administration or governing board. . . . The association has, in effect, cut its members adrift and let them survive as best they could in rough weather.[90]

Gaines said it was time to act quickly to "support our rhetoric with tangible aid." He asked council to authorize his committee to investigate the possibility of establishing a support fund for librarians and the feasibility of a program of action to discourage violations of the Library Bill of Rights. The "program of action" suggested by the IFC did not pose the same threat as "sanctions" (suggested by Daniel Gore), but it was all that seemed possible at this time. Council approved IFC's request, with the advice to include a study of the possible effect this move might have on ALA's tax-exempt status.[91]

A "program of action" was approved by council at Kansas City in 1968, with responsibility centered in the IFC. According to this plan, when IFC found firm evidence of violation of the Library Bill of Rights, it could (1) publish the facts of the case, (2) recommend suspension or exclusion from ALA membership of the individuals and institutions involved, (3) aid in finding jobs for victims, and (4) list in an official publication those institutions or individuals judged to be in violation of the Library Bill of Rights.[92] The support fund asked for by Gore and then by the IFC took longer to achieve. When set up, it became the Freedom to Read Foundation, described as a device to prevent the entire program of ALA from being placed in jeopardy of taxation if the Internal Revenue Service ruled against the association's involvement in intellectual freedom.[93] Since the foundation itself was tax exempt, an additional agency had to be established to accomplish what the IFC was calling for in the nature of a defense fund. This was the LeRoy Merritt Humanitarian Fund, which was designed to provide "instant response" by the association.[94] Since it was not tax exempt, however, its contributions remained small, and therefore its operations were hampered.

One immediate result of the Intellectual Freedom Committee's attempt to expand its scope and activities was a jurisdictional dispute with other groups within ALA. The Office of Intellectual Freedom was the arm of the IFC, but other organizations with some responsibilities in this area were the Library Administration Division (LAD) and the Association of College and Research Libraries (ACRL). The potential for trouble between ALA units, and certainly the potential for delay, seemed to be very great.[95]

In spite of this unresolved situation, ALA did become involved directly in an investigation. On December 7, 1969, the Office of Intellectual Freedom received a "Request for Action" from Joan Bodger, a former children's consultant for the Missouri State Library. She charged that the Missouri State Library, the University of Missouri, and the Missouri State Library Commission had violated the Library Bill of Rights. An initial inquiry indicated the need to investigate further; the Committee on Intellectual Freedom sent a team to Missouri which came to the conclusion that Mrs. Bodger's rights had indeed been violated. The form of censure decided on by the committee was publication of the findings; sanctions were not voted because the policy on sanctions accepted at the Detroit conference did not include a procedure for removing sanctions.[96] It was assumed that the victim in the case would be gratified to be publicly defended in the state and in the library press. It was furthermore believed that such publicity might cause other possible offenders to have greater regard for the rights of librarians.

While librarians were often still critical of ALA's hesitancy to move quickly and decisively in intellectual freedom cases, it was becoming clear that a more active role was being taken by the Committee on Intellectual Freedom and the Office for Intellectual Freedom. Further, the leadership seemed far more willing to actively protest violation. This was clearly shown in 1970 and 1971, when quick action and publicity helped to stop problems. The former problem was the attempts by Treasury Department agents to check public library circulation records of books containing information on explosives. The checks occurred in several areas of the country simultaneously, with the Milwaukee and Atlanta areas being the principal targets.

David Clift appeared on several national news programs with strong statements opposing the activities. Although the executive board later supported Clift, some of the public reaction was very negative and personal. Clift indicated that the experience taught him a lesson: "The executive board's public statements should come from its members. I got caught and there was no retreat."[97] A preliminary statement was later made by the executive board, and this was followed up by a Policy on the Confidentiality of Library Records, approved by the council at the 1971 midwinter meeting.

The second problem was the surfacing again of loyalty oaths, or "negative oaths" required in some states before a person could become a candidate for a position. The resolution presented by the Intellectual Freedom Committee and passed by the council said in part:

> We condemn loyalty oaths as a condition of employment and investigations which permit the discharge of an individual without a fair hearing. . . . We also condemn negative loyalty oaths as a condition of election or appointment of library trustees.[98]

While there was no implementing machinery to enforce this resolution, the decisive and direct statement could leave no question about the association's stand. It was indicative of the stronger positions being taken on intellectual freedom by ALA—possibly not as active or as effective as the IF officials tried to picture, but nevertheless, a vast improvement over what the situation had been.

PUBLISHING ACTIVITIES

During the final years of Clift's tenure, there was progress in other areas—and failure, too. Publishing continued to take on an increasingly significant role to the membership and to the library world. This change was nowhere more apparent than in the association's official publication, the *ALA Bulletin* (changed in 1970 to *American Libraries*). During most of the magazine's history, its role was not only secondary, but it was never even clearly determined. However, the *Bulletin* had certainly functioned as the voice of the ALA establishment. This changed rather drastically under the editorship of Gerald R. Shields, who transformed the publication into a relevant, interesting, and intelligent journal. Its biting comments, strong editorials, and offbeat journalistic style were not always well received by either the membership or the ALA leadership, but *American Libraries* certainly had a vitality that had almost always been lacking in the old *Bulletin*. Some speculated how long the irreverent spirit would last:

> One wonders just how long ALA is going to let its editor give 'em hell, but in the meantime, he's doing much to revitalize the profession. One suspects he's gone so far that even the ALA executive board would hesitate to put on the brakes.[99]

It seems clear that Shield's policy of mixing reporting and spicy editorial comments did, indeed, cause some displeasure within the ALA leadership. The response, however, was to adopt a new policy statement for *American Libraries*. The executive board assumed, perhaps, that its editor would read the statement and take the hint. The statement noted that the editor has a "particular responsibility" to publish full and accurate information about the association:

> He must assume an obligation to represent the best interests of the association and all of its units fairly and as fully as possible. The ALA Publishing Board encourages publication in the news columns of *American Libraries* of news . . . and it also encourages signed interpretive comment in its editorial columns . . . analysis and interpretation should appear over the signature of the Editor.[100]

The board obviously did not enjoy the irreverent comments mixed in with the business, and the reporting of the 1972 annual conference reflected this policy.

Another indication of ALA's growing interest in publishing was a major agreement made in early 1967 to publish the pre-1955 imprints of the National Union Catalog in book form. The British firm of Mansell Information/Publishing Ltd. was selected to undertake this major work. When completed, the 16 million cards in the files at the Library of Congress would compose 610 volumes—the largest single publication undertaken since the invention of printing. Although the project was sponsored by the association, the editorial costs were to be borne by the publisher and the work carried out by the Library of Congress.[101]

While foundation support of ALA's activities was clearly on the wane, there were occasional successes. For example, the Knapp Foundation in 1968 added $1,163,718 to support its school libraries project. But this was a notable exception to the clear decline of foundation aid. Legislative victories were there, although they were obviously financially hurt by the nation's commitment to the Vietnam War and an administration's selection of priorities. In 1971, for example, the strongest support of National Library

Week came from the White House. President Richard Nixon praised the nation's libraries for their leadership in many areas and for providing "a useful groundwork for constructive civic action to improve the quality of life."[102] Yet at almost the same time, his administration was drastically cutting support of the Library Services and Construction Act in its funding of city outreach services, state level library services, and books for college libraries.[103]

ARBITRATION AND INVESTIGATION

In three areas of arbitration and investigation, it appeared that ALA was somewhat successful. The first was an investigation of Joslyn Williams's charges that the Library of Congress was guilty of race discrimination. The investigation was ordered by the Joint Committee on the Library and carried out by the Staff Committee on Mediation, Arbitration and Inquiry (SCMAI). In spite of lack of cooperation by the library, SCMAI found "a pattern of action for which it could conceive no other motivation than racial discrimination."[104] The report found racial bias in salaries, due process, work evaluation and assignments, and promotion. SCMAI included a list of recommended steps to alleviate the situation: adopt a vigorous affirmative action program, implement a human relations program, and seek additional funds from Congress to improve employment opportunities. Joslyn Williams, who had initiated the study by his allegations, appeared before council when the SCMAI report was accepted and said:

> This is by no means a report that had I been given the opportunity of writing, I would have written, but that's understandable. My allegations were far stronger than the report itself. However, this is a report which is far greater in all honesty than I expected when I first came to the American Library Association. Truly, the American Library Association at this juncture . . . can be proud of itself.[105]

Two days later, Keith Doms, ALA president, received a telegram from L. Quincy Mumford that disputed the SCMAI report. It was, Mumford said, lacking in specifics, it contained distortions, and it failed to recognize the library's accomplishments in race relations. Those who had complained before SCMAI should, he said, now come forward and make those charges public.[106] Charges and countercharges continued in an unresolved situation for several years.

The second case involved Zoia Horn, a librarian charged with contempt of court for refusing to testify in the Harrisburg Seven antiwar conspiracy trial. The issue had originally surfaced at the 1971 conference at Dallas, when SRRT requested that ALA give wide publicity to its support of Mrs. Horn and make full financial resources available to her. No direct ALA support had been given, but the SRRT Action Council had granted her $500 and the LeRoy C. Merritt Humanitarian Fund had made a similar contribution "to help defray hardship occasioned by her opposition to threats to intellectual freedom."[107] On March 17, 1972, the executive board in effect turned down the request and indicated that it felt Mrs. Horn had no legal ground for her action:

> The executive board recognizes that Mrs. Horn is acting as a private citizen on a point of conscience . . . the board, having reviewed the facts available to it, does not find a valid basis of support of her action in challenging a duly constituted court of law. . . .[108]

Several months later, however, as more evidence came to light, the council reversed this stand, with the executive board concurring in the change. A new statement was issued that recognized that Mrs. Horn's actions were "a protest against infringement of academic and intellectual freedom." It pointed out that the Library Bill of Rights encourages librarians to cooperate with those who are resisting censorship and restrictions on access to information. Those principles were the basis of Mrs. Horn's actions, in the opinion of the council, and therefore the association commended her "commitment and courage in defense of the principles of intellectual freedom."[109]

The third area of investigation was even more delicate than that of the Library of Congress. It involved Peter Doiron's dismissal from his position as editor of *Choice*, the book selection journal of ACRL. David Clift took the extraordinary procedure of flying to Hartford, Connecticut (*Choice* offices are in Middletown, twenty miles away), and sending ALA's personnel manager, Lucene Hardin, to inform Doiron that he was to meet with Clift at 1:00 P.M. that day, July 29, 1971, at the Hotel Sonesta in Hartford. When Doiron and Miss Hardin arrived at the hotel, they found Clift and J. Donald Thomas, executive secretary of ACRL, in the lobby. The four went to Miss Hardin's room, where Clift told Doiron that he had the alternative of being fired or resigning. He handed Doiron a letter stating that his employment was terminated as of that date and giving the reasons for the dismissal. Doiron was not allowed to return to his office during working hours, and when he went there the following afternoon to remove his personal property, he found that the lock was being changed.[110]

No one at ACRL other than the executive secretary knew of the decisions before receiving a copy of Doiron's termination letter. This included the *Choice* editorial board, the officers of ACRL, and the ACRL Publications Committee. As a result, there was a storm of protest against what appeared to be an arbitrary and precipitous action on the part of Clift. The criticism hurt the executive director, and, in the many letters he wrote in response, he tried to explain that Doiron had been warned during the 1970 midwinter meeting that his performance was unsatisfatcory. Clift also summarized the reasons for the termination:

> his failure in communication; his complete disregard of personnel procedures; and his slowness in proceeding with the expansion of *Choice*.
> I think you know me well enough to know that this action was not precipituous [sic]. The record of Peter's poor performance in his position is thoroughly documented. If we have not spread the facts on the record, it was only in order to avoid embarrassing Peter's career.[111]

Doiron conducted a successful effort to have his case reviewed by established procedures within the association; in the process, the "dirty linen" was not only washed but also hung out in public view for almost one year. One must conclude from reading the available record that Clift probably acted correctly in releasing Doiron after an earlier warning, but that the executive director erred in his method of doing so. He not only damaged his own reputation in the process, but also put the executive board in the extremely awkward position of having to defend his action. At the 1972 conference in Chicago, Keith Doms announced the final disposition of the case: Both sides agreed that (1) due process had been denied in firing Doiron; (2) the editorial competence of Doiron was not at issue; (3) the termination, which the board found justified, was based on administrative factors.[112]

THE PROBLEMS OF GROWTH

During this period, the association once again grappled with the persistent problem of where it should be located, although most members probably thought the matter had been settled rather permanently when the organization had moved into its new home in 1963. Located at the same address as the old headquarters, but providing an attractive and efficient setting, the new building seemed to be everything the growing organization would need for a considerable period. The spaciousness and modernity of headquarters provided a symbol for a forward-looking association and was perhaps a solid indication that, in spite of all its problems, ALA was going to remain as a single organization.

The first public sign of problems came during the Detroit conference in 1965. President Edwin Castagna, in reviewing the association's condition, said:

> Speaking of growing pains brings to mind ALA headquarters. What happened in our original planning that our building just a few years old is already crowded? . . . the increase of staff, the addition of new projects . . . the necessity for more storage space for publications, and the certainty for further expansion make it essential that we now prepare ourselves for proposals both to lease additional space on a temporary basis in the neighborhood of our building, and then to acquire property upon which a larger addition to the building will be constructed.[113]

The basic problem, of course, was growth. When planning had started on the building about 1960, ALA had a membership of 21,000; it had twelve divisions served by nine executive secretaries, and a total staff of slightly more than 100 people. When the building was first occupied in 1963, membership was at 26,000, there were ten executive secretaries, and a total staff of 143. When Castagna pointed out the need for additional headquarters space in 1966, there were 32,000 members, fourteen divisions, and a staff of 166. In addition, lack of adequate planning was surely evident: the mailroom was too small for mass mailing, there was no provision for data processing and storage. A tentative step in planning was taken by incoming president Robert Vosper in 1966 when he appointed a subcommittee of the executive board to determine space needs and to develop plans for meeting the problem. Although the subcommittee was able to make suggestions for improvements, this was clearly a "Band-Aid" approach.[114]

During the 1966 conference in New York, the council, the executive board, and the Space Needs Committee held a joint breakfast meeting at which they discussed possible alternatives. Without arriving at any consensus, they talked over the relative merits of moving to the suburbs or to Washington as well as the advisability of constructing a building, which might offer headquarters space to other library associations. The executive board, after deciding to develop a plan for expansion, committed itself to full membership decision:

> . . . the Executive Board recognized the importance of membership participation in the important decisions which must be made, step by step, as planning proceeds. Above all, Board, committee, and staff are anxious that this be a shared experience. Membership

thinking is solicited as planning progresses. No one directly engaged in this project has anything to gain by producing a report
that is a surprise.[115]

Less than a month later, at the New Orleans midwinter meeting in 1967,
president Mary Gaver announced that ALA had purchased a parcel of
land adjacent to the headquarters building from the Roman Catholic Arch-
diocese of Chicago. President Gaver judged the purchase "a sound investment and not as pre-determining in any way the future decision of membership as to the location" of the association's headquarters.[116]

In spite of the promise of full membership involvement in the step-by-step
planning, the next public mention of the matter was the report of the Subcommittee on Space Needs at San Francisco in June: "ALA's programs will
best be served through a Washington location."[117] It suggested, though,
that membership first be polled through a mail vote. That same day, the
council voted to move headquarters from Chicago to Washington. In doing
so, it became entangled in a parliamentary question that made the council
appear dictatorial and hasty in its judgment. A sizable element in the council wanted that body to advise the membership that the council's best judgment was that the move to Washington should be approved. The parliamentarian said the council could not do this; she ruled that since the
council was the policy-making body of the association, its advice to the
membership would be binding. That decision may well have destroyed any
chance for the move to be accepted by the membership. Within hours of
the council decision, a petition was being circulated to place the issue on a
mail ballot for membership.

To support the decision to move, a number of important factors were
advanced: (1) there was greater ALA involvement in Washington than in
1957, the year the previous move had been rejected; (2) the offices ALA
then had in three cities could be consolidated; (3) midwinter meetings no
longer required one central location; (4) jet aircraft had reduced travel time,
eliminating the need for a centrally located headquarters.[118] The arguments
against moving were the same as in 1957, and this time there was the added
belief that the council had acted undemocratically and without any membership input to the decision. The membership vote was also similar to the
1957 ballot: a majority of three thousand voted to set aside the council's
decision. The West, the Midwest, and the South voted solidly to stay in
Chicago; only the Eastern seaboard plus Alaska, Hawaii, and Canada supported the council.[119] So the question of moving out of Chicago was settled,
at least temporarily. However, judging from ALA's previous history, the
question seems certain to surface once again.

With the decision made to stay in Chicago, the leadership was forced to look into the alternatives available there. A new building or an addition was obviously necessary, but it was unclear at this point in which direction ALA should proceed. In 1968 the planning firm of J.F.N. Associates was engaged to study and report on present and future space needs of head-quarters in Chicago. The firm's first recommendation was to forget about any plans for an addition to the present structure; it would be too expensive and too ineffective a solution for future planning. The firm recommended building on land already owned by ALA; the structure should be large enough to take the association through the 1980s and have rental space to help defray its cost. On the advice of ALA's bankers, two firms were asked to develop independent economic analyses of a proposed new office building. Both firms concurred that such a building on the Huron Street property would be a profitable investment.[120] Within the next few years, the association engaged in several agreements with companies (Real Estate Research Corporation and Collaborative Development Ltd.) in an attempt to develop a multistory office building on the property. The result, after many months of planning and the expenditure of thousands of dollars, was the threat of a lawsuit and termination of the agreements.[121] At the close of Clift's tenure, the building issue was still unresolved.

RETIREMENT OF CLIFT

Unlike previous occasions when a new executive director (secretary) was selected, ALA had a great deal of time to look for a successor to David Clift. After twenty-two years, Clift retired on August 15, 1972, but his re-tirement was well known in advance. Therefore a Search Committee was announced by Roger H. McDonough, representing the executive board, at the Detroit conference in 1970. It was a five-member committee appointed by the executive board, composed of ALA members who were not members of the board and who were broadly representative of the membership.

The committee began its work by asking for nominations from the pro-fession, in order to ensure membership participation in the decision. That process resulted in the nomination of 130 people for the position. The Search Committee explored the possibility of including nonlibrarians as candidates but finally concluded that "recourse to a non-librarian should be had only when all reasonable options fail" to produce a candidate from within the profession. The committee also initially set lower and upper age limits of thirty and fifty-five, but when serious challenges were raised about this requirement, it was dropped.[122]

Over half the people nominated for the position declined when approached by the Search Committee. The situation seemed so serious that, by the end of 1971, President Keith Doms suggested consideration of the possibility of appointing an interim executive director. He said that the basic problem was that the search process had so far been unsuccessful in identifying any qualified person who wanted the job.[123] Fortunately the situation improved with the assumption of the search by a special subcommittee of the executive board. In March, 1972, a list of six men who met the qualifications of the board was presented to the board for a final decision. The six were Don S. Culbertson, Stefan Moses, Robert Sheridan, Gerald Shields, William Summers, and Robert Wedgeworth.[124] The subcommittee recommended that the choice be between Culbertson and Wedgeworth. On March 17, 1972, Wedgeworth was offered the position by the board, and he accepted.

Wedgeworth was the editor of *Library Resources and Technical Services,* the official journal of the Resources and Technical Services Division of ALA. He had held positions in both public and academic libraries; at the time of his appointment, he was a doctoral candidate and assistant professor at Rutgers—The State University of New Jersey. He was young, articulate, and capable. It was a choice that seemed particularly appropriate in providing leadership for the difficult times ahead. The selection of Wedgeworth also seemed to be a rather deliberate attempt to pick a leader very different from what Clift had been. Clift had accomplished a great deal during his tenure, and the association had grown tremendously. He had been, as Grace Stevenson said, "the right man for the times during which he served."[125] Nevertheless, there were also problems, such as his handling of Peter Doiron's dismissal from *Choice.* As had been the case towards the end of Carl Milam's tenure, there was a growing sense of disenchantment, or restlessness, with Clift. His quiet manner, poised control, and sense of humor were of course appreciated by many, but nevertheless, there were rumblings about ineffective leadership and lack of direction from the executive director. Strong assistants, such as Grace Stevenson and Ruth Warncke, it was suggested, were really providing what leadership was available. Whatever truth there may have been to these charges, it was clear that Wedgeworth would offer an entirely different approach to the management of the association. His more forceful manner, his style of presentation, and perhaps even the fact that he is black suggested that the interaction between the association and its director would be entirely different from what it had been.

This had undoubtedly been one of the most difficult periods of ALA history—an era when sheer survival seemed at times to be seriously in doubt. Society was in a tailspin, the library world desperately trying to be relevant, and the association caught in between. Responding too slowly for the growing activist segment of the membership and too rapidly for those more comfortable with the old organization, ALA found it hard to please anyone. Still uncomfortable from the last reorganization, the leadership realized that even expert help had not been enough to avoid problems. More changes would surely be needed to meet the demands. In this, of course, the problems of the association were very much a reflection of the problems facing the American society in the 1970s. Criticism of policies, demands for change, and rebellion against authority were all characteristics of the period, and each was well represented in the association. It was a difficult and challenging time for a young man to assume leadership in a divided profession.

SUMMARY AND CONCLUSIONS

With the end of David Clift's tenure, and the conclusion of the period covered by this study, it is appropriate to summarize the major events and to offer some conclusions based on this research. As the history of ALA is reviewed, one notes that, through the years, the problems of the organization and the profession have tended to remain constant. Many of the issues raised at the first meetings of the association also confronted librarians in 1972. Examples of these problems are cooperative cataloging, distribution of public documents, library education, and inadequate public support of libraries. That is not to say that little has been accomplished during the organization's almost one hundred years of existence. Many problems, both old and new, have been resolved. But the major issues often need greater resources than have ever been available to librarians.

In addition, new problems have been raised, and ALA has had to change in order to meet these challenges. In the process, the association has expanded its role far beyond anything foreseen by its founders. In attempting to meet the library needs of the American people, the association developed during this period into a multifaceted organization that is the most comprehensive national library association in existence.

Partly by design and partly because of its own inadequacies, ALA has spawned many other organizations of librarians. Especially during the early years, the membership looked on each new library group with considerable pride. John M. Cory, when he was executive secretary, spoke of his membership in fifteen different library associations and offered the opinion that "a reasonable diversity and multiplicity of library associations is logical, healthy, and inevitable."[126] Long before 1972, however, a common complaint among librarians concerned the fragmentation of the profession and the association into too many organizations. In a field as diverse as librarianship, some fragmentation should be expected, and is healthy, as Cory said, but perhaps not to the extent that it had been allowed to develop. Some of the splintering possibly could have been prevented or alleviated at various points in ALA's history, but it was not. There was no overall planning in the establishment of organizations, nor was there any serious attempt to prevent duplication until relatively recently. The development of the Special Libraries Association is perhaps the outstanding example. It originated because of the failure of ALA to respond adequately, in the view of SLA's founders, to the needs of special librarians. It grew in spite of some open hostility and several attempts by ALA to engulf the structure and the membership. John Lapp, an early editor of *Special Libraries*, wrote much later that "our chief battle in the early days was to keep our association from being absorbed in the American Library Association."[127] ALA's relations with most of the associations, however, were excellent and without tension. As the largest group of its kind, ALA has during its history sought, achieved, and deserved recognition as the leading library organization. In terms of membership, activities, and programs, it has been unrivaled as the association that could speak for librarians.

Largely as a result of its size and activities, the association itself is a bureaucratic delight: over sixty committees and subcommittees, thirteen major divisions; these in turn are divided into hundreds of committees, groups, sections, and other segments of the association. The council, as the policy-making body, has been so large (212 members before the change in 1972) that it often could not move quickly and effectively. Size alone required the council to turn over to the executive board the power to act in many situations. As David Clift pointed out after retiring:

> It is evident that a large segment of power has been concentrated in one group—the Executive Board. I see no way out. You can't have the Council do it because they meet two times a year; furthermore, there is no way to get them to read what they have to read in order to act.[128]

What a devastating comment to make of librarians; yet the minutes of the council often demonstrate the truth of this criticism. Since this comment was made when the council was still very large, it may be that the tremendous amount of material necessary for each meeting was not supplied far enough in advance.

A frequent criticism of the association throughout its history has been the lack of involvement of the membership. Cory thought that the fact that only about 3 percent of ALA members could participate at any one time helped encourage other organizations to grow.[129] However, some critics have charged that a hierarchy of older librarians developed rather early, and the structure has been perpetuated ever since, thus limiting meaningful participation by most members. The long-established policy of automatically putting past-presidents on the council continued this problem almost to the end of the period covered. Until recently, even committee memberships centered in relatively few people, who served in the same capacities year after year. The vast majority of members have apparently felt relatively uninvolved in the affairs of the organization. Much of this is of their own choosing, if one may judge from typical results of association elections. In 1972, for example, only 29 percent of the membership voted in the presidential balloting, and a much smaller percentage voted in the other races. As Grace Stevenson has pointed out:

> Ultimately the onus of responsibility for what the ALA is and does is on the individual member. In the past . . . there have been heated strident voices attacking ALA as if it were some remote and indifferent monster. The association is what its members make it— no more, no less.[130]

In spite of many membership complaints about ALA's lack of democracy, it appears that Clift was partially right when he indicated that part of ALA's problem, at least in mobilizing to meet a problem, was that it was too democratic. "It's much easier to get things done when you aren't democratic."[131] While this is undoubtedly correct, the membership has often felt far removed from the decision-making process. Only in a relatively few cases can it be said that the membership has directly exercised authority. Usually this has been a reaction to a decision made by another body. Needless to say, in modern times the size of the membership has necessitated a delegation of authority, but this fact has not removed the complaint.

A factor that may have contributed to the feeling of uninvolvement has been the evolution of a powerful executive secretary (director). When ALA decided to limit the president to one year in office, it effectively assured the removal from that office of most functions and authority. This change was combined with the selection of very strong-willed executive secretaries who enjoyed long terms. Perhaps the only exception to this was John MacKenzie Cory, who apparently believed in limiting the powers of the secretary by limiting his term of office. Cory, however, was completely unsuccessful in changing the established policies. Thus, the single most powerful individual in the association has been the secretary, and he has not been chosen directly by the membership. Clift admitted this when he said:

There is too much power in the Executive Director, or at least too much power went through his hands. I expect that it might be a good idea to restrict the term of office, but you have to pay a price. You spend the first third (of the term) deciding what to do after.[132]

However, the executive secretary has added an important element to ALA administration. By the very fact that the secretaries have remained in office for long periods of time, the leadership has gained continuity. And only through such continuity could the association have developed any long-range policies and goals. The presidents set the annual goals, but it was the executive director who established the overall thrust of the organization.

As a socially oriented organization, ALA has been hampered by basic questions of what a professional organization should be doing. How active should it be as a welfare organization, as a guardian of human rights, and as a sentinel for intellectual freedom? The membership has never been able to arrive at satisfactory answers. ALA's expanded role during the two world wars helped to establish a precedent for its role as a welfare organization; yet there was immediate retrenchment following the close of each emergency. The disastrous failure of the Enlarged Program discouraged further peacetime activities in this area. The role of ALA in human rights was almost negligible during most of the period.

Like other professional organizations, ALA adopted the role of a socially activist organization late, hesitantly, and with a great deal of foot dragging. The social revolution of the late 1960s, reflected in the rise of special socially oriented groups within ALA, was clearly viewed with hostility by a large segment of the membership and leadership. Rather than an unconcern for the rights of members, however, this lack of support seemed to indicate a feeling that the problems were outside the sphere of a professional association and that society alone could solve them. In that respect, ALA may well have had distinguished company, for other major professional organizations were also undergoing stirrings of conscience, perhaps coupled with the same conviction that the issues were beyond the scope of a single organization.

In the area of intellectual freedom ALA had little criticism from membership until very late in the period. Its Library Bill of Rights provided librarians with a strong statement that could be used to fight censorship. The resolution against the use of loyalty oaths was strong at first, but many members felt it was then weakened through revision. When the problem surfaced once again, there could be no doubt where the association stood on the oath as a condition of employment. The statement on labeling was similarly an unqualified condemnation that left no room for interpretation.

The association was willing to take a stand on most matters concerning intellectual freedom because these issues seemed to be an integral part of the library profession. Librarians also found, through the *Newsletter on Intellectual Freedom*, that very often the intense glare of national publicity was enough to discourage many would-be violators of the freedom to read.

ALA was vulnerable to frequent criticism that it delighted in "paper policies" that did not have to be or could not be enforced. When moves developed to put teeth into the statements, they were sometimes met with delaying tactics or rejection. In this connection, a 1969 committee report on the organizational structure stated the case very bluntly:

> Thirty months after a fire begins we have permission and resources to put it out—a poor analogy, perhaps, but by that time, in all too many cases, the barn is either in ashes or the fire has gone out without assistance and much of the immense effort required to move this ponderous machine called ALA has been expended to no real purpose.[133]

It was through the combined efforts of such diverse groups as the Committee on Intellectual Freedom, the Office for Intellectual Freedom, and SRRT that significant accomplishments in this area were finally made. Leaders such as Robert Downs, LeRoy Merritt, David Berninghausen, and many others also helped to make ALA a significant adversary of oppressors of the freedom to read.

Through the development of various standards, the association has been very effective in raising the quality of library service throughout the country. Occasionally other organizations, such as the National Education Association, have contributed in this effort, but the standards have been mainly the work of librarians. These guidelines have had a pronounced effect in convincing authorities of the need for larger budgets, better buildings and equipment, and more qualified personnel. Peggy Sullivan noted the important role of standards for school libraries when she wrote:

> Among the most cited standards are those emanating from the ALA's American Association of School Librarians since World War II. The 1960 publication, *Standards for School Library Programs*, came at the ideal time for implementation when significant federal funds were first given to school library programs with the passage of the 1963 Elementary and Secondary Education Act.[134]

In establishing these goals, ALA has performed a real and valuable service to librarianship.

As a political organization, the association has also demonstrated some notable successes through its lobbying efforts. Major victories have included an active role in securing the passage of the following: the Printing Act of 1895, various postal measures, the Library Services Act, the National Defense Education Act, the Depository Act of 1962, the Academic Facilities Act, the Higher Education Act, the Elementary and Secondary Education Act, the Medical Library Assistance and Hospital Construction Act, and the measure establishing a National Commission on Libraries and Information Science. What this federal legislation has "meant to libraries is visible all over the land in new buildings, improved collections, larger staffs, bookmobiles, and a broader concept of library service," in the words of Grace Stevenson.[135] Yet a listing of major successes does not reveal the whole story. It is certain that constant lobbying and contact with members of Congress has produced additional results that are not so noticeable but are still very important. A greater awareness of librarians and libraries, as well as a respect for the abilities of librarians in marshaling facts, are among the possible effects of these lobbying efforts.

Foremost in the ALA's efforts has been the Washington office with its *Newsletter*. Among the outstanding directors have been Paul Howard, Julia Bennett, and Germaine Krettek. The office, and especially Miss Krettek, were often given credit by members of Congress for their favorable attitude toward libraries. Her persistence and diligence during fourteen years at the head of the Washington office paid off in achieving gains and helping to prevent unfriendly legislation. In many cases, ALA has worked with other organizations, in a loosely formed coalition, to "increase the strength —or clout, if you will—of each organization that joins the common effort."[136]

While the successes of the Washington office have often been spectacular, the association has shown one of its most persistent problems to be its relationships with the divisions. Divisions, like the separate library associations mentioned earlier, were often formed willingly and with the encouragement of ALA. Given the wide diversity of interests of librarians, the divisions would seem to be a necessary and integral part of the association. As the divisions grew in membership, there was a corresponding growth in desire for authority, autonomy, and a greater share in the financial resources. The association was unwilling to grant these concessions until confronted with the threat of secession. The possibility of the loss of ACRL in particular was real enough so that a number of changes were made. Ironically, though, according to the management firm that studied ALA in 1954, some of the changes were not beneficial as far as the total organization was concerned. The last reorganization made further changes, yet it was clear at the end of the period that no satisfactory permanent solution had been achieved. The eventual secession of ACRL, AASL, and the urban librarians remains a distinct possibility.

On the other hand, one of the greatest strengths of the association has been its publishing program. It was recognized early as an integral and important need of such a professional organization; it has improved in quality since the early criticism of John Cotton Dana. This is especially true of the periodicals that emanate from both headquarters and the member organizations. Leading the way has been *American Libraries,* which during most of its life as the *ALA Bulletin* was "a rather stodgy and un-inspired journal."[137] Librarians in general have been extremely critical of their own press; Eric Moon has said that the "deadliest disease afflicting the library press is proliferation."[138] So it should come as no surprise that some of ALA's periodicals should be criticized for their lack of content. As with membership involvement in ALA, much of the blame must be placed on librarians. However, there has been a distinct improvement, and the association can justly be proud of such other publications as *College and Research Libraries, RQ,* and *Booklist.*

The international role played by ALA has also been strong and signifi-cant. There was an almost missionary spirit in carrying the American meth-ods of librarianship to other nations, and many countries benefited from the association's work. Both Carl Milam and David Clift had very strong in-terests in the international programs and actively worked to extend the organization's projects. New libraries were founded, and existing libraries were improved with foundation support. Although seemingly one-sided in terms of benefits, the enterprises actually formed an international exchange. As Lester Asheim, former director of the ALA International Relations Office, has written, "American librarianship has as much to gain as to give by participation in the one world of librarianship."[139] However, the benefits to be gained from this exchange are not as easily grasped as those of some other activities of ALA:

> It is exceedingly difficult for members at the proverbial grassroots levels to recognize the values of international improvements, and they are often suspicious of the world-traveling leaders who en-courage them to see this as a responsibility.[140]

Therefore when foundation support disappeared, so did most of the international programs because of lack of funding. Although most of these programs did not draw on membership monies directly, they were not entirely without cost to the association. The foundation funding rarely cov-ered the complete overhead expenses, and the programs drew away ener-

gies that could have been expended on much-needed domestic library service. As with some social issues, there was the serious question of whether a
professional association should be involved in some of the activities. In
spite of problems and questions, however, the association was able to accomplish far more than if it had been completely limited to internal sources
of funding.

While library education has not been discussed here in any depth because
of the research already done, several comments in this area are appropriate.
Through the accreditation process, the level of library education has been
steadily improved. There has also been a change in the philosophy behind
the statement of standards for library schools. As evidenced in the latest
standards (effective January, 1973), the emphasis is on qualitative guidelines rather than the previous quantitative statements. The accreditation
program, however, has yet to exercise strong direction over the majority
of library education programs in the United States. When Churchwell wrote
of the "lack of control over the agencies which were capable of developing
library education programs," he was describing the situation as it was in
1939.[141] But it is essentially the same today. Of the 400 institutions offering
some training for librarians, only 55 had been accredited by ALA in 1972.

The association has been criticized for the fact that far more librarians
are being prepared for the profession than the field is capable of handling.
The mythical need of a hundred thousand librarians reported in the late
1960s has been completely discredited, but unfortunately the library education agencies of the country continue to produce graduates as if the figure
were still viable. In a period of restricted employment, this has made ALA's
lack of leadership in limiting output a common complaint. Yet it is uncer-
tain by what authority such a move might be taken. Furthermore, output of
graduates is clearly only part of a complex problem.

Finally, during its recent history, ALA has spent an inordinate amount
of time on its own organizational structure. It has reorganized itself five
times during the previous four decades. The last reorganization officially
took place in 1957, but its implementation continued almost unabated for
the following fifteen years. There is no question about the sincerity of the
soul searching that has gone into the attempts at coming up with the solution. Part of the problem, of course, is in trying to determine what are the
ultimate goals of the organization. This was pointed out in 1967 when the
Committee on Organization (COO) reminded ALA:

> Reorganization is not the answer as long as the Association's basic
> objective does not change and so long as the membership demands
> continue in their present direction. A new skin surrounding the

same old pieces re-disguised by new names or titles will soon be as misshapen and confining as the one we have now and nothing new will have been served.[142]

It is clear now that neither ACONDA nor the previous reorganization provided the basic changes that were necessary. In part that is because of the remarkable tendency of ALA to commission a study with broad goals and then to pick and choose from the recommendations. That is a piece-meal, Band-Aid approach that has not worked in the past and is not likely to be any more successful in the future.

Among the many suggestions for change has been the persistent call for a federation or "umbrella" type of organization. The federation had been one of the alternate suggestions of ACONDA, but by the time its revised report came out, ACONDA already had some second thoughts. It became aware that, although some organizations like ACRL and AASL might very well thrive as separate organizations, other smaller divisions such as the Association of State Librarians or the Association of Hospital and Institution Libraries might flounder.[143] In spite of obvious flaws, the federation plan has been popular with many members, and there has been a persistent effort to move in that direction. In its ultimate form, it would be an umbrella type organization, with ALA working with other library associations as equals. It may be the hardest structure to achieve, for ALA would have to give up a number of prerogatives.[144] In some respects, the umbrella organization is similar to what the Council of National Library Associations tried to achieve and never could.

Given an organization's natural tendency to resist change, it may well take a major secession to force a substantive structural realignment. If that happens, it may be too late to effect a federation; instead there may be a combination arrangement comprising the structure of 1972 along with several large independent organizations tied very loosely to ALA. Although such an arrangement would lack the "grand design" of a federation, it would be a pragmatic solution and would seem to have a broader appeal than a true federation. Unfortunately, ALA has spent a tremendous amount of time, effort, and money on studying itself. "There cannot," wrote Grace Stevenson in 1972, "be many more organizations more given to self-examination."[145] These expenditures in the future must be weighed against what else might be accomplished within the goals and objectives of ALA. In spite of their costs, we may assume that there will be further studies and reorganizations:

These upheavals appear to be cyclical and they keep ALA viable, though one could wish they might take place with a little less rancor and more understanding of the association's history and why we are what and where we are.[146]

In the area of working conditions, the attitude of ALA has slowly changed, just as have the attitudes of many librarians. Concern for adequate salaries has long been important in the association, as can be seen by the appointment of a Salaries Committee as early as 1922. Its mission was "to supply ammunition to the librarian in his fight for . . . better salaries."[147] Until 1943 the committee continued to publish its annual statistics in the hope of improving working conditions. Statistics were not enough, however, and the gains made through unionization by some professionals caused librarians to have second thoughts about unions. Mary Gaver, in her 1967 speech as outgoing president, spoke to this point:

> Closely related to the ramifications of manpower is a concern we had all year that ALA has not concerned itself aggressively enough in matters of employee welfare, a matter which professional associations generally ignore or treat with lofty disdain, as you must be aware. . . . it would appear that most of the effective work in this area has been done by unions, not by professional associations.[148]

Library unions enjoyed a steady growth during the last five years of this study, and they grew because ALA left them room to grow. Like other professional organizations, ALA has yet to resolve the problem of a satisfactory stand on collective bargaining. A solution would seem to be imperative if the association is to prevent a serious erosion of membership. Gail Schlachter has written in this regard that

> as collective organization and militant behavior become more of a norm in American society, collective organization and militancy will likely become more acceptable and common among professional workers, including librarians.[149]

The options would seem to be either to continue basically disregarding this trend and lose members, or to forget the traditional distaste for collective bargaining so as to win back members lost.

In retrospect, the American Library Association has been a remarkable institution during its almost one hundred years: often resistant to change, sometimes utterly unpredictable, frequently right in the vanguard of American thought, and always determined in its principles. It has been, on occasion, an organization that has seen nothing wrong with being outspokenly liberal one moment and terribly conservative the next. It, like other professional organizations, will never be completely satisfactory because it must be all things to all members. The membership is so diverse that ALA cannot possibly answer the call of every member. ALA will surely always be behind the demands of its outspoken dissenters, and just as surely, far in advance of its conservative constituency. In spite of its flaws, it will continue, as the field's major organization, to make outstanding contributions to librarianship and to American life.

APPENDIX A

CONFERENCES
OF THE
AMERICAN LIBRARY ASSOCIATION

DATE	PLACE	DATE	PLACE
1876	Philadelphia	1898	Lakewood-on-Chautauqua, N.Y.
1877	New York	1899	Atlanta
1877	London (International)	1900	Montreal
1878	No meeting	1901	Waukesha, Wis.
1879	Boston	1902	Boston and Magnolia, Mass.
1880	No meeting	1903	Niagara Falls, N.Y.
1881	Washington	1904	St. Louis
1882	Cincinnati	1905	Portland, Ore.
1883	Buffalo	1906	Narragansett Pier, R.I.
1884	No meeting	1907	Asheville, N.C.
1885	Lake George, N.Y.	1908	Lake Minnetonka, Minn.
1886	Milwaukee	1909	Bretton Woods, N.H.
1887	Thousand Islands, N.Y.	1910	Mackinac Island, Mich.
1888	Catskill Mountains, N.Y.	1910	Brussels (International)
1889	St. Louis	1911	Pasadena
1890	Fabyans (White Mountains)	1912	Ottawa
1891	San Francisco	1913	Kaaterskill, N.Y.
1892	Lakewood, N.J.	1914	Washington
1893	Chicago	1915	Berkeley, Calif.
1894	Lake Placid, N.Y.	1916	Asbury Park, N.J.
1895	Denver and Colorado Springs	1917	Louisville
1896	Cleveland	1918	Saratoga Springs, N.Y.
1897	Philadelphia	1919	Asbury Park, N.J.
1897	London (International)	1920	Colorado Springs

DATE	PLACE	DATE	PLACE
1921	Swampscott, Mass.	1947	San Francisco
1922	Detroit	1948	Atlantic City
1923	Hot Springs, Ark.	1949	Regional conferences
1924	Saratoga Springs, N.Y.	1950	Cleveland
1925	Seattle	1951	Chicago
1926	Atlantic City	1952	New York
1927	Toronto	1953	Los Angeles
1928	West Baden, Ind.	1954	Minneapolis
1929	Washington	1955	Philadelphia
1930	Los Angeles	1956	Miami
1931	New Haven	1957	Kansas City
1932	New Orleans	1958	San Francisco
1933	Chicago	1959	Washington
1934	Montreal	1960	Montreal
1935	Denver	1961	Cleveland
1936	Richmond, Va.	1962	Miami Beach
1937	New York	1963	Chicago
1938	Kansas City	1964	St. Louis
1939	San Francisco	1965	Detroit
1940	Cincinnati	1966	New York
1941	Boston	1967	San Francisco
1942	Milwaukee	1968	Kansas City
1943	No meeting	1969	Atlantic City
1944	No meeting	1970	Detroit
1945	No meeting	1971	Dallas
1946	Buffalo	1972	Chicago

APPENDIX B

PRESIDENTS
OF THE
AMERICAN LIBRARY ASSOCIATION

PRESIDENTS	YEARS
Justin Winsor	1876–85
William Frederick Poole	1885–87
Charles Ammi Cutter	1887–89
Frederick Morgan Crunden	1889–90
Melvil Dewey	1890–July, 1891
Samuel Swett Green	July–Nov., 1891
William Isaac Fletcher	1891–92
Melvil Dewey	1892–93
Josephus Nelson Larned	1893–94
Henry Munson Utley	1894–95
John Cotton Dana	1895–96
William Howard Brett	1896–97
Justin Winsor	July–Oct., 1897
Herbert Putnam	Jan.–Aug., 1898
William Coolidge Lane	1898–99
Reuben Gold Thwaites	1899–1900
Henry James Carr	1900–01
John Shaw Billings	1901–02
James Kendall Hosmer	1902–03
Herbert Putnam	1903–04
Ernest Cushing Richardson	1904–05
Frank Pierce Hill	1905–06
Clement Walker Andrews	1906–07
Arthur Elmore Bostwick	1907–08

257

PRESIDENTS	YEARS
Charles Henry Gould	1908–09
Nathaniel Dana Carlile Hodges	1909–10
James Ingersoll Wyer	1910–11
Theresa West Elmendorf	1911–12
Henry Eduard Legler	1912–13
Edwin Hatfield Anderson	1913–14
Hiller Crowell Wellman	1914–15
Mary Wright Plummer	1915–16
Walter Lewis Brown	1916–17
Thomas Lynch Montgomery	1917–18
William Warner Bishop	1918–19
Chalmers Hadley	1919–20
Alice S. Tyler	1920–21
Azariah Smith Root	1921–22
George Burwell Utley	1922–23
Judson Toll Jennings	1923–24
Herman H. B. Meyer	1924–25
Charles F. D. Belden	1925–26
George H. Locke	1926–27
Carl B. Roden	1927–28
Linda A. Eastman	1928–29
Andrew Keogh	1929–30
Adam Strohm	1930–31
Josephine Adams Rathbone	1931–32
Harry Miller Lydenberg	1932–33
Gratia A. Countryman	1933–34
Charles H. Compton	1934–35
Louis Round Wilson	1935–36
Malcolm Glenn Wyer	1936–37
Harrison Warwick Craver	1937–38
Milton James Ferguson	1938–39
Ralph Munn	1939–40
Essae Martha Culver	1940–41
Charles Harvey Brown	1941–42
Keyes D. Metcalf	1942–43
Althea H. Warren	1943–44
Carl Vitz	1944–45
Ralph A. Ulveling	1945–46
Mary U. Rothrock	1946–47
Paul North Rice	1947–48
E. W. McDiarmid	1948–49
Milton E. Lord	1949–50
Clarence R. Graham	1950–51
Loleta Fyan	1951–52
Robert Downs	1952–53
Flora B. Ludington	1953–54
L. Quincy Mumford	1954–55
John S. Richards	1955–56

PRESIDENTS	YEARS
Ralph R. Shaw	1956–57
Lucille Morsch	1957–58
Emerson Greenaway	1958–59
Benjamin Powell	1959–60
Francis Lander Spain	1960–61
Florinell Morton	1961–62
James Bryan	1962–63
Frederick Wagman	1963–64
Edwin Castagna	1964–65
Robert Vosper	1965–66
Mary Gaver	1966–67
Foster Mohrhardt	1967–68
Roger McDonough	1968–69
William Dix	1969–70
Lillian Bradshaw	1970–71
Keith Doms	1971–72
Katherine Laich	1972–73

NOTES

CHAPTER 1

1. This discussion is based on the official proceedings of the conference as published in *Norton's Literary and Educational Register for 1854* (New York: Norton, 1854).

2. William F. Poole, in *A.L.A. Papers and Proceedings* (New York: American Library Assn., 1886), p. 1.

3. Jewett to Grant, August 16, 1853, American Library Association Archives, University of Illinois, Urbana.

4. Louis A. Fagan, *Life of Sir Anthony Panizzi*, 2 vols. (London: Remington, 1880), 1: 98.

5. Several other sources indicate that there were eighty-two men present.

6. *Norton's Register*, p. 54.

7. For a full discussion of this proposal, see Joseph A. Borome, *Charles Coffin Jewett* (Chicago: ALA, 1951), pp. 45–71.

8. *Norton's Register*, p. 55.

9. Ibid., p. 94.

10. *See* Samuel S. Green, *The Public Library Movement in the United States, 1853–1893* (Boston: Boston Book Co., 1913), p. 10.

11. George B. Utley, *The Librarians' Conference of 1853* (Chicago: ALA, 1951), p. 3.

12. R. R. Bowker, "Postcript," *Library Journal*, 21: 52 (February, 1896).

13. The author has been identified as Prof. Friedrich Max-Muller, former curator of the Bodlein Library.

14. Diary of Melvil Dewey, Melvil Dewey Papers, Columbia University Libraries, New York. Dewey had met with Justin Winsor one month earlier, on April 22, 1876, to talk over his plan for a journal and other library matters.

15. The following discussion is based on "The A.L.A. Scrapbook," in Edward

G. Holley, *Raking the Historic Coals; the A.L.A. Scrapbook of 1876* (Urbana: Beta Phi Mu, 1967).

16. Poole to Winsor, May 18, 1876, Justin Winsor Collection, Boston Public Library.

17. Poole to Winsor, May 24, 1876, Winsor Collection.

18. Spofford to Leypoldt, May 29, 1876, ALA Archives.

19. Poole to Winsor, May 31, 1876, ALA Archives.

20. Cutter to Poole, June 5, 1876, ALA Archives.

21. Dewey to Poole, June 5, 1876, ALA Archives.

22. Poole to Dewey, June 15, 1876, ALA Archives.

23. "Papers and Proceedings of the American Library Association," *American Library Journal* 1: 143 (October, 1876).

24. Samuel S. Green, "Personal Relations Between Librarians and Readers," *American Library Journal* 1: 74–81 (November 30, 1876).

25. Samuel R. Warren, ed., *Public Libraries in the United States of America* (Washington, D.C.: Bureau of Education, 1875–76). See also Frances Miksa, "The Making of the 1876 Special Report on Public Libraries," *Journal of Library History* 8: 30–40 (January, 1973).

26. "Papers and Proceedings of the American Library Association," *American Library Journal* 1: 170 (October, 1876).

27. Among the committees established were: Cooperation Committee, Committee on Poole's Index, and Committee on Sizes of Books.

28. Melvil Dewey, "The American Library Association," *American Library Journal* 1: 245–46 (March 31, 1877).

29. "The Librarians' Convention," *New York World*, September 7, 1877, p. 4.

30. [Editorial], *American Library Journal* 1: 12–13 (September 30, 1876).

31. "Publishers Note," *Library Journal* 4: 461 (December, 1879).

32. Dewey was an early and ardent advocate of spelling reform. The change in spelling appeared for the first time in the January, 1880, issue of *Library Journal.*

33. Dewey, who was twenty-five years old, was a notable exception.

CHAPTER 2

1. For an excellent discussion of Winsor's contributions, see Joseph Alfred Borome, "The Life and Letters of Justin Winsor" (Ph.D. diss., Columbia University, 1950).

2. William E. Foster, "Five Men of '76," *Papers and Proceedings of the 1926 Conference* (Chicago: ALA, 1926), p. 312.

3. [Editorial], *American Library Journal* 1: 1 (March 31, 1877).

4. The apparent intent of this rule was to limit the membership of committees to current members of the executive board. It contributed to the policy of restricting leadership roles to a relatively few members.

5. "Report of the Committee on Sizes," *American Library Journal* 1: 180 (January 31, 1877).

6. "Report on a New Edition of Poole's Index," *American Library Journal* 1: 182 (January 31, 1877).

7. Fletcher was then librarian of the Watkinson Library in Hartford, Conn., and was later librarian of Amherst College.

8. *American Library Journal* 1: 176 (January 31, 1877).

9. Two early examples of this can be seen in the discussions of the 1877 and the 1885 conferences.

10. "The Proceedings," *Library Journal* 2: 5 (September, 1877).

11. Ibid.

12. Ibid.

13. *Library Journal* 2: 14 (September, 1877).

14. Samuel S. Green, *Public Library Movement in the United States,* p. 60.

15. *Transactions and Proceedings of the Conference of Librarians* (London: Trubner, 1878), p. 1.

16. Ibid., p. 177.

17. Ibid., p. 179.

18. Ibid., p. 181.

19. "Publishers' Title Slips," *Library Journal* 3: 112 (May, 1879).

20. "The Proceedings," *Library Journal* 4: 282 (July–August, 1879).

21. "Library Progress in 1878," *Library Journal* 3: 367 (December, 1878).

22. "Incorporation of the A.L.A.," *Library Journal* 5: 307 (November–December, 1880).

23. Ibid.

24. John Y. Cole, "Smithmeyer and Pelz: Embattled Architects of the Library of Congress," *The Quarterly Journal of the Library of Congress* 29: 285 (October, 1972).

25. "The Proceedings," *Library Journal* 6: 140 (November, 1881).

26. "Secretary's Report," in *Papers and Proceedings of the A.L.A. Conference* (New York: American Library Association, 1881), 112.

27. "The Proceedings," *Library Journal* 6: 135 (February, 1881).

28. Ibid., p. 131.

29. [Editorial], *Library Journal* 7: 289 (December, 1882).

30. "The Proceedings," *Library Journal* 10: 309 (September–October, 1885).

31. Larned was librarian of the Young Men's Library Association of Buffalo, New York.

32. "The Proceedings," *Library Journal* 10: 311 (September–October, 1885).

33. Winsor to Dewey, February 20, 1885, Dewey Papers, Columbia University Libraries, New York.

34. Fremont Rider, *Melvil Dewey,* p. 70.

35. Green, *Public Library Movement,* p. 78.

CHAPTER 3

1. "The Proceedings," *Library Journal* 19: 145 (October, 1894).

2. Ibid.

3. "Papers and Proceedings of the 21st Meeting" (New York: ALA, 1899), p. 1.

4. William E. Foster, "Five Men of '76," *Papers and Proceedings of the 1926 Conference*, 314–15.

5. This change was made permanent by being added to the 1893 constitution. However, Charles A. Cutter did serve a second consecutive term prior to the adoption of the amendment.

6. Samuel S. Green, *The Public Library Movement in the United States*, p. 183.

7. Evans to Poole, December 30, 1887, Poole Papers, Newberry Library, Chicago.

8. Melvil Dewey, "Report of the Committee on Arrangements," *Library Journal* 12: 429 (September–October, 1887).

9. The documents relating to the establishment of the first library school are collected in *School of Library Economy of Columbia College, 1887–1889: Documents for a History* (New York: School of Library Service, Columbia University, 1937).

10. Melvil Dewey, "Apprenticeship of Librarians," *Library Journal* 4: 16 (May 31, 1879).

11. W. Boyd Rayward, "Melvil Dewey and Education for Librarianship," *Journal of Library History, Philosophy, and Comparative Librarianship* 3: 299 (October, 1968).

12. Green, *Public Library Movement*, p. 109.

13. "A.L.A. Proceedings," *Library Journal* 12: 288 (September–October, 1887).

14. Poole to Dewey, December 28, 1883, Melvil Dewey Papers, Columbia University Libraries, New York.

15. See William L. Williamson, *William Frederick Poole and the Modern Library Movement* (New York: Columbia University Pr., 1963) for a thorough discussion of the Poole-Dewey clashes.

16. "Proceedings, 1883," *Library Journal* 8: 290 (September–October, 1883).

17. Sarah K. Vann, *Training for Librarianship before 1923: Education for Librarianship Prior to the Publication of Williamson's Report on Training for Library Service* (Chicago: ALA, 1961), p. 27.

18. "The Proceedings," *Library Journal* 12: 426 (September–October, 1887).

19. For an extensive discussion of the problem, see Vann, *Training for Librarianship*.

20. W. T. Peoples to George W. Cole, January 18, 1889, ALA Archives. Peoples was librarian of the New York Mercantile Library and Cole was at the Newberry Library.

21. "Conference of Librarians," *Library Journal* 13: 318 (September–October, 1888).

22. "Librarians and Library Architecture," reprinted in *Library Journal* 13: 339 (November, 1888).

23. *Papers and Proceedings of the 10th General Session* (New York: ALA, 1888), p. 143.

24. "Conference of Librarians," *Library Journal* 13: 309 (September–October, 1888).

25. "The Proceedings," *Library Journal* 20: 78–79 (December, 1895).

26. "The Proceedings," *Library Journal* 14: 217 (May–June, 1889).

27. Ibid., p. 284.

28. Ibid.

29. "Mr. W. F. Poole's Remarks at the Publishers' and Booksellers' Dinner," *Library Journal* 15: 164–65 (December, 1890).

30. Evans to Poole, October 14, 890, Poole Papers.

31. "Special Meeting of the Executive Committee," *Library Journal* 16: 200 (July, 1891).

32. Green, *Public Library Movement*, p. 237.

33. George W. Cole, "Notes on the Library Exhibit of the Columbian Exposition," *Library Journal* 16: 238 (August, 1891).

34. Green to Poole, May 21, 1892, Poole Papers.

35. Larned to Poole, May 3, 1892, Poole Papers.

36. Dewey to Poole, May 5, 1892, Poole Papers. For a more complete discussion see Dennis Thomison, "The A.L.A. and Its Missing Presidents," *Journal of Library History* 9: 362–66 (October, 1974).

37. "The A.L.A. Council," *Library Journal* 17: 386 (September, 1892).

38. "The Lakewood Conference," *Library Journal* 17: 119 (April, 1892).

39. "The Proceedings," *Library Journal* 17: 119 (August, 1892).

40. Poole to Winsor, May 22, 1893, Massachusetts Historical Society, Boston.

41. "Minutes, Executive Board, July 25, 1892," *Library Journal* 17: 120 (September, 1892).

42. "Central Card Cataloging," *Library Journal* 18: 509 (December, 1893).

43. "The A.L.A. Index," *Library Journal* 18: 50 (February, 1893).

44. "The Proceedings," *Library Journal* 19: 116–18 (October, 1894).

45. Dewey to Hill, February 16, 1894, ALA Archives.

46. "The Proceedings," *Library Journal* 21: 93 (December, 1896).

47. [Editorial], *Library Journal* 21: 395 (September, 1896).

48. "Eighteenth Annual Conference, Cleveland, September 1–8, 1896," *Library Journal* 21: 416 (September, 1896).

49. Ibid., 418.

50. "The Three Library Events of 1897," *Library Journal* 22: 3 (January, 1897).

51. [Editorial], *Library Journal* 22: 90 (February, 1897).

52. For more extensive coverage, see Budd L. Gambee, "The Role of American Librarians at the Second International Library Conference," *Library History Seminar Proceedings*, No. 4 (Tallahassee: Florida State University Pr., 1971).

53. "The Second International Library Conference, London, July 13–16, 1897," *Library Journal* 22: 399 (August, 1897).

54. "Differences in English and American Library Methods," *Library Journal* 22: 380 (August, 1897).

55. Hayes, the son of the nineteenth president of the United States, was a banker and a library trustee.

56. Rutherford Hayes, "The Presidency of the American Library Association," *Library Journal* 23: 23 (January, 1898).

57. Herbert Putnam, "Address of the President," *Library Journal* 23: 1 (August, 1898).

58. For a more complete discussion, see Dennis Thomison, "The A.L.A. and Its Missing Presidents."

59. Henry Carr to William C. Lane, January 14, 1899, ALA Archives.

60. For a more extensive study of this incident, see Thorvald Solberg, "A Chapter in the Unwritten History of the Library of Congress from January 17 to April 5, 1899," *Library Quarterly* 9: 285–96 (July, 1939). See also David Mearns, *The Story Up to Now: The Library of Congress 1800–1946* (Washington, Library of Congress, 1947), pp. 164–69.

61. William C. Lane, "The Appointment of a Librarian of Congress," *Library Journal* 24: 99 (March, 1899).

62. Charles Soule to Carr, February 14, 1899, ALA Archives.

63. J. C. M. Hanson, "The Library of Congress and its New Catalogue: Some Unwritten History," in W. W. Bishop and Andrew Keogh, eds., *Essays Offered to Herbert Putnam* (New Haven: Yale University Pr., 1929), p. 188.

64. Lane to Carr, March 26, 1899, ALA Archives.

65. See George S. Bobinski, *Carnegie Libraries: Their History and Impact on American Public Library Development* (Chicago: ALA, 1969) for an extensive discussion of the Carnegie endowments. A more general and comprehensive study of Carnegie is Joseph Wall's *Andrew Carnegie* (New York: Oxford University Pr., 1970).

66. Letter, Carr to Soule, March 19, 1900, ALA Archives.

67. Soule to Carr, March 21, 1900, ALA Archives.

68. Carr to Haines, July 10, 1900, ALA Archives.

69. "American Library Association," *Library Journal* 25: 285 (June, 1900).

70. Ibid., p. 291.

71. "American Library Association," *Library Journal* 26: 22 (January, 1901).

72. Haines to Carr, June 8, 1901, ALA Archives.

73. June 9, 1900, ALA Archives.

74. Henry Carr, "Being a Librarian," *Library Journal* 26: 1 (August, 1901).

75. C. H. Hastings, "The Card Distribution Work of the Library of Congress," *Library Journal* 27: 156 (July, 1902).

76. John S. Billings, "Some Library Problems of To-Morrow," *Library Journal* 27: 9 (July, 1902).

77. [Editorial], *Library Journal* 20: 374 (November, 1895).

78. Carr to Thwaites, April 19, 1900, ALA Archives.

79. Thwaites to Carr, April 21, 1900, ALA Archives.

80. Charles W. Eliot, "The Division of a Library into Books in Use and Books Not in Use, with Different Storage Methods for the Two Classes of Books," *Library Journal* 27: 55 (July, 1902).

81. "Committee on Relations with the Book Trade," *Library Journal* 28: 67 (February, 1903).

82. Mary Plummer, "Report of the Committee on Library Training," *Library Journal* 28: 83–101 (July, 1903).

83. "Library Training," *Library Journal* 28: 976 (August, 1903).

84. "Report on Standards of Library Training," *Library Journal* 30: 123 (September, 1905).

85. Edward M. Fleming, *R. R. Bowker: Militant Liberal* (Norman: University of Oklahoma Pr., 1952), p. 355.

86. W. I. Fletcher, "Report of the A.L.A. Publishing Board," *Library Journal* 30: 107 (September, 1905).

87. "American Library Association," *Library Journal* 32: 266 (June, 1907).

88. Arthur Bostwick, *A Life with Men and Books* (New York: Wilson, 1939), p. 195.

89. George Iles, "A Headquarters for Our Association," *Library Journal* 28: 24 (July, 1903).

90. Melvil Dewey, "A National Headquarters for the Library Association," *Library Journal* 28: 757 (November, 1903).

91. Iles, "Headquarters for Our Association," p. 758.

92. Arthur Bostwick, "Organization and Administration," *Library Journal* 28: 761–62 (November, 1903).

93. Iles, "Headquarters for Our Association," p. 28.

94. Virgil Massman, "From out of a Desk Drawer . . . The Beginnings of ALA's Headquarters," *ALA Bulletin* 28: 478 (April, 1969). Temporary offices had previously been established at 10½ Beacon Street, Boston, on April 22, 1905. Boston was the home of the secretary of the Publishing Board, Nina E. Browne, and although this was not given as a reason for selecting that city, it may have been the major reason.

95. "Minutes, Executive Board, May 27, 1907," ALA Archives. Also see "American Library Association," *Library Journal* 32: 505–06 (November, 1907).

96. "Minutes, Executive Board, June 27, 1908," ALA Archives.

97. [Editorial], *Public Libraries* 13: 309 (October, 1908).

98. "Minutes, Executive Board, June 28, 1909," ALA Archives.

99. "American Library Institute," *Library Journal* 33: 483 (December, 1908),

100. "Revision of the A.L.A. Constitution," *Library Journal* 33: 255 (July, 1908).

101. "Bretton Woods Conference," *ALA Bulletin* 3: 224 (October, 1909).

102. Anthony T. Kruzas, *Business and Industrial Libraries in the United States, 1820–1940* (New York: Special Libraries Assn., 1965), p. 8.

103. D. N. Handy, "John A. Lapp, Editor," *Special Libraries* 8: 109 (September, 1917).

104. "International Conference of 1910," *Library Journal* 35: 35 (January, 1910).

105. "International Congresses," *Library Journal* 35: 426 (October, 1910).

106. "Report of the Committee on Library Training," in *Papers and Proceedings of the 34th Annual Conference of the A.L.A.* (Chicago: ALA, 1912), p. 113.

107. "Social Side of the Conference," in *Proceedings of the 34th Conference,* p. 205.

108. Bostwick, *A Life with Men and Books*, p. 212.

109. *Papers and Proceedings of the Kaaterskill Conference, 1913* (Chicago: ALA, 1913), p. 343–44.

110. F. P. Hill, "Opening of the A.L.A. Exhibit at Leipzig," *Library Journal* 39: 593 (August, 1914).

111. [Editorial], *Library Journal* 39: 657 (September, 1914).

112. "Reduction in Library Budgets," *Library Journal* 39: 801 (November, 1914).

113. Plummer to J. I. Wyer, August 3, 1915, ALA Archives.

114. President Plummer was ill at the time and died on September 21, 1916.

115. [Editorial], *Library Journal* 41: 569 (August, 1916).

116. "Our Libraries and the War," *Library Journal* 42: 607 (August, 1917).

117. "Library War Service," *Library Journal* 42: 875 (November, 1917).

118. "Library War Service," *Library Journal* 42: 771 (October, 1917).

119. "Library War Service," *Library Journal* 43: 168 (March, 1918).

120. "Library War Service," *Library Journal* 43: 417 (June, 1918).

121. Ibid.

122. Matthew Dudgeon, "What Men Read in Camps," *Library Journal* 43: 593 (August, 1918).

123. "Library War Service," *Library Journal* 43: 643 (June, 1918).

124. Frank Stockbridge, "The Library War Service Fund Campaign," *Library Journal* 43: 643 (September, 1918).

125. "Special Libraries Association Plans for War Service," *Library Journal* 42: 773 (October, 1917).

126. C. C. Williamson, "Presidential Address," *Special Libraries* 9: 101 (September, 1919).

127. *Proceedings, ALA General Session, June 22, 1922* (Chicago: ALA, 1922), p. 18.

128. "American Library Association War Service Committee," *Library Journal* 44: 21 (January, 1919).

129. [Editorial], *Library Journal* 44: 202 (April, 1919).

130. "Library War Service," *Library Journal* 44: 240 (April, 1919).

131. "Progress Overseas," *Library Journal* 44: 166 (March, 1919).

132. Harry Clemons, "Statement of ALA Representatives in Siberia," *ALA Bulletin* 13: 222 (July, 1919).

133. Carl H. Milam, "Statement of the Acting General Director, ALA War Service," *Papers and Proceedings of the Asbury Park Conference* (Chicago: ALA, 1919), p. 264.

134. Herbert Putnam, "Statement of the General Director, ALA War Services," *ALA Bulletin* 13: 261 (July, 1919).

CHAPTER 4

1. "Minutes, Executive Board, January 11, 1919," ALA Archives.

2. William Warner Bishop, "The American Library Association at the Cross-roads," *ALA Bulletin* 13: 100 (July, 1919).

3. Chalmers Hadley, "The Library War Service and Some Things It Has Taught Us," *ALA Bulletin* 13: 109 (July, 1919).

4. "Report of the Committee of Five on Library Service," *ALA Bulletin* 13: 326 (July, 1919).

5. Charles C. Williamson, "Some Present Day Aspects of Library Training," *ALA Bulletin* 13: 120 (July, 1919).

6. "Council," in *Papers and Proceedings of the Asbury Park Conference* (Chicago: ALA, 1919), p. 368–70.

7. For a thorough discussion of Bishop's role, see Claude Glenn Sparks, "William Warner Bishop, A Biography" (Ph.D. diss., University of Michigan, 1967).

8. [Editorial], *Library Journal* 44: 687 (November, 1919).

9. "A.L.A. Constitution," *ALA Bulletin* 15: 57 (May, 1921).

10. Chalmers Hadley, "The Proposed Enlarged Program of the A.L.A.," *Library Journal* 44: 753 (December, 1919).

11. "Publicity for the A.L.A. Enlarged Program," *Library Journal* 44: 788 (December, 1919).

12. "Preliminary Report of Committee on Enlarged Program for American Library Service," *Library Journal* 44: 647 (October, 1919).

13. Ibid., p. 648.

14. Ibid., p. 649.

15. Ibid., p. 651.

16. Ibid., p. 652.

17. Ibid., p. 659.

18. "At Chicago," *Library Journal* 45: 55 (January 15, 1920).

19. "The Enlarged Program Proceedings," *ALA Bulletin* 14: 7 (January, 1920).

20. Ibid., p. .8

21. "Minutes, Executive Board, March 20, 1920," ALA Archives.

22. "American Library Association Special Conference Not to Be Called," *ALA Bulletin* 14: 95 (March, 1920).

23. "Circular Letter on the Enlarged Program," *Library Journal* 45: 363–64 (April 15, 1920).

24. [Editorial], *Library Journal* 45: 453 (May 15, 1920).

25. "American Library Association," *Library Journal* 45: 796 (October 1, 1920).

26. "American Library Association," *Library Journal* 45: 990 (December 1, 1920).

CHAPTER 5

1. [Editorial], *Library Journal* 45: 271 (March 15, 1920).

2. Hawthorne Daniel, *Public Libraries for Everyone* (Garden City, N.Y.: Doubleday, 1961), p. 27.

3. For a comprehensive discussion of Milam's earlier work, see Peggy Sullivan,

"Carl H. Milam and the American Library Association" (Ph.D. diss., University of Chicago, 1972).

4. Milton J. Ferguson, "Humanizing the A.L.A.—Chicago, 1922," *Library Journal* 47: 912 (November 1, 1922).

5. [Editorial], *Library Journal* 46: 367 (May 15, 1921).

6. [Editorial], *Library Journal* 47: 15 (January 1, 1922).

7. [Editorial], *Library Journal* 47: 466 (May 15, 1922).

8. Ola Wyeth, "The A.L.A. Library in Coblenz," *Library Journal* 46: 353 (April 15, 1921).

9. "The Launching of the Ala," *Library Journal* 46: 25 (January 1, 1921).

10. [Editorial], *Library Journal* 47: 30 (January 1, 1922).

11. *A.L.A. Handbook* (Chicago: ALA, 1922), p. 10.

12. "American Library Association," *Library Journal* 47: 32 (January 1, 1922).

13. [Editorial], *Library Journal* 47: 169 (February 15, 1922).

14. "The John Newbery Medal," *Library Journal* 47: 399 (May 1, 1922).

15. [Editorial], *Library Journal* 48: 476 (May 15, 1923).

16. "Proceedings, Council, June 22, 1922," ALA Archives.

17. "Report of the Committee on Library Training," typewritten, ALA Archives, p. 1.

18. The original members of the Temporary Board were Linda Eastman, Andrew Keogh, Harrison W. Craver, Malcolm Wyer, Sarah Bogle, and Adam Strohm, chairman.

19. Carl M. White, *A Historical Introduction to Library Service: Problems and Progress to 1951* (Metuchen, N.J.: Scarecrow Pr., 1976), p. 168.

20. Frank K. Walter, A Dynamic Report, *Library Journal* 48: 709 (September 1, 1923).

21. Anne W. Howland, "Drexel Institute," *Library Journal* 48: 903 (November 1, 1923).

22. Sarah K. Vann, *Training for Librarianship before 1923*, p. 2.

23. Charles C. Williamson, *Training for Library Service* (New York: Carnegie Corp., 1923), p. 30. See also Sarah K. Vann, *The Williamson Reports: A Study* (Metuchen, N.J.: Scarecrow Pr., 1971) and Charles C. Williamson, *The Williamson Reports of 1921 and 1923* (Metuchen, N.J.: Scarecrow Pr., 1971).

24. "Proceedings, Council, January 2, 1924," ALA Archives.

25. "A.L.A. News," *ALA Bulletin* 18: 95 (May, 1924).

26. "Board of Education for Librarianship," *ALA Bulletin* 19: A6 (November, 1925).

27. "Proceedings, Council, March 7, 1926," ALA Archives.

28. Jesse Shera, *The Foundations of Education for Librarianship* (New York: Becker and Hayes (Wiley), 1972), p. 246.

29. William N. C. Carlton, "The American Library in Paris, Inc.," *Library Journal* 46: 823 (October 15, 1921).

30. George B. Utley, "The Expanding Responsibilities of the American Library Association," *Library Journal* 48: 450 (May 15, 1923).

31. "Proceedings, Executive Board, July 5, 1924," ALA Archives.

32. "Annual Reports, 1923–24," *ALA Bulletin* 18: 204 (July, 1924).

33. "Proceedings, Executive Board, June 20, 1927," ALA Archives.

34. See also Richard K. Gardner, "Education for Librarianship in France, an Historical Study" (Ph.D. diss., Case Western Reserve University, 1968).

35. [Editorial], *Library Journal* 49: 679 (August, 1924).

36. This account is based on "The President's Address," made to the SLA Annual Conference on June 24, 1924. There is no mention of the incident in ALA literature. Mimeographed, ALA Archives.

37. Ibid.

38. "Minutes, Executive Board, January 2, 1924," ALA Archives.

39. [Editorial], *Library Journal* 49: 536 (June 1, 1924).

40. *New York Times*, May 19, 1924, p. 16.

41. "Proceedings, Executive Board, December 29, 1925," ALA Archives.

42. "Proceedings, Council, March 7, 1926," ALA Archives.

43. [Editorial], *Library Journal* 51: 529 (June 1, 1926).

44. [Editorial], *Library Journal* 51: 917 (October 15, 1926).

45. "The A.L.A. Fiftieth Anniversary Exhibit," *Library Journal* 51: 1122–23 (December 15, 1926).

46. [Editorial], *Library Journal* 51: 917 (October 15, 1926).

47. Melvil Dewey, "Our Next Half-Century," *Library Journal* 51: 889 (October 15, 1926).

48. "Proceedings, Council, April 23, 1923," ALA Archives.

49. [Editorial], *Library Journal* 49: 428 (May 1, 1924).

50. [Editorial], *Library Journal* 53: 316 (April 1, 1928).

51. Forrest B. Spaulding, "Two Days at A.L.A. Headquarters," *ALA Bulletin* 23: 35 (February, 1929).

52. "Proceedings, Executive Board, December 27, 1928," ALA Archives.

CHAPTER 6

1. "A.L.A. News," *ALA Bulletin* 21: 82 (June, 1927).

2. *New York Times*, November 5, 1927, p. 1.

3. Note that the formation of a Canadian Library Association had also been announced at the 1900 annual conference of ALA. Both announcements were premature, however, and the CLA was not organized until 1946.

4. George Locke, "Presidential Address," in *Papers and Proceedings of the Toronto Conference, 1927* (Chicago: ALA, 1927), p. 269.

5. Craver to Bogle, November 2, 1927, ALA Archives.

6. Dana to Council, December 20, 1927, ALA Archives.

7. "Proceedings, Executive Board, December 28, 1927," ALA Archives.

8. "Proceedings, Council, December 30, 1927," ALA Archives.

9. "On A.L.A. Activities," *Library Journal* 53: 557 (June 15, 1928).

10. "Proceedings, Executive Board, December 27, 1928," ALA Archives.

11. *New York Times*, June 22, 1929, p. 18.

12. Arthur Bostwick, *A Life with Men and Books*, pp. 211–12.

13. Frances E. Cady, "The President's Address," *Special Libraries* 17: 310 (November, 1926).

14. "Proceedings, Council, December 29, 1927," ALA Archives.

15. R. H. Johnson in "Proceedings, Council, December 29, 1927," ALA Archives.

16. "American Library Association," *Special Libraries* 19: 52 (February, 1928).

17. [Editorial], *Library Journal* 53: 96 (January 15, 1928).

18. [Editorial], *Special Libraries* 20: 117 (May–June, 1929).

19. "Acting President's Address," *Special Libraries* 20: 160–61 (May–June, 1929).

20. "Editorial Forum," *Librarian Journal* 54: 714 (September 1, 1929). Before his election as pope, he had served as librarian of the Ambrosian Library and the Vatican Library.

21. "Minutes, Association of American Library Schools, May, 1929," ALA Archives.

22. "Report of the Activities Committee on the Board of Education for Librarianship," typewritten (Chicago: 1930), ALA Archives.

23. Dana to Council, May 29, 1928, ALA Archives.

24. "Minutes, Executive Board, December 28, 1930," ALA Archives.

25. Windsor to Williamson, January 29, 1931, ALA Archives.

26. Indicative, too, of her power was her nickname, "the Colonel House of the ALA," which referred to President Woodrow Wilson's close associate.

27. Louis Shores, "Limiting the Library School Output," *Library Journal* 54: 65 (January 15, 1929).

28. "Board of Education for Librarianship," typewritten (Chicago: 1930), ALA Archives. The board discouraged the founding of library schools at the University of Tulsa, Virginia College, and Ohio University.

29. Sydney B. Mitchell to Sarah Bogle, January 17, 1931, ALA Archives.

30. James Ingersoll Wyer, "Oversupply among Librarians," *ALA Bulletin* 26: 753 (October, 1932).

31. Quoted in "Editorials," *Library Journal* 57: 856–57 (October 15, 1932).

32. Sydney B. Mitchell, "Ways and Means of Limiting Library School Output," *ALA Bulletin* 26: 425 (July, 1932).

33. [Editorial], *Library Journal* 57: 1044 (December 15, 1932).

34. The board of education agreed, however, that, "when normal employment conditions return," there would be a need for an accredited library school in Los Angeles. See "Southern California Library School," *Library Journal* 58: 318 (April 1, 1933).

35. "Minutes, Executive Board, January 1, 1931," ALA Archives.

36. "The A.L.A. Activities Committee Report," *ALA Bulletin* 24: 633 (December, 1930).

37. "The Library Quarterly," *ALA Bulletin* 24: 600 (October, 1930).

38. "Minutes, Council, December 28, 1928," ALA Archives.

39. *Papers and Proceedings of the 1930 ALA Conference* (Chicago: ALA, 1930), p. 373.

40. [Editorial], *Library Journal* 56: 124 (February 1, 1931).

41. *Chicago Tribune*, July 18, 1931, p. 1.

42. "Notes from New Haven," *ALA Bulletin* 25: 369 (July, 1931).

43. "A.L.A. Activities Committee Report," *ALA Bulletin* 24: 676 (December, 1930).

44. Asa Don Dickinson, letter to editor, *Library Journal* 56: 549 (June 15, 1931).

45. "The President Asks Your Support," *ALA Bulletin* 25: 3 (January, 1931).

46. "A.L.A. Faces Serious Situation," *Library Journal* 56: 136 (February 1, 1931).

47. "Communication from the Executive Board, to the Members of the A.L.A.", mimeographed, June 25, 1931. ALA Archives.

48. "Endowment Fund Passes the Goal," *ALA Bulletin* 25: 366 (July, 1931).

49. "A.L.A. News," *ALA Bulletin* 25: 714 (December, 1931).

50. Frederick Keppel, memo, March 5, 1936, Carnegie Corporation Archives, quoted in Peggy Sullivan, "Carl H. Milam and the American Library Association," p. 198.

51. "Notes from New Haven," *ALA Bulletin* 25: 368 (July, 1931).

52. "A.L.A. News," *ALA Bulletin* 25: 714 (December, 1931).

53. "Editorial Forum," *Library Journal* 55: 870 (November 1, 1930).

54. See the *New York Times*, January 21, 1905, p. 5, for a discussion of the club's restrictions. Dewey's connection with this club, and its well-known restrictions, led to a reprimand from the Board of Regents and his resignation from his position of secretary of the board.

55. Ernest C. Cushing to Dewey, July 15, 1931, ALA Archives.

56. Bostwick, *A Life with Men and Books*, p. 217.

57. Circular letter to "a fu personal friends" from Dewey, December 10, 1931, ALA Archives.

58. "Melvil Dewey," *Library Journal* 57: 153 (February 1, 1932).

59. Frank P. Hill, "Melvil Dewey," *Library Journal* 57: 153 (February 1, 1932).

60. See Edward M. Fleming, *R. R. Bowker, Militant Liberal*.

61. "A.L.A. Regional Conference," *Library Journal* 57: 949 (November 15, 1932).

62. "A.L.A. Salaries Cut," *Library Journal* 57: 660 (August, 1932).

63. "Employment Prospects for 1933," *ALA Bulletin* 27: 103 (February, 1933).

64. "Finances of the Association," *ALA Bulletin* 28: 860 (December, 1934).

65. Carl H. Milam, "Libraries and the Emergency," *ALA Bulletin* 28: 281 (June, 1934).

66. "Proceedings, Executive Board, October 7, 1940," ALA Archives.

67. "Proceedings, Executive Board, December 28, 1941," ALA Archives.

68. Rebecca Rankin, "Unemployment among Librarians," *ALA Bulletin* 29: 148 (March, 1935).

69. "Midwinter Brevities," *ALA Bulletin* 29: 10 (January, 1935).

70. R. E. Dooley, "Financial Statement," *ALA Bulletin* 29: 305 (June, 1935).

71. Ralph R. Shaw, "The American Library Association—Today and Tomorrow," *ALA Bulletin* 29: 483 (August, 1935).

72. "Resolution United Association," *Library Journal* 60: 606 (August, 1935).

73. Rankin, "Unemployment among Librarians."

74. "A.L.A. Activities Committee Report," *ALA Bulletin* 24: 609 (December, 1930).

75. "Report of the Second Activities Committee," *ALA Bulletin* 28: 859–65 (December, 1934).

76. Clarence B. Lester, "The Need for Federal Aid," *Library Journal* 60: 106 (February 1, 1935).

77. Charles H. Compton, "Answers to Questions on Federal Participation in Library Development," *Library Journal* 60: 366 (May 1, 1935).

78. "A National Plan for Libraries," *ALA Bulletin* 29: 91 (February, 1935).

79. Putnam to Milam, January 21, 1935, ALA Archives.

80. "Will Seek $50,000,000–$100,000,000 Federal Support," *ALA Bulletin* 29: 40 (January, 1935).

81. "Minutes, Council, June 24, 1935," ALA Archives.

82. Carleton B. Joeckel, "The New Federal Library Agency," *ALA Bulletin* 30: 529 (July, 1936).

83. [Editorial], *Library Journal* 61: 387 (May 15, 1936).

84. Letter to editor, *Library Journal* 61: 467 (June 15, 1936).

85. *New York Times*, October 19, 1936, p. 1.

86. "Report of the Committee on Racial Discrimination," typewritten (Chicago: 1936), ALA Archives.

87. "Minutes, Executive Board, December 28, 1936," ALA Archives.

88. "Proceedings, Council, December 28, 1940," ALA Archives.

89. "A.L.A. News," *ALA Bulletin* 34: 208 (March, 1940).

90. Mary M. Taggert, letter to editor, *ALA Bulletin* 34: 195 (March, 1940).

91. "Minutes, Council, May 31, 1940," ALA Archives.

92. "Where to Stay in Cincinnati," *ALA Bulletin* 34: 195 (March, 1940).

CHAPTER 7

1. [Editorial], *ALA Bulletin* 31: 39 (January, 1937).

2. "Library Progress," *New International Yearbook* (New York: Dodd, Mead, 1937), p. 410.

3. "The Reorganization of the A.L.A.," *ALA Bulletin* 32: 674 (October 1, 1938).

4. Clarence E. Sherman, "Should A.L.A. Conference Be Held Biennially?" *ALA*

Bulletin 33: 237 (April, 1939). The association in 1931 had turned down the idea of having biennial conferences.

5. "Final Report of the Third Activities Committee," typewritten (Chicago: 1930), ALA Archives.

6. "Tentative Report of the Third A.L.A. Activities Committee," *ALA Bulletin* 33: 428 (June, 1939).

7. Luther Dickerson to Harrison Craver, memo reporting on conversations with presidential adviser Harry Hopkins, ALA Archives.

8. Committee members were William Warner Bishop, H. M. Lydenberg, Linda A. Eastman, Louis R. Wilson, and Harrison W. Craver.

9. Luther Dickerson to Harrison Craver, confidential report of conversations with Hopkins, May 16, 1938, ALA Archives.

10. Milam to Craver, June 30, 1938, ALA Archives.

11. Craver to Delano, August 25, 1938, ALA Archives.

12. Milam to Parker, September 10, 1938, ALA Archives.

13. Craver to Milam, June 29, 1938, ALA Archives.

14. Craver to Roosevelt, February 9, 1939, ALA Archives.

15. Frankfurter to Roosevelt, May 3, 1939, ALA Archives.

16. Milam to Ferguson, memo, June 7, 1939, ALA Archives.

17. *New York Times*, June 8, 1939, p. 2.

18. Open letter to Roosevelt, June 19, 1939, ALA Archives.

19. Craver to Milam, June 7, 1939, ALA Archives.

20. Munn to MacLeish, July 1, 1939, ALA Archives.

21. MacLeish to Munn, July 5, 1939, ALA Archives.

22. Milam to MacLeish, July 13, 1939, ALA Archives.

23. M. Llewellyn Raney, letter to editor, *Library Journal* 64: 522 (July, 1939).

24. Cora Beatty to Milam, memo, August 4, 1939, ALA Archives.

25. For a detailed discussion of his contributions, see Eva Goldschmidt, "Archibald MacLeish, Librarian of Congress," *College and Research Libraries* 30: 12–24 (January, 1969). For a more detailed discussion of ALA's role, see Betty Schwartz, "The Role of the American Library Association in the Selection of Archibald MacLeish as Librarian of Congress," *Journal of Library History* 9: 241 (July, 1974), and Dennis Thomison, "F.D.R., the ALA, and Mr. MacLeish: The Selection of the Librarian of Congress, 1939," *Library Quarterly* 42: 390 (October, 1972).

26. Beatrice Rosell to Executive Board, *ALA Bulletin* 34: 477–78 (September 1, 1940).

27. "Repudiation by ALA," *Library Journal* 65: 599 (July, 1940).

28. "Communication to President Roosevelt," *ALA Bulletin* 34: 415–16 (June, 1940).

29. Except for the first sentence of the telegram, included in "Communication to President Roosevelt."

30. Irene Fetty, letter to editor, *ALA Bulletin* 34: 479 (September, 1940).

31. *Papers and Proceedings of the Cincinnati Conference* (Chicago: ALA, 1940), p. 5.

32. "Minutes, Council, May 27, 1940," ALA Archives.

33. The committee's first members were Forrest P. Spaulding, Jens Nyholm, and Hiller C. Wellman.

34. Leon Carnovsky, "Can the Public Library Defend the Right to Freedom of Inquiry?" *ALA Bulletin* 38: 255 (July, 1944).

35. "Proceedings, Council, October 14, 1944," ALA Archives.

36. Kimball Young, "Censorship in Wartime," *ALA Bulletin* 38: 441 (November, 1944).

37. "Proceedings, Executive Board, October 5, 1938," ALA Archives, p. 488.

38. Ibid., p. 489.

CHAPTER 8

1. *Collier's Encyclopedia*, 1968 ed., s.v. "World War II."

2. "National Defense Activities," *ALA Bulletin* 35: 57 (February, 1941).

3. "Progress Report on A.L.A. Emergency Activities," *ALA Bulletin* 35: 140 (March, 1941).

4. Charles H. Brown, "Librarians Interested in National Defense," *Library Journal,* 66: 1026 (December, 1941).

5. "National Defense Book Campaign," *Library Journal* 66: 1082 (December 15, 1941).

6. "Victory Book Campaign," *Library Journal* 67: 74 (January 15, 1942).

7. John M. Connor, "The Victory Book Campaign," *ALA Bulletin* 36: 377 (June, 1942).

8. "Minutes, Council, June 26, 1942," ALA Archives.

9. December 12, 1942, ALA Archives.

10. Louis J. Bailey, "Victory Book Campaign, 1943," *Library Journal* 68: 945 (November 15, 1943).

11. "Proceedings, Executive Board, October 6, 1941," ALA Archives.

12. "Library Progress," *New International Yearbook* (New York: Dodd, Mead, 1941), p. 332.

13. "Libraries and Good Neighborliness," *Library Journal* 66: 977 (November 15, 1941).

14. Morrow had served as U.S. Ambassador to Mexico and had negotiated the settlement of Mexican confiscation of United States oil interests.

15. "Proceedings, Executive Board, October 6, 1941," ALA Archives.

16. "Annual Report of the Board of Education for Librarianship," *ALA Bulletin* 36: 688–89 (October 15, 1942).

17. Carl H. Milam, "Report of the Executive Secretary," *ALA Bulletin* 36: 688 (October 15, 1942).

18. Ellsworth R. Young, "American Library in Paris," *ALA Bulletin* 36: 43 (January, 1942).

19. Milam, "Report of the Executive Secretary," *ALA Bulletin* 36: 653.

20. "Report of the Third Activities Committee," *ALA Bulletin* 33: 389 (July, 1939).

21. "An Important Resolution," *Special Libraries* 32: 201 (July–August, 1941)

22. "Proceedings, Executive Board, October 7, 1941," ALA Archives.

23. "Proceedings, Executive Board, December 28, 1941," ALA Archives.

24. Hill was then president of the American Association of Law Libraries.

25. "Unity in the Profession," *Library Journal* 67: 166 (February 15, 1942).

26. Ibid.

27. Charles H. Brown, "Report of the President," in *Papers and Proceedings of the 1942 Annual Conference* (Chicago: ALA, 1942), p. 648.

28. "Minutes, Council, December 28, 1941," ALA Archives.

29. "Proceedings, Executive Board, October 12, 1944," ALA Archives.

30. "Minutes, Executive Board, June 27, 1942," ALA Archives.

31. "The Librarian in Wartime," *ALA Bulletin* 37: 358 (October 15, 1943).

32. "Report of the Personnel Division," *ALA Bulletin* 37: 365 (October 15, 1943).

33. Williamson's report is quoted in "Librarian Shortage," *Library Journal* 68: 126 (January 15, 1943).

34. "Annual Report," *ALA Bulletin* 37: 361 (October 15, 1943).

35. "Minutes, Executive Board, October 15, 1942," ALA Archives.

36. Anita M. Hostetter, "Planning the A.L.A. Institutes," *ALA Bulletin* 37: 72–73 (March, 1943).

37. Carl H. Milam, "Report of the Executive Secretary," *ALA Bulletin* 37: 312 (October 15, 1943).

38. Milam to Ferguson, March 10, 1939, ALA Archives.

39. Milam to Charles I. Gosnell, May 10, 1940, ALA Archives.

40. Althea Warren, "Salute to the Dawn," *ALA Bulletin* 37: 245 (September, 1943).

41. Shaw to Milam, July 28, 1943, ALA Archives.

42. Warren to Charles H. Brown, November 10, 1943, ALA Archives.

43. "A.L.A. Grants Received During 1942," *ALA Bulletin* 37: 59 (February, 1943).

44. "Highlights from the A.L.A. Report," *Library Journal* 68: 955 (November 15, 1943).

45. Carl Vitz, "Demobilization and the Library," mimeographed, (Chicago, 1943).

46. "Minutes, Executive Board, October 9, 1943," ALA Headquarters Library.

47. *Post-War Standards for Public Libraries* (Chicago: American Library Association, 1943), pp. 75–76.

48. Althea Warren, "Changes Ahead," *ALA Bulletin* 38: 414–15 (October 15, 1944).

49. Carl Vitz, "The Time to Plan Is Always Now," *ALA Bulletin* 38: 411–12 (October 15, 1944).

50. Carl Vitz, "Librarian of Congress," *ALA Bulletin* 39: 252 (July, 1945).

51. Carl Vitz, "President's Report," *ALA Bulletin* 39: 327 (October 15, 1945).

52. Julian P. Boyd to author, June 6, 1974.

53. MacLeish to author, n.d.

54. Carl H. Milam, "News from the Executive Secretary," *ALA Bulletin* 39: 165 (May, 1945).

55. "A.L.A.'s New Home," *ALA Bulletin* 39: 208 (June, 1945).

56. Paul Howard, "The Washington Scene," *Library Journal* 70: 1129 (December 1, 1945).

57. Paul Howard, "A.L.A. Washington Office Established," *Library Journal* 70: 970 (October 15, 1945).

58. "A Matter That Concerns Us All," *ALA Bulletin* 39: 2 (January, 1945).

59. Muriel E. Perry, "The Library Development Fund," *ALA Bulletin* 39: 454 (November, 1945).

60. "Minutes, Council, October 14, 1944," ALA Archives. However, the idea goes back at least several years. In 1942, President Charles Brown wrote to a friend following a proposal in an Executive Board meeting that a Washington office be established, "[I am] opposed to keeping a representative in Washington to pester government officials, but I shall probably go down to defeat on this issue."

CHAPTER 9

1. Anita M. Hostetter, "Enrollments in Library Schools," *ALA Bulletin* 39: 100 (February, 1945).

2. Margery C. Quigley, "The Librarian in Wartime and After: Board of Education for Librarianship," *ALA Bulletin* 39: 381 (October 15, 1945).

3. Paul Howard, "Whither A.L.A.?" *ALA Bulletin* 40: 304 (October 1, 1946).

4. "A.L.A. Activities Committee Report," *ALA Bulletin* 24: 660 (December, 1930).

5. "Final Report of the Third Activities Committee," *ALA Bulletin* 33: 783 (December, 1939).

6. Blanche McCrum, "The A.C.R.L.: Milestone, 1946," *ALA Bulletin* 40: 118 (April, 1946).

7. Ellsworth to Milam, January 10, 1946, ALA Archives.

8. Charles H. Brown, "The A.C.R.L. and the A.L.A.," *Library Journal* 71: 1005–1006 (August, 1946).

9. "Report of the Committee on the Relations of the ACRL to the ALA," typewritten (Chicago, 1946).

10. "Minutes, Council, June 17, 1946," ALA Archives.

11. Carl Milam, "Executive Secretary's Report to Council," *ALA Bulletin* 40: 233 (July, 1946).

12. John M. Cory, "Memo to Members," *ALA Bulletin* 45: 237 (July–August, 1951).

13. "Minutes, Council, January 30, 1952," ALA Archives.

14. Robert B. Downs, "One Library World," *ALA Bulletin* 46: 215 (July–August, 1952).

15. "Annual Report of Board of Personnel Administration," *ALA Bulletin* 41: 383 (October 15, 1947).

16. "Annual Report of Office of Placement and Personnel Records," *ALA Bulletin* 41: 387–88 (October 15, 1947).

17. "Annual Report of Board of Education for Librarianship," *ALA Bulletin* 41: 378–79 (October 15, 1947).

18. "Undergraduate Courses in Library Science," *ALA Bulletin* 41: 70 (March, 1947).

19. Ibid.

20. Harriet E. Howe, "The New Program at the University of Denver," *ALA Bulletin* 41: 450–53 (November, 1947).

21. "Library Schools' Opportunity," *Library Journal* 74: 1642 (November 1, 1949).

22. Jerrold Orne, "Unrecognized Library School Offers Training Opportunities," *Library Journal* 74: 1626 (November 1, 1949).

23. "Minutes, Council, July 13, 1951," ALA Archives.

24. Anita M. Hostetter, "Accrediting Programs of ALA Board of Education for Librarianship," *ALA Bulletin* 46: 51 (February, 1952).

25. "Program Letter No. 3," (National Commission on Accrediting, January 29, 1953), ALA Archives.

26. "Proceedings, Council, December 28, 1934," ALA Archives.

27. "The National Plan," *ALA Bulletin* 41: 249 (August, 1947).

28. Carl Milam, "Executive Secretary's Report," *ALA Bulletin* 41: 337 (October 15, 1947).

29. "Public Libraries Study Announced," *Library Journal* 72: 583 (April 15, 1947).

30. "The Public Library Inquiry," *ALA Bulletin* 41: 433–34 (November, 1947).

31. Paul Rice, "A.L.A. Finances," *ALA Bulletin* 42: 294 (July–August, 1948).

32. Harold Brigham, "Placement Service Suspended," *ALA Bulletin* 42: 294 (July–August, 1948).

33. "Minutes, Executive Board, September 28, 1949," ALA Archives.

34. "A.L.A. Sells Two Buildings," *ALA Bulletin* 43: 50 (January, 1949).

35. John Cory, "Memo to Members," *ALA Bulletin* 43: 5 (January, 1949).

36. "Minutes, Executive Board, December 27, 1945," ALA Archives, p. 204.

37. "Preliminary Report of the Fourth Activities Committee to the Council," *ALA Bulletin* 42: 306 (July–August, 1948).

38. Ibid., 295.

39. "Proceedings, Council, January 29, 1948," ALA Archives.

40. "Minutes, Executive Board, February 1, 1948," ALA Archives.

41. Carl H. Milam, "From the Corner Office," *ALA Bulletin* 42: 103 (March, 1948).

42. "Carl Milam," *Library Journal* 70: 348 (April 15, 1945).

43. Ralph Munn, "Carl Milam—The Administrator," *ALA Bulletin* 42: 3 (September 15, 1948).

44. Louis R. Wilson, "Carl H. Milam," *Library Journal* 70: 331 (April 15, 1945).

45. See Peggy Sullivan, "Carl H. Milam and the American Library Association."

46. "Carl Milam's Successor," *ALA Bulletin* 42: 241 (May, 1948).

47. This discussion is based on the minutes of the council and on Leslie Poste, "No Top Brass in A.L.A.," *Library Journal* 74: 334 (March 1, 1949).

48. "Minutes, Council, January 23, 1949," ALA Archives.

49. "Minutes, Council, January 22, 1949," ALA Archives.

50. "A.L.A.'s Presidency," *Library Journal* 74: 425 (March 15, 1949).

51. Poste, "No Top Brass," p. 336.

52. "Minutes, Council, January 20, 1949," ALA Archives.

53. "Official Report of Returns of 1949 Election," *ALA Bulletin* 43: 264 (September, 1949).

54. Carl H. Milam, "News from the Executive Secretary," *ALA Bulletin* 39: 167–68 (May, 1945).

55. Lucile Deaderich, "Pickups," *ALA Bulletin* 39: 248 (July, 1945).

56. Carl H. Milam, "News from the Executive Secretary," *ALA Bulletin* 39: 60 (January, 1945).

57. John M. Cory, "Memo to Members," *ALA Bulletin* 44: 444 (December, 1950).

58. Margaret C. Scoggin, "The International Youth Library," *ALA Bulletin* 44: 39 (January, 1950).

59. "Japanese Library School," *ALA Bulletin* 44: 458 (December, 1950).

60. David H. Clift, "Memo to Members," *ALA Bulletin* 50: 411 (July–August, 1956).

61. David H. Clift, "Memo to Members," *ALA Bulletin* 50: 335 (June, 1956).

62. "ALA's New International Relations Office," *ALA Bulletin* 51: 446 (June, 1957).

63. Ruth Warncke, "Library Community Project," *ALA Bulletin* 49: 2 (April, 1955).

64. David H. Clift, "Memo to Members, *ALA Bulletin* 50: 622 (November, 1956).

65. "Council on Library Resources," *ALA Bulletin* 50: 662 (November, 1956).

66. Clift, "Memo to Members," *ALA Bulletin* 50: 622 (November, 1956).

67. Louis B. Wright, et al., *The Democratic Experience* (Glenview, Ill.: Scott, Foresman, 1968), p. 451.

68. "Minutes, Council, June 18, 1948," ALA Archives.

69. Berninghausen, "Book-banning and Witchhunts," *ALA Bulletin* 42: 204–7 (May, 1948).

70. "Minutes, Council, June 18, 1948," ALA Archives.

71. Verner W. Clapp, "Disloyalty by Imputation or by Due Process," *Library Journal* 75: 678 (April 15, 1950).

72. W. Holloway, "Bull by the Tail . . .," *Library Journal* 75: 679 (April 15, 1950).

73. "It Is the Loyalty Oaths That Are Subversive," *Library Journal* 75: 82 (January 15, 1950).

74. "Loyalty Oath Dismissal," *ALA Bulletin* 44: 149 (May, 1950).

75. "It Is the Loyalty Oaths That Are Subversive," *Library Journal* 75: 82 (January 15, 1950).

76. David K. Berninghausen, "Loyalty by Choice or Coercion," *ALA Bulletin* 44: 17 (January, 1950).

77. "Minutes, Council, July 21, 1950," ALA Archives.

78. "Labeling—A Report of the Committee on Intellectual Freedom," *ALA Bulletin* 45: 241 (July–August, 1951).

79. "Minutes, Council, July 13, 1951," ALA Archives.

80. *New York Times,* June 15, 1953, p. 1.

81. *New York Times,* June 16, 1953, p. 1.

82. *New York Times,* June 17, 1953, p. 1.

83. *New York Times,* June 26, 1953, p. 16.

84. Eisenhower to Downs, June 24, 1953, ALA Archives.

85. Robert Downs, "The ALA Today—A 1953 Stocktaking Report to the Council, June 27, 1953, Los Angeles," *ALA Bulletin* 47: 397 (October, 1953).

86. "Overseas Library Statement Adopted by ALA Council, June 25, 1953," *ALA Bulletin* 47: 487 (November, 1953).

87. *Freedom to Read Statement,* reprint from the Office for Intellectual Freedom, ALA Headquarters, Chicago, unpaged.

88. Ibid.

89. Ibid.

90. "Council Sessions—Second Council Session," *American Library Association 73rd Annual Conference Proceedings, Minneapolis, Minnesota, June 20–26, 1954* (Chicago: ALA, 1954), p. 3.

91. *New York Times,* December 6, 1955, p. 1.

92. This is quoted in "Editorial," *Newsletter on Intellectual Freedom* 4: 2 (January, 1956).

93. Paul Bixler, Secretary of the Intellectual Freedom Committee, to Edward Reed, Fund for the Republic, February 9, 1956, ALA Archives.

94. Milam to Paul Bixler, undated, ALA Archives.

95. John M. Cory, "Report to Council," *ALA Bulletin* 45: 47 (February, 1951).

96. This policy was discontinued by action of the executive board and council at the 1952 midwinter meeting.

97. Loleta Fyan, "A Welcome to David H. Clift," *ALA Bulletin* 45: 249 (July–August, 1951).

98. John M. Cory, "ALA Membership—Past and Future," *ALA Bulletin* 45: 197 (June, 1951).

99. John M. Cory, "Memo to Members," *ALA Bulletin* 45: 237 (July–August, 1951).

100. *New York Times,* June 20, 1956, p. 1.

101. Julia Bennett, "Congress Appropriates $2,050,000 for Grants for the Library Services Program," *Washington Newsletter* 8: 1 (July 27, 1956).

102. "Minutes, Executive Board, June 17, 1956," ALA Archives.

103. U.S. Congress, Senate, Committee on Rules and Administration, *Nomina-*

tion of Lawrence Quincy Mumford to be Librarian of Congress, 83rd Cong., 2nd sess., 1954, p. 145.

104. Ibid., 61.

105. David H. Clift, "Memo to Members," *ALA Bulletin* 48: 188 (April, 1954).

106. "Minutes, Council, February 4, 1954," ALA Archives.

107. *New York Times*, March 29, 1954, p. 21.

108. "Statement for an Enlarged Program for a Headquarters Library," mimeographed, September, 1955, ALA Archives.

109. "Minutes, Executive Board, November 11, 1955," ALA Archives.

110. "Proceedings, Council, June 24, 1957," ALA Archives.

111. The vote in favor of Washington was 2,100, and for Chicago 5,749.

112. The following discussion is based on "Management Survey," *ALA Bulletin* 49: 411–64 (September, 1955).

113. Ibid., p. 454.

114. "Special Committee on Reorganization," *ALA Bulletin* 51: 680 (October, 1957).

115. "Management Survey," p. 441.

116. Ralph R. Shaw, "The President's Report," *ALA Bulletin* 51: 174 (March, 1957).

117. The dues structure was not immediately affected by the reorganization.

118. Shaw, "President's Report," p. 173–79.

CHAPTER 10

1. "The SCAD Report: The Place of the ACRL in the Reorganized ALA," *College and Research Libraries* 19: 246 (May, 1958).

2. "Minutes, Council, January 31, 1957," ALA Archives.

3. "Minutes, Council, March 4, 1957," ALA Archives.

4. "Report of the Committee of Council on the Proposed Revision of ALA Bylaws Article VI, Section 2 (b)," March 13, 1959, ALA Archives.

5. Lucile M. Morsch, "Authority of the Divisions to Act for ALA," *ALA Bulletin* 53: 596 (July–August, 1959).

6. "Council-Division Relations: A Report of the Committee on Organization," *ALA Bulletin* 54: 523 (June, 1960).

7. "Minutes, Executive Board, January 31, 1957," ALA Archives.

8. "Highlights of the Midwinter Meeting," *ALA Bulletin* 53: 235 (March, 1959).

9. "Minutes, Executive Board, November 17, 1959," ALA Archives.

10. The executive board on November 15, 1958, confirmed the change in Clift's title, which he had requested on July 31, 1958.

11. Clift to officers, July 10, 1959, ALA Archives.

12. "Minutes, Executive Board," November 17, 1959, and March 21, 1960, ALA Archives.

13. Samray Smith, "A Look at the New Headquarters," *ALA Bulletin* 57: 655 (July–August, 1963).

14. Verner W. Clapp, "LTP—The Rattle in an Infant's Fist," *American Libraries* 3: 799 (July–August, 1972).

15. David H. Clift, "Memo to Members," *ALA Bulletin* 52: 802 (December, 1958).

16. David H. Clift, "Memo to Members," *ALA Bulletin* 52: 586 (September, 1958).

17. For a discussion in greater detail of the various federal programs, see: Genevieve M. Casey, ed., "Federal Aid to Libraries: Its History, Impact, Future," *Library Trends* v. 24 (July, 1975); Edmon Low, "Federal Consciousness and Libraries," *American Libraries* 3: 717–24 (July–August, 1972); Richard M. Leach, "A Broad Look at the Federal Government and Libraries" in *Libraries at Large: Tradition, Innovation, and the National Interest*, ed. by Douglas M. Knight and E. Shepley Nourse (New York: Bowker, 1969).

18. John Pierson, "Do Libraries Need Federal Aid? White House Says No, but Librarians Say They'll Suffer," *Wall Street Journal*, February 27, 1973, p. 42.

19. David H. Clift, "Memo to Members," *ALA Bulletin* 57: 216 (March, 1963).

20. Edmon Low, "Federal Consciousness and Libraries," *American Libraries* 3: 723 (July–August, 1972).

21. Clift to Benjamin Powell, August 3, 1960, ALA Archives.

22. Ibid.

23. "Report to Executive Board, Council Committee on Institutional Membership," October 29, 1965, ALA Archives.

24. "Minutes, Executive Board, March 27, 1960," ALA Archives.

25. "Proceedings, Council, March 27, 1960," ALA Archives.

26. "Highlights of the Midwinter Meeting," *ALA Bulletin* 55: 233 (March, 1961).

27. Ibid.

28. Everett T. Moore, "The Freedom to Use Libraries," *ALA Bulletin* 55: 303 (April, 1961).

29. "ALA and the Segregation Issue," *ALA Bulletin* 55: 486 (June, 1961).

30. John Wakefield, letter to editor, *Library Journal* 86: 732 (February 15, 1961).

31. Executive Board to Kennedy and Shriver, telegrams, January 4, 1961, ALA Archives.

32. Shriver to Clift, January 12, 1961, ALA Archives.

33. Frederick G. Kilgour to Clift, March 16, 1961, ALA Archives. Kilgour heard the news from a friend, Mrs. Hajo Holborn, whose son was in the new administration.

34. This is reinforced by Mrs. Spain, who believed it to be a trial balloon to get ALA's reaction. Quick response and the presentation of ALA's philosophy on the position, according to Mrs. Spain, prevented a change. Spain to author, September 23, 1973.

35. David Clift, personal interview with author, August 3, 1973.

36. A memorandum on the role of the Library of Congress prepared by Douglas Bryant, associate director of the Harvard University Library.

37. Gordon P. Martin and Irving Lieberman, "Library 21: ALA's Exhibit at the Seattle World's Fair," *ALA Bulletin* 56: 230 (March, 1962).

38. "Library 21's Electronic Library Previewed in New York," *Library Journal* 87: 1568 (April 15, 1962).

39. David H. Clift, "Memo to Members," *ALA Bulletin* 56: 982 (December, 1962).

40. "Proceedings, Council, February 1, 1962," ALA Archives.

41. Ibid.

42. Ibid.

43. Ibid.

44. "Proceedings, Council, June 19, 1962," ALA Archives. The statement was adopted on June 19 and approved, with an amendment, by the membership on June 22.

45. This was reported in the "Minutes, Executive Board, November 1, 1962," ALA Archives.

46. Quoted in "Moments at Midwinter," *Library Journal* 88: 967 (March 1, 1963).

47. All four associations had rejoined the parent organization by mid-1966.

48. "Minutes, Membership meeting, July 3, 1964," ALA Archives.

49. "Problems of Consistency," *Library Journal* 89: 2966–67 (August, 1964).

50. "Minutes, Executive Board, August 5, 1964," ALA Archives.

51. "Proceedings, Council, January 27, 1965," ALA Archives.

52. Ibid.

53. Ibid.

54. "Constitutional Rites," *Library Journal* 80: 1079 (March 1, 1955).

55. Principal funding came from ALA general funds, H. W. Wilson Co., New World Foundation, and the R. R. Bowker Co.

56. *Access to Public Libraries* (Chicago: ALA, 1963).

57. "The Access to Public Libraries Study," *ALA Bulletin* 57: 743 (September, 1963).

58. "Minutes, Executive Board, November 23, 1963," ALA Archives.

59. Frederick Wagman, March 12, 1964, ALA Archives.

60. "Minutes, Council, January 30, 1964," ALA Archives.

61. "Report of the Council Committee on Freedom of Access to Libraries," mimeographed, July 15, 1966, ALA Archives.

62. Clift, interview with author, August 3, 1973.

63. "Minutes, Membership Meeting, July 6, 1965," ALA Archives.

64. "Highlights of the Midwinter Meeting," *ALA Bulletin* 60: 241 (March, 1966).

65. "Minutes, Council, January 30, 1966," ALA Archives.

66. "Report of the Council Committee on Freedom of Access to Libraries," mimeographed, July 15, 1966, ALA Archives.

67. "Minutes, Council, June 28, 1968," ALA Archives.

68. Eric Moon, "Business—Not Quite as Usual," *Library Journal* 93: 2797 (August, 1968).

69. Kenneth Duchac, "A Plea for Social Responsibility," *Library Journal* 93: 2798–99 (August, 1968).

70. "Minutes, Council, June 28, 1968," ALA Archives.

71. Ibid.

72. Ibid.

73. Kenyon C. Rosenberg and Daniel Suvak, "ALA Committee Membership: A Statistical Survey," *Library Journal* 98: 842–44 (March 15, 1973).

74. John Berry III, "The New Constituency," *Library Journal* 94: 2725–28 (August, 1969).

75. Ibid., p. 2734.

76. "Minutes, Membership Meeting, June 25, 1969," ALA Archives.

77. But when the committee received its official title, the word "activities" was included.

78. "Minutes, Council, June 27, 1969," ALA Archives.

79. Ibid.

80. "Final Report of the Activities Committee on New Directions for ALA and Subcommittee Reports," June, 1970, ALA Archives.

81. Ibid.

82. David Clift, "Report to the Executive Board, 1970–71," mimeographed, August 18, 1970, ALA Archives.

83. ACONDA Revised Recommendations on Democratization and Reorganization," mimeographed, 1971, ALA Archives, p. 2.

84. "Recommendations from ANACONDA," mimeographed, 1971, ALA Archives.

85. "ALA Goals for Action, 1967," *ALA Bulletin* 61: 952 (September, 1967).

86. "The Library Bill of Rights," *Library Journal* 92: 984 (March 1, 1967).

87. "Minutes, Council, June 27, 1967," ALA Archives.

88. "San Francisco Conference '67," *Library Journal* 92: 2709 (August, 1967).

89. "Kansas City Conference: Growing Pains and Generation Gaps," *ALA Bulletin* 62: 822 (July–August, 1968).

90. "Minutes, Council, June 25, 1968," ALA Archives.

91. Ibid.

92. "Minutes, Council, June 27, 1969," ALA Archives.

93. "Headin' for the Last Roundup," *American Libraries* 2: 243 (March, 1971).

94. Ibid.

95. David Berninghausen, "Defending the Defenders of Intellectual Freedom," *American Libraries* 2: 119–20 (January, 1971). This apparent weakness was removed in a revision adopted by council at Los Angeles in 1971.

96. Ibid.

97. Clift, interview with author, August 3, 1973.

98. "Minutes, Council, December 1, 1970," ALA Archives.

99. Bill Katz, "Magazines," *Library Journal* 96: 1949 (June 1, 1971).

100. "Minutes, Executive Board, April 30, 1972," ALA Archives.

101. David Clift, "Memo to Members," *ALA Bulletin* 61: 238 (March, 1967).

102. "Nixon on NLW 1971: Praise for Libraries," *Library Journal* 96: 1914 (June 1, 1971).

103. "New Austerity Threat: The Nixon 1972 Budget," *Library Journal* 96: 1181 (April 1, 1971).

104. "Three Request for Action Reports," *American Libraries* 2: 278 (March, 1972).

105. "Minutes, Council, July 5, 1965," ALA Archives.

106. Mumford to Doms, telegram, January 27, 1972, ALA Archives.

107. "Minutes, Executive Board, March 17, 1972," ALA Archives.

108. Ibid.

109. David H. Clift, "Memo to Members," *American Libraries* 2: 511 (May, 1972).

110. Doiron to Gerald Shields, August 5, 1971 (photocopied and distributed to executive board members), ALA Archives.

111. Based on the following letters photocopied and distributed to executive board members: Doiron to Shields, August 5, 1971; Clift to Executive Board, September 10, 1971; Clift to Doiron, July 28, 1971; Clift to Thomas R. Buckman, September 8, 1971; Clift to George S. Bobinski, September 7, 1971, ALA Archives.

112. "Minutes, Council, June 27, 1972," ALA Archives.

113. "Minutes, Council, July 5, 1965," ALA Archives.

114. Katherine Laich, "ALA Headquarters Space Problem Grows," *ALA Bulletin* 60: 502 (May, 1966).

115. Katherine Laich, "Keep the Lines Open," *ALA Bulletin* 60: 1162 (December, 1966).

116. "Minutes, Council, January 12, 1967," ALA Archives.

117. "Minutes, Council, June 27, 1967," ALA Archives.

118. Ibid.

119. "Keep ALA in Chicago Says Membership Vote," *Library Journal* 92: 4092 (November 15, 1967).

120. "Report of the Space Needs Committee to Council," mimeographed, January, 1969, ALA Archives.

121. Ibid.

122. Executive Director Search Committee to Executive Board, mimeographed, May 24, 1971, ALA Archives.

123. Keith Doms to Executive Board, mimeographed, November 29, 1971, ALA Archives.

124. Report, Subcommittee on Candidates for Position of Executive Director, to Executive Board, mimeographed, March 6, 1972, ALA Archives. However, Summers had by this time already withdrawn his name from consideration. There were no women in the group of candidates, but many had been nominated earlier for consideration. Among them were Katherine Laich, Lillian Bradshaw, and Margaret Monroe, all of whom declined to be considered.

125. Theodore Waller, "David H. Clift—A Very Partial Profile," *American Libraries* 2: 708 (July–August, 1972). The entire issue is a festschrift to Clift.

126. John M. Cory, "The American Library Association in the National Library Economy," *Catholic Library World* 21: 13 (October, 1949).

127. John A. Lapp, "My Contributions to the Special Library Movement: A Symposium by Some of Our Founders," *Special Libraries* 23: 210 (May–June, 1932).

128. Clift, interview with author, August 3, 1973.

129. Cory, "National Library Economy," p. 14.

130. Grace T. Stevenson, "ALA—The Fight for Library Service," *American Libraries* 2: 716 (July–August, 1972).

131. Clift, interview with author, August 3, 1973.

132. Ibid.

133. "Minutes, Council, June 24, 1969," ALA Archives.

134. Peggy Sullivan, "Library Associations," *Library Trends* 25: 146 (July, 1976).

135. Stevenson, "Fight for Library Service," p. 716.

136. Eileen D. Cooke, "The Role of ALA and Other Library Associations in the Promotion of Library Legislation," *Library Trends* 24: 141 (July, 1976).

137. J. Periam Danton, "The Library Press," *Library Trends* 25: 163 (July, 1976).

138. Eric Moon, "The Library Press," *Library Journal* 94: 4104 (November 15, 1969).

139. Lester Asheim, "As Much to Learn as to Teach," *Library Journal* 89: 4465 (November 15, 1964).

140. Sullivan, "Library Associations," p. 148.

141. Charles D. Churchwell, *The Shaping of American Library Education,* ACRL Publications in Librarianship No. 36 (Chicago, ALA, 1975), p. 101.

142. "Final Report to Council, Committee on Organization," mimeographed, June, 1969, ALA Archives.

143. "ACONDA Revised Recommendations on Democratization and Reorganization," January, 1967, ALA Archives.

144. Edward G. Holley, "Federation: An Idea Whose Time Has Come?" *Library Journal* 99: 338 (February 1, 1974).

145. Stevenson, "Fight for Library Service," p. 715.

146. Ibid.

147. Charles Compton, "Annual Reports: Salaries," *ALA Bulletin* 16: 217 (July, 1922).

148. "Minutes, Membership Meeting, June 25, 1967," ALA Archives.

149. Gail Schlachter, "Quasi Unions and Organizational Hegemony Within the Library Field," *Library Quarterly* 43: 191 (July, 1973).

SELECTED BIBLIOGRAPHY

The research for this history has depended mainly on the archives of the American Library Association, now at the University of Illinois. The correspondence of some of the early officers has been preserved there, as well as many of the official records of the association. Minutes and proceedings of the executive board and the council were made available by the headquarters library staff. These accounts were not always verbatim, however, and frequently it was necessary to depend on unofficial accounts reported on in the library press. The footnotes serve as an extended bibliography for that period of the association's history. However, as a matter of convenience, I have also included the following publications as being especially important in understanding the role of ALA, and in my preparation of this history.

BOOKS

Access to Public Libraries. Chicago: American Library Association, 1963.

Bobinski, George S. *Carnegie Libraries: Their History and Impact on American Public Library Development.* Chicago: American Library Association, 1967.

Carroll, C. Edward. *The Professionalization of Education for Librarianship, With Special Reference to the Years 1940–1960.* Metuchen, N.J.: Scarecrow Press, 1970.

Churchwell, Charles D. *The Shaping of American Library Education.* ACRL Publications in Librarianship, no. 36. Chicago: American Library Association, 1975.

Davis, Donald G., Jr. *The Association of American Library Schools, 1915–1968: An Analytical History.* Metuchen, N.J.: Scarecrow Press, 1974.

Final Report of the Activities Committee on New Directions for ALA, and Subcommittee Reports. Chicago: American Library Association, 1970.

Fleming, Edward M. *R. R. Bowker: Militant Liberal.* Norman: University of Oklahoma Press, 1952.

Green, Samuel S. *The Public Library Movement in the United States, 1853–1893.* Boston: Boston Book Co., 1913.

Hadley, Chalmers. *John Cotton Dana: A Sketch.* Chicago: American Library Association, 1943.

Holley, Edward G. *Charles Evans, American Bibliographer.* Urbana: University of Illinois Press, 1963.

————. *Raking the Historic Coals: The A.L.A. Scrapbook of 1876.* Urbana: Beta Phi Mu, 1967.

Knight, Douglas M., and E. Shepley Nourse. *Libraries at Large: Tradition, Innovation, and the National Interest.* New York: Bowker, 1969.

Literary and Educational Register for 1854. New York: Norton, 1854.

Mearns, David. *The Story Up to Now: The Library of Congress, 1800–1946.* Washington: Library of Congress, 1947.

Rider, Fremont. *Melvil Dewey.* Chicago: American Library Association, 1944.

Vann, Sarah K. *Training for Librarianship before 1923: Education for Librarianship Prior to the Publication of Williamson's Report on Training for Library Service.* Chicago: American Library Association, 1961.

————. *The Williamson Reports: A Study.* Metuchen, N.J.: Scarecrow Press, 1971.

White, Carl M. *A Historical Introduction to Library Education: Problems and Progress to 1951.* Metuchen, N.J.: Scarecrow Press, 1976.

————. *The Origins of the American Library School.* Metuchen, N.J.: Scarecrow Press, 1961.

Williamson, Charles C. *The Williamson Reports of 1921 and 1923.* Metuchen, N.J.: Scarecrow Press, 1971.

Williamson, William L. *William Frederick Poole and the Modern Library Movement.* New York: Columbia University Press, 1963.

DISSERTATIONS

Borome, Joseph Alfred. "The Life and Letters of Justin Winsor." Ph.D. dissertation, Columbia University, 1950.

Gardner, Richard K. "Education for Librarianship in France, an Historical Study." Ph.D. dissertation, Case Western Reserve University, 1968.

Maddox, Lucy. "Trends and Issues in American Librarianship as Reflected in the Papers and Proceedings of the American Library Association, 1876–1885." Ph.D. dissertation, University of Michigan, 1958.

Sparks, Claude Glenn. "William Warner Bishop, a Biography." Ph.D. dissertation, University of Michigan, 1967.

Sullivan, Peggy. "Carl H. Milam and the American Library Association." Ph.D. dissertation, University of Chicago, 1972.

PERIODICAL ARTICLES

Casey, Genevieve M., ed. "Federal Aid to Libraries: Its History, Impact, Future." *Library Trends* v.24 (July, 1975).

Cooke, Eileen D. "The Role of ALA and Other Library Associations in the Promotion of Library Legislation," *Library Trends* 25: 137–53 (July, 1976).

Davis, Donald G., Jr. "Education for Librarianship." *Library Trends* 25: 113–33 (July, 1976).

Gambee, Budd L. "The Role of American Librarians at the Second International Library Conference" in *Library History Seminar Proceedings*, no.4. Tallahassee: Florida State University, 1971.

Low, Edmon. "Federal Consciousness and Libraries." *American Libraries* 3: 717–24 (July–August, 1972).

Miksa, Frances. "The Making of the 1876 Special Report on Public Libraries." *Journal of Library History* 8: 30–40 (January, 1973).

Solberg, Thorvald. "A Chapter in the Unwritten History of the Library of Congress from January 17 to April 5, 1899." *Library Quarterly* 9: 285–96 (July, 1939).

Sullivan, Peggy. "Library Associations." *Library Trends* 25: 135–52 (July, 1976).

INDEX